The Crisis in Marxism

THE
CRISIS

Jack Lindsay

IN
MARXISM

BARNES & NOBLE BOOKS
TOTOWA, NEW JERSEY

To my son PHILIP
without whose persistent interest I should not have written this book

First published in the U.S.A. 1981 by
BARNES & NOBLE BOOKS
81 Adams Drive, Totowa, New Jersey 07512
ISBN 0-389-20185-5
Printed in England by
T. H. Brickell & Son Ltd, Shaftesbury, Dorset
and bound in England by Butler & Tanner Ltd

CONTENTS

1 The Crisis in Marxism

There are various ways in which the term 'Crisis in Marxism' can be applied. In a broad way we can refer it to the period after 1917 when all Communist Parties assumed that the strategies of Lenin, in his particular historical situation, constituted a model for the bringing about of any fundamental social change; when in the 1920s the revolutionary forces in Central Europe and Germany failed to bring about any such change; when in the 1930s, with the political crisis represented by Hitler, none of the parties succeeded in dominating the situation. The one time when the parties in Europe made genuine headway was during the resistance struggles against Hitler; but these gains were not effectively consolidated, partly through the tactics of the United States in supporting reactions and partly through the inability of the party leaderships to learn the relevant lessons and change their outlooks and methods fast enough in the needed ways. There were, indeed, important theoretical advances made by Gramsci in the 1920s and 1930s, and his work is now beginning to bear fruit. But though it has important bearings on the crisis we are considering, which we shall later assess, it cannot be said to solve it in any simple way.

There is also a wider sense in which the creation and growth of Marxism must always involve a crisis of some sort. For each advance as well as each setback cannot but stir up new problems and set the past developments in a new focus, so that urgent issues of re-unification and redirection keep emerging. There is thus always liable to be a conflict between past formulations and those more adequate to the new phases of struggle.

Indeed in this sense Marx's whole career itself is a movement from one crisis to another after the first bringing-down of the Hegelian dialectic to earth and the grappling with the question of what changes were needed in it if it were to express material processes in their fullness. In failing to develop fully and directly his philosophic system, despite the magnificent advances in his early works and much of the *Grundrisse*, he bequeathed as many unsolved problems as

1

thoroughly worked-out analyses. Lenin made many brilliant advances again, but also heaped up a large number of pressing but unsolved problems. And these developments of Marxism took place in a rapidly and often violently changing world. Consider the differences of 1848 and 1948, of 1917 and 1977, and we see obviously enough how no formulations of the earlier years could be expected to clarify effectively the situation in the later ones, however illuminating they may have been in their context.

I am not saying that there were not present in Marxism from the mid-1840s many important revelatory elements. Merely that the critical task of assessing those elements and realising them afresh in changed circumstances, with an ever-widening range of problems, applications, expansions, continued to be extremely pressing and has grown ever more pressing as the contradictions of capitalism have kept on worsening and the potentialities of movement on to a level of vastly enriched humanity have increased—yet without the needed resolutions and comprehensions being attained.

So we may say that in one sense it is natural enough that there should continue to be a crisis in Marxism. But we cannot halt comfortably at that conclusion. The crisis in Marxism we are considering is also one of inadequacy, of inability to recognise outworn formulations and to keep abreast of history in all its complexity and richness. As a result there has so far been nothing like an effective gathering of the forces capable of resolving the inner conflicts of the capitalist system. Yet all the while those conflicts have been dangerously intensified, as we shall discuss later. Since Marxism at any moment seeks ways of overcoming the existing contradictions and conflicts inside society, it attempts (or should attempt) to bring about a higher unity of thought and action than has been so far achieved. The unity of thought and action implies a living link between the ideas of necessary change and the means whereby those changes can be effected. To achieve this link, no small group is sufficient, even if a lonely thinker (like Gramsci in his prison-cell) may at times be able to make a valuable contribution. Broadly, there must be a link of Marxist thought with groups or organisations large enough, and strategically placed in society, so as to have powerful and steady effects moving towards the necessary changes. The problem of gaining a true unity of thought and action at any given moment is thus charged with many difficulties and subject to many dislocating pressures, so that the crisis-nature of the situation is sharpened.

The claim here being made is that Marxism alone is capable of fully grasping what is happening in history, what is at stake, and how the next stage of human development can be brought about. If that is so,

2

movements inspired by Marxism can alone achieve the necessary unity of thought and action for that next stage. Marxism is Historical Materialism. That is as close as Marx or Lenin got to a succinct definition. By Historical Materialism they meant a philosophy and science of history which grasped the essential forces and structures at work in human development, indeed in all process. The forces and structures must be realised inside history, revealed in their immanent action and shown as sufficient explanation of the changes and movements investigated. The method used may be defined as Dialectical Materialism. The system of dialectical logic is derived from Hegel but brought down to earth, rejecting the idea of mind or spirit as self-sufficient cause and seeking in material conditions and in social processes the essential driving forces and structurations, without attempting to reduce in any simple way the highly complex intellectual, emotional, cultural elements of human life to such bases. These rough-and-ready definitions must suffice us here for the moment. In struggling to apply them, Marx himself, and Engels, came up against many problems which they had to set aside, or deal with cursorily, as they carried on with their main task, the analysis of the nature and structure of capitalism, its working-out, its contradictions, and the ways in which its inner conflicts could be validly resolved. The essential aspect of dialectical logic we may state as the recognition that in all living systems there is a unity and conflict of opposites, which maintains inner balances, breaks them down, and finally drives the system to the point where breakdown or resolution on a higher level must occur.

Put like that, Marxism and its tasks sound clear enough; but we have only to glance at the working-out to see that, even where there has been general agreement on what constitutes Marxist method, there have often been wide divergences in conclusions as to the precise state of capitalist development and the tactics required. There is nothing magical then in dialectical principles, formally accepted, and their application to any social situation, even if in a general way the key-forces in conflict have been identified. This point is abundantly brought out by the fact that since 1917 no party dedicated to socialism has known how to build mass-bases and to spread effectively an understanding of what is at stake in a capitalist world torn by unresolved contradictions. Such a failure means an inadequate unity of theory and practice, an inability to work out an adequate theory which would at every point be linked with effectively transformatory action.

There are two main fields in which this transformatory action must work. First, the world of direct political factors in all their multiple forms, with all their varying levels—the State and the legal system, the

3

political groupings that range from national parties to small local organisations, trade unions and the many organisations of employers, bankers, and so on. Secondly there is the world of cultural activity that embraces all literary, artistic, musical expression and performance, the spheres of entertainment and of sport, the mass-media and the newspapers, a vast concert of pop-singers or a piano played in a pub, the National Theatre or a game mimed by children in a class-room. It also embraces scientific activity in all its multiple forms.

We need then to confront with our revolutionary unity of theory and practice a world of which we are a part, a world that is in many respects alien and hostile, a world that has many aspects in harmony with the revolutionary aim. Every system, every society, has its living unity as well as its inner conflicts and contradictions. The neglect of this obvious fact, with all stress being put on the conflicts, led Marxists to underestimate badly the, problems of transforming a society. Gramsci has given us the convenient term hegemony to define the multiple ways, political and cultural, by which a ruling class maintains its dominance. Hegemony includes both coercion, direct and indirect, and consensus, the ways in which people are brought to accept the system under which they live, and to adapt themselves to it. People in a given system may argue about this or that detail, seek certain reforms and so on, struggle for more wages and better conditions; but unless they squarely confront and question the system in all its essentials, they are securely held by the hegemonic controls.[1]

A party seeking revolutionary change, seeking the full resolution of the contradictions between socialised production and individual (or monopolistic) ownership, must attempt to affect the situation at all levels, to make men aware not only of the coercions, but also of the forms of consensus, composed of conscious and unconscious elements, that bind them to the system. Only along such lines can the hegemonic controls be broken or weakened. To wait merely for a moment of crisis when the contradictions more or less break down automatically the system is a counsel of despair; there is no proof that such a moment will come of its own accord and enable a revolutionary party to take over the power of the State. In Russia in 1917 what broke down was a semi-feudal State, and what broke it down was the impact of war, not the destructive effect of its own inner workings; Lenin did not seize power from a bourgeois State, or from a semi-feudal one. He stepped into the political vacuum which the war situation had brought about and which the Russian bourgeoisie were far too weak and embryonic to fill. In making this point one is not underestimating the brilliant tactics of Lenin, which made the swiftest and most effective

4

use of the given situation.

In China, though the situation was more complex and took longer to work out, in general the same point can be made. It was the Japanese invasion that broke down the Chinese State, such as it was, and made possible the ultimate success of Mao Tse Tung. Nowhere has a developed bourgeois State broken down through its inner contradictions; nowhere has power been seized from the bourgeoisie by a revolutionary proletariat. In the years immediately following the 1914-18 war, Germany was in a very demoralised condition, but sufficient State power survived the war, together with considerable bourgeois hegemony (both coercion and consensus), to obstruct and defeat the revolutionary forces, despite the successes in Russia. Yet throughout this period the leading Marxists, including Lenin, looked for a breakthrough in Germany and Central Europe. The lessons of the failure of the revolutionary forces were never in the least faced, analysed, understood. Now, with the development of nuclear fission and the incredible increase of destructive war-powers, any strategy that looks to a revolutionary breakthrough as the result of a war-situation is mere madness. (Only in backward colonial countries, with movements of national liberation, does the question of military struggle have any meaning.)

We must turn to Gramsci for the beginnings of an analysis that makes possible a successful struggle in advanced industrialised countries. The importance of his work is not lessened by the fact that there are confusions or inadequacies in the full theoretical working-out of his positions: the precise relations and demarcation of coercion and consensus, of the State and civil society (the one the core of coercion, the other the sphere of consensus). Further, the concentration on forms of hegemony must not lead us to the attitude that the whole struggle is one of breaking down the forms of consensus that bind people to a class society, as if it involved solely or primarily a strategy of a war of position. The struggle to gain more and more an effective position must be linked at all points with the strategy of a war of movement, of political attack aimed at transforming the State and its organs of coercion, its economic bases in monopoly-forms of industry, and so on. But when the worst is said, Gramsci has given us the clues to successful struggle in advanced industrial societies, with a socialist concept which is simultaneously present in immediate objectives and ultimate goals. The fusion of the two strategies necessarily involves a continuous extension or deepening of democratic liberties, since the socialist element in the positions gained through political onward movement must by its nature keep eliminating the coercive elements, thus preparing the way

5

for fully-realised socialist democracy and the withering-away of the State.

Where Marxism does not effectively develop, it will either stand still or draw in more and more distortions from its bourgeois environment. Theory, we must always remember, cannot develop in isolation; for Marxism there must always be a unity of theory and practice. Otherwise we find a tendency to idealism or mechanism, or to a mixture of the two.

To stand still is to become codified into a rigid set of rules that steadily lose whatever connection with the real world they once had. Except in a very general and ineffective way, Marxist dialectic in the socialist countries has become a sort of scholasticism, obstructing any movement of thought to grapple with the fundamental problems of development in our world, inside or outside socialism. A number of formal definitions (of capitalism, of socialism, and so on) continue to be used, but what they cover is purely pragmatic attempts to deal with the issues of our world, attempts that show varying degrees of intelligence but are not Marxist in method. This is not to say that elements of dialectical thinking do not survive in a relatively haphazard way, in creative literature and the arts, or in certain aspects of social relationships. Once the repressive controls were lifted, there would be a rapid rebirth of Marxist ideas and methods. We need not spend much time on this point, apart from noting that (after the admission of the appalling repressions and murders under Stalin) the failure of Marxist theory-practice reached its culmination in the 1968 invasion of Czechoslovakia. Here is a position that must be reversed before a revival of Marxism in the USSR is possible.

Our theme here is rather the ways in which Marxism has been side-tracked or distorted through the failure to make a correct evaluation of 1917 and the following years. First of all a rough and rapid glance at writings attempting to develop Marxism after Marx and Engels may be of some use. The impact of Marx on European thought was inevitably through *Capital*, through his transformation of political economy. His early philosophic manuscripts were not published till the 1930s. The essential positions there set out stayed with him to the end, but appeared in *Capital* only in limited ways, in the concepts of the fetishism and the alien nature of commodities. William Morris in the 1880s developed Marxist concepts of the creative nature of work and its role in communist society, in the achievement of human wholeness; but he had no effect on the tradition until recently. Marx and Engels were followed by several thinkers who tried to develop historical materialism: Labriola in Italy, Mehring and Kautsky in the Germanic area, Plekhanov, son of a landowner of Tambov. They sought mainly to systematise the work of Marx and Engels and to widen the study of art and religion; none of them was a political leader. Then with the expansion of capitalism and the growth of conflicts leading to the first world war we meet a number of thinkers more actively involved in politics: Lenin, Rosa Luxemburg, Hilferding, Trotsky, Bauer, Preobrazhensky, Bukharin, Marxist methods were applied in fields of analysis. Lenin made the first attempt to apply the general theory of *Capital* to an actual social formation, in his study of the Russian economy, 1899. In the same year Kautsky analysed the changes in American and European agriculture. Hilferding published his *Finance Capital* in 1910, dealing with the growing power of banks, monopolies, state machinery, trusts. Bauer published *The Nationalities Question* in 1907. Luxemburg and Bukharin tackled the question of Imperialism, followed by Lenin with his study in 1916. Meanwhile the year 1905 in Russia had produced works on political strategy like Trotsky's *Results and Prospects*, and Lenin worked out the first systematic construction of a political theory of class struggle, of the organisation of a socialist party. Then came the 1917 revolution, which stimulated works by Lenin, Trotsky, Bukharin and others. [2]

With the 1920s we enter a different phase. In Russia Marxism settled down into Stalinist orthodoxy, which was promulgated by the Communist International. The enemies were mainly Trotsky with his theory of permanent revolution, or the Revisionists who, one way or another, had given up the idea that revolution was round the corner and must be tackled along the lines of 1917. Stalinism was a definite ideology, a distortion of Marxism, which we shall discuss further in the next chapter. For the moment we shall glance at the new turns taken by Marxist theory at the hands of various intellectuals. The advent of the Russian revolution and the long turmoil in Central Europe that issued in Hitler's triumph had very much widened the interest of intellectuals in what was happening and liable to happen. In 1923 was set up at Frankfurt the Institute of Social Research to promote Marxist studies. It worked in the 1920s with the Marx-Engels Institute of Moscow, which in its early days was directed by Ryazanov. From it came Adorno, Marcuse, Horkheimer, and others.

A new kind of Marxist intellectual was being born. As well as the Frankfurt school there were other Germans such as Bloch, Korsch, or Benjamin; there was Lukacs the Hungarian, whose ideas were largely formed at Heidelberg. In Italy there were Gramsci and Della Volpe. In France, with its tradition of Anarcho-Syndicalism, Proudhonism, and so on, the first original Marxists in this period were scholars like Lefebvre, Cornu and Politzer. In England in the 1930s there were

Marxists such as Caudwell and George Thomson, concerned with the nature and history of culture; and there was growing up an important school of Marxist historiographers, which was to include Christopher Hill and Edward Thompson. With the advent of Hitler several of the Frankfurt School went to America but Adorno and Horkheimer returned to Germany after the war, though Marcuse stayed on in California. Now the vanguard thinkers were rather in France and Italy than in Germany: Della Volpe and Colletti, Sartre and Althusser. (Sartre, though an Existentialist, had his links with Marxism from the 1950s). The main section of this book will deal with the developments of what we may call intellectual Marxism since the 1920s, Marxism which, unable to shelve political issues and questions, has been largely concerned with problems of philosophy, art, knowledge, theory (often in a highly abstracted form). However many criticisms we may have to make of these developments, they have their positive side and in any event raise questions that urgently need to be tackled. The range and scope of Marxism is very much widened. Often the very way in which direct political issues are dodged or avoided leads into a fuller and more soundly based approach to those issues.

In the extent to which many of the thinkers to be considered have been driven to rather abstract analyses of what we may call the theory of theory, losing touch with the unity of theory-practice which lies at the root of Marxism, we see the effects of the dilemmas and blind alleys of so much of the directly political Marxism after 1917. With the Russian Revolution it seemed that a general overthrow of the bourgeoisie could not be far off; but the failure of any further revolutions to mature (apart from the Chinese) and the continual disproof of the theses that the end of capitalism was near, led to varying degrees of disillusion with what was being set out as orthodox Marxism (in effect Stalinism). German Fascism seemed the final organisation of capitalism in decay (as Palme Dutt's influential book on the subject set out in the late 1930s). But the defeat of Hitler brought about no real revolutions; and the consolidation of post-1945 capitalism under U.S. domination, with the vastly speeded-up growth of international monopoly-forms and State intrusion in industry and finance, has been seen as integrating the proletariat into the system rather than compacting them as a challenging counter-force (we shall discuss later how far this position can be defended). Thus we find Adorno and Marcuse driven into positions where they completely lose faith in any proletarian revolt, and Horkheimer indeed ending as a defender of capitalist competition. On the one hand what has seemed a complete failure of orthodox Marxism to show a revolutionary way forward has led to a retreat into extreme intellectualism, often expressed in an almost hermetic jargon, which seeks to find an uncontaminated doctrine by concentrating on theory, on what I have called the theory of theory. Althusser is the outstanding figure here. On the other hand the result has been a turn into what is at root a kind of anarchism, giving a new twist to Trotsky's theory of permanent revolution. It is felt that what is needed is somehow to set off the liberating explosion, which will then spread throughout society.

2 Man and Nature

But first there are some general points that need to be clarified, and we may begin with a few quotations that set out briefly what we may call axioms of historical materialism. Marx and Engels in *The German Ideology* state that the forces bringing about social change—and we might add, bringing society itself into existence and keeping it going—are 'real active men, as they are conditioned by a definite development of their productive forces and of their intercourse corresponding to these.' They form their ideas and aims 'on the basis of their real life-process.' Engels, in *Socialism, Utopian and Scientific*, remarks: 'The production of the means to support human life, and, next to production, the exchange of things produced . . . is the basis of every social order.' He goes on, 'In every society that has appeared in history, the distribution of the products and with it the division of society into classes, is determined by what is produced, and how it is produced and how the product is exchanged.'

Man is the sole animal that produces by the use of tools and machines. In that fact lies his essence, that which distinguishes him from all other animals and without which he would not be man—though we must add that the invention, use, and development of the tool is at every point linked with the creation and development of language.

Marx declares in *Capital*, 'Man opposes himself to nature as one of her own forces, setting in motion arms and legs, head and hands, the natural forces of his body, in order to appropriate nature's productions in a form adapted to his own wants. By thus acting on the external world and changing it, he at the same time changes his own nature. He develops his slumbering powers and compels them to act as in obedience to his will.'

We must never forget that all productive activity takes place inside the world of nature and is concerned with appropriating and trans-ferring nature one way or another. So, if we treat production as a thing in itself, we are in fact abstracting it and turning it into something that could not exist. Production is always the transformation of nature and involves man in an active relation with nature. Herein lies the creative aspect of humanity. In treating of economic activity we are in fact dealing with one side of an activity which in its totality involves a creative and transforming relation to nature: which simultaneously draws human beings more and more into the depths of nature and its systems, and sets them over and against nature. We may validly treat of the varying modes of production that make up human history as long as we never forget the relation to nature. But the moment we see economic activity as a thing in itself without this wider interrelation we falsify the whole situation.

The last sentence of the passage cited from Engels seems to assume that human history has always been that of classes. But the period in which class societies have existed is only a very small section of the time covered by human evolution. For the vastly longer period there were groups cooperating in the transformation of nature through the tool and the word. The tool and its accompanying forms of communication are what constitute the human essence. With the advent of class societies the situation grows ever more complex, but the human essence remains the same.

All forms of communication (that is, in the last resort, of culture) are thus linked with the productive sphere. Exactly how they are linked and how the connection operates is one of the crucial problems of Marxism; and of it many illuminating and many mechanistic things have been said. One of our main tasks here is to sort out and evaluate those comments.

One simple point that emerges from the fact that productive activity is always also a transformation of nature is the insistence that we cannot treat it apart from the level of technology reached; and that level in turn cannot be separated from the level of science. In turn, scientific theory and practice cannot be separated from the whole cultural life of society. There is no simple dividing line between the economic productive world and the other spheres of social and intellectual activity and expression. To attempt to limit the situation to an economic Base on which a social, political, cultural Superstructure is erected, is to oversimplify the situation hopelessly. It sets out in mechanistic terms a complex of movements that are always dialectically interrelated. It is valid however to assert, as we did above, that economic productive activity is central, is the main determinant of human history and development. We have yet to examine the ways in which the various factors interact and merge with one another; the endless series of mediating factors involved in the total movement of society. However, by keeping steadily before us the fact that productive activity is always a transformation of nature, we have taken the

12

first necessary step towards achieving a dialectical grasp of the human situation.

It follows that we must never abstract productive relations from the forces of production, must never seek to separate at any given moment the people interconnected in the process of production from the actual situation of work and all it involves, as if we could thereby grasp a significant structure explaining the whole mode of production. What then emerges is a dead pattern which explains nothing.

It may be objected that the terms *Base* and *Superstructure* were used by Marx and Engels, and constitute a generally accepted part of Marxism. But in fact the terms were used only casually, in a sort of rough shorthand, to underline the point that productive activity is the essential human activity, and were never worked out or applied in any coherent and extended way. Marx in the *Preface to The Critique of Political Economy* commented that the problem was to relate the economic structure of society to the 'the legal and political superstructure to which correspond definite forms of social consciousness.' The reason lay in the fact that: 'The mode of production in material life determines the general character of the social, political, and spiritual processes of life.' Engels expanded these ideas in a letter to Bloch in 1890:

According to the materialist conception of history the determining element [*Moment*] in history is *ultimately* the production and reproduction in real life. More than this neither Marx nor I have ever asserted. If therefore somebody twists this into the statement that the economic element is the only determining one, he transforms it into a meaningless, abstract and absurd phrase. The economic situation is the basis, but the various elements of the superstructure—political forms of the class struggle and its consequences, constitutions established by the victorious class after a successful battle, etc.—forms of law—and then even the reflexes of all these actual struggles in the brains of the combatants: political, legal, philosophical theories, religious ideas and their further development into systems of dogma—also exercise their influence upon the course of the historical struggles and in many cases preponderate in determining their *form*. There is an interaction of all these elements, in which, amid all the endless *host* of accidents (i.e., of things and events whose inner connection is so remote or so impossible to prove that we regard it as absent and can neglect it), the economic movement finally asserts itself as necessary. Otherwise the application of the theory to any period of history one chose would be easier than the solution of a simple equation of the first degree.

From the very rare and occasional use of the terms it is ridiculous to make Marx or Engels responsible for a theory of Base and Superstructure. Timpanaro correctly notes the confusions brought about by the fact that Marx starts off with ideas of law and religion mainly in his mind, constructions eminently devoid of objective validity and profuse in universalist pretensions. Marx was seeking to de-mystify those pretensions; but when his terms are transferred to the realms of science, art, and so on, they are liable to make them seem mere subjective projections of socio-economic realities. In fact he was clearly thinking of the relation of the socio-economic Base and the State: in which connection the image of a Superstructure is not so adequate. But once we try to construct a Superstructure in which all culture is embedded, the image becomes ridiculously inadequate and distorts the whole problem. [1]

Plekhanov, pioneer in the attempt to work out a Marxist theory of culture, never has recourse to the terms. Nor does Lenin. The person who made them important elements in his version of Marxism was Stalin. He puts his position most clearly in his discussion of language. There he defines the Superstructure as having a sphere of action that is 'narrow and restricted,' since it is not directly connected with productive activity. It is indirectly connected 'through the economy, through the base.' It reflects changes in the development of the productive forces, not immediately and directly, 'but only after changes in the base, through the prism of changes wrought in the base by the changes in production.' While the base is 'the economic structure of society at a given stage of development,' the superstructure consists of 'the political, legal, religious, artistic, and philosophical views of society and the political, legal and other institutions corresponding to them.' (Science is not mentioned; it presumably does belong to the superstructure.) Stalin continues:

The superstructure is a product of the base; but this does not mean that it merely reflects the base, that it is passive, neutral, indifferent to the fate of its base, to the fate of the classes, to the character of the system. On the contrary, no sooner does it arise than it becomes an exceedingly active force, actively assisting its base to take shape and consolidate itself, and doing everything it can to help the new system finish off and eliminate the old base and the old classes. It cannot be otherwise. The base creates the superstructure precisely in order that it may serve it, that it may actively help it to take shape and consolidate itself, that it may actively strive for the elimination of the old moribund base and its old superstructure.

That is, he stresses that the superstructure is not passive or neutral in order to put it ever more securely at the service of the economic base. He sets out here the theory underlying his ruthless subordination of all elements of culture to the socialist base as he understood it. The theses on culture by Zhdanov were the direct expression of his position as here stated. It followed that Marxism, historical science, 'can become as precise a science as, let us say, biology.' With a socialist base, it was

14

assumed, the direct relation of politics, the State and culture became clear, precise, visible, lacking all the old mystifications. On *a priori* grounds Stalinism felt itself capable of telling empirical scientists what they ought to discover; there was no room for dissent. Under both socialism and capitalism 'the laws of social development are objective ones, operating independently of the consciousness and will of human beings.' The only difference was that under socialism 'the party, the state, and society as a whole have the opportunity, unknown in past history, of comprehending those laws, consciously applying them in their activities,' and thus 'accelerating the course of societal development.' Freedom was simply the recognition of Necessity.

Stalin's use of dialectical formulas was arbitrary, twisted any way that suited his political policy. Thus in his speech to the 16th Congress on the State he made a quite false and irresponsible use of the unity-of-opposites formula. He was defending the thesis that the way forward to Communism was via the strengthening of the State:

It may be objected that such a way of stating the question is 'contradictory.' But do we not meet with similar contradictions in the question of the State? We are for the withering away of the State. And yet we also believe in the proletarian dictatorship, which represents the strongest and mightiest form of State power that has existed up to now. To keep on developing State power in order to prepare the conditions *for* the withering away of State power—that is the Marxist formula.

Certainly it is contradictory, but in no sense an example of Marxist dialectics, of the mutual penetration of opposites. It is merely an abstract formula used to evade criticism of the repressive State apparatus being built up. A true statement might have been: We want to wither away the State as quickly as possible, but in a situation of imperialist encirclement there are special problems—however at every phase we will test out the situation to see how far we can develop the taking-over of State-functions by the ordinary citizens, and so on. But to make some such formulation would have been to stir a critical spirit among the people, who would have pressed for the implementation of socialist democracy as far as possible. We see how the term Dictatorship of the Proletariat was used to muffle the problem, to cast an illusion of socialist functioning over the procedures of the repressive bureaucracy. Stalinism thus appears as a definite ideology or distortion of Marxism. (In many of the formulations of the 1930s, such as those of Vyshinsky, the period of the Dictatorship, before the withering-away began, assumed the dimensions of a geological epoch.)

Before we pass on, it is of interest to note that it was Stalin's account of Language that gave Althusser the first basis of his structuralist positions. Accepting the base-superstructure system, he was deeply affected by the isolation of science from the rest of the cultural field:

Paradoxically, it was no other than Stalin, whose contagious and implacable system of government and thought had induced this delirium, who reduced the madness to a little more reason. Reading between the lines of the few simple pages in which he reproached the zeal of those who were making strenuous efforts to prove language a superstructure, we could see that there were limits to the use of the class criterion, and that we had been made to treat science, a status claimed by every page of Marx, as merely the first-comer among ideologies. We had to retreat, and, in semi-disarray, return to first principles.

As we shall see later, Althusser was thus led to an abstraction, a fetishism, of science, not to an attempt to find a fuller and truer relation of science to human process. [2]

An important role in producing confusion and in preventing an effective grappling with the problems of politics and culture is played by the dual use made of the term 'economic.' On the one hand the economic sphere is the broad and dynamic one of productive activity in the sense described here earlier; on the other hand it is seen as limited to the economic relations in a given system. To use the old terms for a moment, if the superstructure is affected by the base, so is the base by the superstructure. If we are dealing with, say, capitalism in its fullness, we cannot treat the economic productive relations apart from the complex cultural and social consequences flowing from the extending and deepening relationship to nature which is involved in the action of the productive forces. But from the angle of political economy we can ignore the living fullness of the situation and deal only with the class relationships, the relations between capitalists and workers, that are involved. (To make this abstraction is not wrong as long as we realise what we are doing. Where it becomes false is when we are attempting to assess the total situation in all its dialectical interconnections.*)

---

* True, the passage from the windmill to the steam-mill does not explain the transition from feudalism to capitalism; but class-struggle in the windmill epoch is very different in its forms and results from class-struggle in that of the steam-mill. If we are considering the totality of the situation we must relate the windmill to the relevant class-struggle; if we are concentrating on the class-struggle we then agree: 'If the productive forces possess a materiality of their own that one cannot ignore, they are organised however always under given productive relations (which does not exclude contradictions between them, nor their unequal development in the bosom of a process that is the effect of this primacy)' Poulantzas. (3)

16

Putting aside then for the moment the static terms Base and Superstructure, we can see economic productive work as the central human activity, to which all the others are related, and can speak of it as in the last resort the determinant factor in human development, yet can avoid seeing it as a sort of machine that controls the other parts. We still have a large number of difficult problems to solve, but we are dealing with a comprehensible system of relationships. While accepting this position, we are not setting economic activity as a thing apart, opposed in any simple way to other human activities, with recourse to some such phrase as 'relative autonomy' to explain the distance from it of the other activities in their origin and functioning.

We may glance at that phrase, 'relative autonomy,' which is much used in order to shelve the problem, for it explains nothing unless we know how a system is autonomous and how it is dependent. When used of spheres of culture it does little more than state that the spheres do not merely reflect directly and passively the situation on the economic levels. There is a certain sense in saying that a legal system enjoys a relative autonomy from the State, as well as being tied in closely to it. But in what sense is the art of Turner relatively autonomous from the socio-economic situation of the years 1775-1850? It has indeed its own freedom of expression as well as its relation to the world in which Turner grew up and developed, its relation to previous art and to the art of its epoch. But the term 'relatively autonomous' does little or nothing to illuminate what the freedom and the connection were, or how they functioned in complex union-and-conflict, involving both the problems of the relation of art and society in general, and the particular set of definitions that make up Turner's art in all its creative originality. The existence of the industrial system has important effects on the art, and inside it, but in no sense is the art 'isomorphic' with the economic situation.

I suggest then that even if we keep the term Base in certain connections for the economic system, we also use the term Mode of Production for the merged relations and forces of production. The term Productive Activity can then be used to define the Mode in its fuller series of relations that involve the transformation of nature and so of humanity itself. Productive Activity extends its scope to take in also all cultural activities, all forms of expression. We can add the term 'economic' when we wish to limit productive activity to the economic sphere.

There is no simple line, then, dividing culture and the mode of production. They are both in different ways included in the concept of Productive Activity. And culture involves not only the arts and sciences, all the forms of self-expression and of knowledge, it is fused in turn with personal life in all its aspects, with the family, and so on. These formulations indeed still leave the various aspects of productivity activity too undifferentiated. But at every moment of analysis we must be ready to find points of linkage and differentiation. We can begin by taking the particular form and content of each section of self-expression, and then the point where they break down in terms of a fuller organic unity. Each man's aesthetic experience, which involves his sensuous being, in turn fuses (for example) with his struggle for knowledge, for the understanding of his place in society and in nature. All these come together to create his identity, his unity as a person and as a member of society.

In the last resort there are no dividing lines. The mode of production in its earliest phases involved tools and forms of communication, science in embryonic forms, and speech in the co-operation of labour; and play, carrying over rhythmic elements from work and nature, developed into ritual, song, art. The productive mode we may call the central and fundamental aspect of the complex of human activities. For there it is that the process of transforming nature begets the basis which human nature needs for its survival and development, and without which the other forms of activity could not emerge and carry on. The level reached by the productive mode, its forms and inner conflicts, are thus crucial for those other forms, though not in any simple and mechanistic way. The relation between one form and another, and the movement inside each of the forms, will be dialectical. The mode of production may be termed the determinant or dominant element in the whole, as long as we clear our minds of all mechanist concepts in the relationship and think in the terms of productive activity which I have sketched.

It is worth noting the German term used by Engels when he wrote of 'the production and reproduction in real life' as the determinant: *Moment*. This lays more emphasis on the dynamic and dialectical nature of the relationship than does the English *element*, which suggests something materially preponderant.[3]

As we saw, the term Superstructure came to Marx's mind when he was thinking of the State and its variously connected institutions, where indeed we may trace a strong relationship to the mode of production and its internal relations. But even here there is no simple reflection, for in all living systems we must look for the law of uneven growth. The State will not automatically reflect the productive relations; it will have its own inertia, its own traditions and hangovers from previous stages. The modern state expresses the needs and powers of the bourgeoisie; but if one can imagine the bourgeoisie in the eighteenth century being able to distance themselves from the actual historical situation and devise abstractly the sort of state system that best expressed their needs, they would certainly have worked out something very different from the national State that emerged from the complex conflicts of history. There are inherited elements going back to feudal and indeed to tribal days; elements that can be used by socialists in their struggle to move beyond the bourgeois State. Yet at any given moment, we may agree that

Productive relations and the relationships that compose them (economic property/ownership) are translated under the form of class *powers*; these powers are organically articulated with the political and ideological relationships that consecrate and legitimise them. Those relationships are not simply added to productive relations already there, do not simply act upon them by a return action in a relation of primary exteriority or in a rhythm of chronological *a priori*. They are themselves present, in a form specific to each mode of production, in the constitution of the productive relations.

(POULANTZAS)

But the State did not exist in pre-class societies, though production, art, and science (in primitive forms) did exist. The State will not exist under communism, though production, art, and science will. We cannot then treat the State in the same way as those other factors. It exists only in a specific period of history (a relatively brief period); it is built up only upon the basis of a class-system in which exploitations and subjections exist as a pervasive characteristic. So it would be defensible to use a specific term for it. I suggest then that we keep the term *Superstructure* for the State and its linked institutions, e.g. those of the law. Such a use does not arouse the resistances or raise the problems that must come up when we talk of a poem as a superstructure of the economic base.

The connection between the State and the mode of production, complex as it can become, is relatively simple beside the relation of the mode and the very wide field of culture: technology, the sciences, the arts, philosophy, literature, and so on. In these as in economic production human beings are transforming nature, transforming themselves. As in economic activity, they produce objects, though not for the same kind of consumption. In both kinds of activities there is a process of objectification involved. Human beings confront the world outside themselves, confront otherness, and make it, one way or another, part of themselves. There is thus no easy dividing line between economic and cultural production. One cannot exist without the other, and yet we see in economic activity a primacy, a centrally organising point, which in the last resort holds human life together, gives it meaning, and provides the basis of development. For this reason we need a distinguishing term for economic activity: the Mode of Production, which unites the relations and the forces of economic production. But we need to see that the activities of culture are also productive activities, involving in their turn a complex of social relations and material forces.

In speaking of man transforming nature in culture and in economic production we may be easily misunderstood and the position oversimplified. The confrontation is not a simple one, for behind every productive act in our world, economic or cultural, there lies a vast past in which human beings have been carrying on the work of transforming the world and themselves. The nature that we confront involves both these past transformations and the immediate acts of objectification that we are seeking to carry out; part of the nature that we are seeking to transform is our own biological inheritance. The problem is highly complicated, but none the less real. Timpanaro has raised the issue ; and though some of his answers are too simple, the question remains.

There are cultural responses to and within biological conditions, and what needs to be estimated, in each case, is the nature of the mix. The deepest significance of a relatively unchanging biological human condition is probably to be found in some of the basic material processes of the making of art: in the significance of rhythms in music and dance and language, or of the shapes and colours in sculpture and painting. Because art is always *made*, there can of course be no reduction of works of this kind to biological conditions. But equally, where these fundamental physical conditions and processes are in question, there can be no reduction either to simple social and historical circumstances. (RAYMOND WILLIAMS)[4]

However, the human transformation of nature is not limited to matters where there is a relatively unchanging biological condition. All our most characteristic activities involve such transformations. Science must keep on deepening and extending its knowledge of the systems of nature and the results affect our attitudes and responses in a myriad ways. Through technology they enter the forces of production, and the sphere of economic activity becomes a reconstruction, on a different level, of the world of natural forces and systems. Society and nature merge in the material of art, in the whole attempt to recreate our sensuous being. And so on. At the same time the social contradictions and conflicts, which pervade the structures of the mode of production, reappear in all the various forms of culture, setting up tensions there and needing their own specific forms of resolution.

In a wider context we must recognise that the basic human need of food which underlies production is biological. Production comes about through an appropriation of nature by biologically-determined agents, even if that nature is ceaselessly transformed by their activities which always appear in a specific form since they occur only in specific historical and social contexts.

It is not that natural determinants gradually disappear and become submerged in social determinants, but that these natural determinants can never be explained wholly in terms of physical and biological properties for they are always materialised as particular cultural products. For example, human beings are naturally determined in various ways by virtue of a common biological structure: they are endowed with certain somatic instincts, a certain physiognomy, a certain level of physical strength, a certain sex and therefore a certain role in reproduction and so on. But it is how these instincts are satisfied, the value conferred on particular physical attributes, the ways in which physical strength is harnessed, the forms in which sexual division is lived and experienced, that are central to any understanding of the concrete effects of these determinations: it is these social features that in a real and important sense render the natural a cultural product. This, however, does not mean that their explanation can be given wholly in terms of social relations. (KATE SOPER)[5]

We must reject then the attempts by a Marxist such as L. Sève to dissolve all facts of existence into an undifferentiated mass of social relations, which are then assimilated to work-relations. On the other hand Timpanaro while raising many real problems, seems to assume that our history is given a materialist explanation by a simple recognition of general biological determinations abstracted from their particular effects at different stages of historical and social process.

We shall have more to say of art later, but here we can cite two ways of failing to tackle the theme. Romano Luperini recently stated:

The study of a work of art should be a cognitive activity, which moving from a viewpoint estranged both in relation to the work and the tradition or system in which the work is set, decomposes the object in its various components, and places it face to face with the real (socio-economic) base from which it is born.

But a simple cognitive study is one that ignores most of the components and cannot possibly do anything about them; by its nature it omits the emotional element and the sensuous definition, and the omission is not made any better by calling it a decomposition. The work is stripped of everything but those aspects that directly correspond to the socio-economic base or productive mode of the moment of its creation. What is then left is not the work of art, but certain aspects of the base with which it can be linked. The work of art, with all its specific elements, is considered irrelevant. Luperini sums up that the social sciences, as well as literature and all manifestations of the superstructure, are eminently historical and have no autonomy from the socio-economic base (or structure in the

21

Marxist sense), the modes of production, the laws of the market, which condition their methods and their very genesis. We may agree that the social sciences and literature are indeed historical, but their relation to the base is dialectical and cannot be demonstrated by any reductive method which merely ends by revealing once again the base and discarding all that differentiates the cultural expressions.

We are little better situated to tackle the problem if we accept the solution offered by Lucien Goldmann, who uses the terms *homology* and *isomorphism* to define the relation between cultural and economic phenomena. He thus hopes to demonstrate structural parallelisms between, say, a tragedy by Racine and the religious ideology of Port Royal, between the form of the nineteenth-century novel and the structure of the market system. In such an analysis some interesting and even important interconnections may be brought out, but in the last resort there is only a mechanistic comparison of different structural levels. The essential differences of art and ideology, art and economics, is not touched. The system is again essentially reductive.

The *Communist Manifesto* noted certain forms of consciousness common to the successive societies so far developed, since all were class-divided (the problem of pre-class societies was ignored). Guido Voghera tried to work out in Marxist terms the idea that certain moral principles were inherent in any society and were thus superstructures of 'sociality in general.' But though any society must have an organising system of ideas and attitudes, it would be rash to attempt to define any clear and constant moral principles common to all societies. The one sure constant is the active relation to nature expressed by the tool, which in turn involves communal or social relations. We may add that though languages vary endlessly in their systems and sounds, there is a common element in that one group, with sufficient knowledge, can understand and make sense of the language of any other group. There may be (as Chomsky says) a development of common physiological forms among human beings (as active agents in nature) which help towards the formation and utterance of languages[6]. But what is crucial is the shared attitude to nature, with consequent effects inside the group (varied as those effects may be), which results in a general intelligibility of languages, an ultimately common structure. Communication by means of language involves the growth of a collective spirit, which is derived in the last resort from shared labour. This collective element (with tool and language) is distinctively human and has persisted at all phases, from the earliest times on through more complex groupings and finally class-societies. It is shared by all persons in all societies and thus represents a human constant.

The first premise of all human history is, of course, the existence of living human individuals. Thus the first fact to be established is the physical organisation of these individuals and their consequent relation to the rest of nature . . . [Human beings] begin to distinguish themselves from animals as soon as they begin to produce their means of subsistence, a step which is conditioned by their physical organisation. Marx (*The German Ideology*).

Marx set out these positions with great power and clarity already in the 1844 Manuscripts. Because he had not yet fully matured his views, many critics have tried to brush the Manuscripts aside as still largely Hegelian or Feuerbachian. His diction indeed still shows strong signs of the early influences of Hegel and Feuerbach, but he has already made the definite break into his distinctive positions, though in a rather generalised and at times oversimplifed way. He has not yet historically applied and worked out his definitions; when he does so, they are modified and made precise. But the key point is that, while using such terms as species-life, which suggest Feuerbach, he has moved decisively past vague, rationalistic concepts of what constitutes humanity to the realisation that the labour-process is the essential thing:

Animals construct only in accordance with the standards and needs of the species to which they belong, while man knows how to produce in accordance with the standards of every species and knows how to apply the appropriate standards to the object. Thus man constructs also in accordance with the laws of beauty.

Through labour man can make nature 'his inorganic body, both as a direct means of life and as the matter, the object, and the instrument of his life-activity.' The orientation of Marx's thinking is turned decisively away from Hegel and Feuerbach in the direction of the *Grundrisse* and *Capital*. Indeed the fundamental concepts of the Manuscripts are so deeply imbedded in his mind that he takes them for granted and writes at times in an expansive way, using terms that could be interpreted as meaning that somehow humanity's active relation to the universe was a predestined aspect of things. In the *Grundrisse* the earth is described as the 'laboratory', the 'primitive instrument', and the 'primitive condition of production', and in *Capital* as 'the original larder' and 'the original tool house'. But he writes in such terms only because the ideas of the Manuscripts so completely fill the background of his mind that he does not feel the need to explain their full bearing and interrelation.[7]

In the *Grundrisse* too he takes up and develops the notion of nature as the inorganic body of man:

What M. Proudhon calls the *extra-economic* origin of property . . . is the pre-bourgeois relation of the individual to the objective conditions of labour, and first of all the natural objective conditions of labour, because as the working Subject is a natural individual, having a natural existence, the first objective condition appears as nature, i.e. as earth, his inorganic body. The individual himself is not only the organic body of nature, but also *this inorganic nature as a Subject.*

What Marx is saying is that under slavery and serious serfdom people still feel an organic part of nature, so that their conditions and forms of work seem part of a natural order. With capitalism and the sale of labour-power like any other commodity there is a sharp break. People feel separated out from nature; but instead of feeling an enhanced creativity they are more than ever subjected to powers they cannot control. Now they are victims, not of a lord's rule, but of the universal power of the cash nexus. Their own creative energies are alienated and enclosed in the objects they produce.

We see how more complex the ideas of the Manuscripts become as they are related to historical moments of development; but the ideas themselves still derive from the Manuscripts:

The slave stands in absolutely no relation to the objective conditions of his labour; it is rather the *labour* itself, in the form of the slave as of the serf, which is placed in the category of *inorganic condition* of production alongside the other natural beings, e.g. cattle, or regarded as an appendage of the earth . . . These *natural conditions of existence*, to which he is related as if they were his own inorganic body, are of a twofold, that is to say of a subjective and an objective nature. He finds he is a member of a family, a clan, a tribe, etc . . . and as such a member he is related to a definite area of nature . . . as his own inorganic existence, as the condition for his own production and reproduction.[8]

These generalisations, however, need to be further analysed and developed. From the outset people as producers feel separated out from nature as well as merged in it. Alienation arises to some degree, expressed directly in the notion of an External Soul or Otherself, which has been cut off, lost. But human powers are still so small in comparison with the vast forces of nature that people do not dare to confront directly the facts of the situation. They emotionally reunite themselves with nature through myth, ritual, art, in which the primal division is explained away and made the basis of a new harmonious or organic system of integrations. Nature is reunited with society; society becomes a form of nature. Despite increasing stresses this situation in general holds till the advent of class society, when religion proper takes over, expressing both the pang of alienation from nature and the inner division of society, and at the same time justifying the situation, making it again natural, a necessary part of the universe which it reflects.

The inner conflict, the class-struggle (in the forms which it takes in early class-societies), indeed invades the religious sphere in various ways, especially at times of social crisis, and modifies the ideological system. But the generalisation we have made remains essentially true till the advent of capitalism, when in early days the struggle is still largely waged in religious terms. Christianity is a special case, testifying to the acute social struggles of the epoch when it was born. Here the sense of social alienation grows so acute that people feel cut off from nature, opposed to it as evil. The problem of the church, as it matured in the third and fourth centuries A.D., was to preserve the basic ideology, use it to drive people ever more deeply into subjection by projecting the sphere of union into another world, and to build a bridge between itself and the power-world. Hence the intense contradictions in the Christian idiom, which made it usable by rebels in times of crisis.

With the full advent of capitalism there was a vast extension of alienation, which indeed now operated on a qualitatively new level. The State and its ideological apparatus had to find ways of doing the work that had been mainly done by religion in the past. The old ideas of a natural (or supernatural) order of things which embraced the whole of society and determined its productive relations were now gone. People were alienated from themselves (their creative powers), their fellows who were in the same situation, and from nature, to which they were opposed as producers. The positive side of the situation lay in the fact that the old ideological systems which imposed a false unity on a divided society had fallen away, and the full reality could be realised and stated; and in the fact that thus people might struggle for a society in which unity was truly concrete. The driving-force that made the struggle for the truth and for genuine unity possible lay in the inner contradictions of the system, which prevented the ideological mystification from lying heavily and organically over the lives of people as the old systems had done. We grasp what Marx meant when he analysed how the previous class-systems had managed to preserve the idea of their society as part of the natural order, and how the particular form of exploitation appeared as a part of that order. In the *Grundrisse* he goes on to say that bourgeois society brings about the '*division* between these inorganic conditions of human existence and this active relation itself, a division first posited in its completeness in the relation between wage-labour and capital.' People enter for the first time into a real 'relationship' with production. The capitalist does not directly appropriate the worker, as if he were a natural thing, but does it through the medium of exchange, as the bearer of abstract labour. The worker becomes a 'purely subjective power of labour', which finds its negation 'as a value existing for itself' in the alienated and objective preconditions of labour.

Incidentally we may note that in *Capital* Marx refers to use-values as a constant in all human societies: 'a necessary condition, independent of forms of society, for the existence of man; an eternal natural necessity, which mediates the metabolism between man and nature, and hence makes possible human life in general.' Again, in his important comments on the purposiveness of labour, he treats labour as a similar constant.

There are two misconceptions developed from these positions of Marx. First, that to speak of human beings achieving and carrying on at all phases a purposive labour-process implies a teleological system : that each stage of the consequent developments was already fated and that the stage we have now reached was inevitable after the first purposive labour-acts were carried out. Secondly, that the separation-out of man from nature implied by the active relationship meant that humanity by its essential drive had embarked on a Conquest of Nature. But Marxism is not teleological and has no triumphalist concept of mankind's destiny in the universe. What it sees as emerging at each step of human development is not some fated next stage, but definite possibilities inherent in the positions already achieved. Failure as well as success is always possible, and in early days there must have been many groups who were unable to cope with their situation. At the present moment the contradictions of bourgeois society and the enormous powers of destruction concentrated in nuclear fission make our future more than ever uncertain. Further, though the human achievement in grasping the natural forces at work in our universe is indeed remarkable, there are obvious limits hedging us all round and all sorts of further forces quite outside any possible control. (The whole concept of an attack on nature, a mastery of nature, and so on, is bourgeois in origin; the communist aim is successful adaptation on a world scale, with human beings harmoniously involved with nature.)

There is yet another distortion of Marxism which is allied to those just set out. This is the theoretical system of what has been called the Praxis school.[9] Here the creative elements of human achievement, their important aspects of potentiality, are abstracted as existing without the limits and modifications imposed on people at each moment of history. As George Petrovic, editor of the Yugoslav periodical *Praxis*, has put it: 'Man is society, freedom, history, and the future.' Or, in the words of an English exponent:

The *reciprocal* action of all aspects of human activity reveals man as producing the conditions that produce him. Human ideas modify, through praxis, the very existential substratum of ideas themselves: history is the unfolding of man shaping his world. (J. COULTER)

All true enough, if seen within the full perspective of the factors involved. But, taken as the whole and simple truth, such views are an idealist abstraction of one aspect of human process. This abstraction, which quite ignores the complexity of history, substitutes the ideas which can only be realised at the end of a long transforming struggle for the immediate principles and methods of the struggle itself. It thus becomes a justification for theories of spontaneous revolt, since 'through praxis, thought is reunited with being, consciousness with sensuous or physical nature, the mind with spontaneity' (LEFEBVRE).[10]

We have here a sort of ultra-left parody of the Marxist concept of the unity of theory and practice. In the latter indeed the old kind of pragmatic test of theory by seeing how adequately it works in some experiment is supplanted by a new dynamic and dialectical relation, in which theory emerges from action and is at the same time expressed and tested in action. But such a testing can only come about if there is an adequate dialectical understanding at work in the thought and in the action it inspires, the action that in turn awakens a new sense of the unity of process. The praxis-position is that once this unity of theory and action begins there is no further problem; the revolution can explode. For praxis, man is already creatively united with the world in which he lives; all dialectical contradictions or oppositions disappear in its theory.

There is one further aspect of man's relations with nature that we need to glance at here: the ecological relation and the question of the pressure of population. Such factors can exercise a decisive influence on economic and social development. Thus the American Indians invented the wheel (certainly as a toy, perhaps for making pottery), but they made practically no use of it. There were no animals suited for hauling heavy loads. Llamas and alpacas were no use; and bison, hard enough to tame in any event, lived far away from the areas where the first stages of farming and State-formation occurred. So America was left far behind the Old World in all lifting, hauling, milling and manufacturing processes in which pulleys, gears, cogs, and screws played an essential role. Or to take another example, in Mesoamerica the hunter-collectors, like their near contemporaries in the Middle East, used to gather grains: in their case, the seeds of amaranth and maize. But the domestication of animals in Tehuacan did not keep pace with an agricultural use of these plants for the reason that all domesticable herd-animals had become locally extinct through climatic changes and overkill. If the people wanted meat they had to

27

move about widely in response to the seasonal habits of their prey (woodland deer, rabbits, turtles, and various small animals and birds). They had no stimulus to carry out the hard work done by the Near-Eastern seed-gatherers in constructing houses, roasting pits, and storage facilities. So they did not arrive at full village life till long after they had taken to growing many species of plants; they waited till they had badly depleted the stocks of the smaller animals that could be hunted. Decisive for the differing developments in America and the Middle East was the fact that the former lacked wheat, barley, peas, and lentils in a wild state as well as the precursors of domesticated sheep, goats, pigs and cattle. [11]

It is necessary to give these few examples since Marxists have been reluctant to look outside society for the explanations of the ways in which different peoples developed. True, we must always look inside society, at the mode of production and its inner relations, to grasp the economic structure; and we must concern ourselves with that structure in its changes if we are to understand human history and its movements. But the ecological conditions, especially in earlier periods (though not only then), can hold back or drive forward those movements, can provide a dynamic force without which the inner changes of society cannot be fully understood.

The same point can be made about the pressure of population. Men did not turn from hunting and food-gathering to agriculture for some abstract reason of choice. It has been shown that the life of hunters was in general much easier than those of the peasants, and the former often knew all about grains before they felt impelled to cultivate the plants that provided them. But the system of the hunters could continue to prosper only if the population was strictly limited. Various methods of curbing population-growth were used, including infanticide, but in the end population-pressure drove men to agriculture, in which they had to work much harder, but could (again within limits) feed a growing population. On through history a detailed analysis shows an important role played by population-pressure in driving societies forward, in forcing people to develop their internal social structures. We can only grasp the problems facing the world today if we relate depleted energy resources to the pressures of population. Thus,

If the rest of the world were suddenly to adopt the energy ratios characteristic of US agriculture, all known reserves of petroleum would be exhausted in eleven years. Or, to put it in a slightly different form: the faster the under developed world industrialises, the sooner the industrial world must develop a new mode of production. (M. HARRIS)

Even if there are more petrol and other resources than that estimate suggests, the problem is still inescapably there, a problem that cannot be overcome by the capitalist mode of production. We need a system in which the new forces of production are linked with new productive relations.

We have now glanced at the problems encountered by Marxism after 1917, in particular the problem of what it is that shapes people (culture in its full far-reaching complexity). We have also considered the relation of humanity to nature, a relation that has been neglected by Marxists, but which is of great importance if we are to realise what productive activity is in its full character. Now we will consider the contributions made to such themes by a number of post-1917 thinkers.

3   Georg Lukacs and The New Start

The great importance of Lukacs' *History and Class-Consciousness* lay
in the fact that it was the first irruption into the post-1917 situation of
a complex philosophic work which crashed through the positions that
had dominated in Marxist thinking and raised a whole set of new
problems. It cut through the dilemmas that had been afflicting the
theoreticians of the Second International, both the evolutionists and
the neo-Kantians, who assumed that Marx's theory was solely a
statement of inevitable historical laws and thus lacked any moral
content. The neo-Kantians argued that the necessary normative
factors or ideals must be important from Kant. Lukacs pointed out
that they accepted the Kantian dualism of what-is and what-ought-to-
be, which had been overcome by Hegel and Marx. Marxism was the
expression and self-knowledge of a social process that changed the
world. The subject (the proletariat) simultaneously comprehended
and transformed reality. Subject and object, freedom and necessity,
actuality and the norm were, then, aspects of a single reality. Such
propositions also ended the conflict between voluntarism and
determinism, the idea that the revolution resulted from human will or
from the objective forces of history.

Lukacs had been one of the group whom he later described as
holding to a romantic anti-capitalism, but his viewpoint had been
tragic, seeing no possible resolution of the worsening human
condition. With 1917 he moved into politics, and in 1919 was
Commissar for Education in the short-lived Hungarian Soviet
Republic. He felt himself at home in the leftist tendencies among
German communists, such as the *Kommunismus* group, which called
for 'partial insurrections' to offset and overcome 'the ideological
crisis and Menshevik lethargy of the proletariat and the halting of
revolutionary development.' In 1967 he called *Kommunismus* the
mouthpiece of 'a messianic sectarianism', and said that at the time he
favoured 'a total break with every institution and mode of life
stemming from the bourgeois world.' The essays composing his book
were written between 1919 and 1922, while the book itself appeared in

31

1923. Inevitably much of its force comes from the way it reveals a severely self-contained system in which a few formulas of dialectical logic are set to work with inexorable consistency. The result can be called at one level historicist: that is, it sees history as a force sufficient in itself, moving towards predetermined goals. [1]

And yet such a description fails badly to do justice to the powerful many-sided effect of the work as a whole. In its two major concepts both the strengths and the weaknesses come together inextricably. First there is the vision of history in the capitalist epoch as leading to the dehumanisation or reification of the proletariat, on whom the direct crushing burden of the system weighs and who are yet thus in the position to achieve consciousness of what is happening—what the human condition has become—and to make a total revolt lifting humanity on to a decisively new level of harmonious integration. Secondly, there is in consequence a pervasive realisation of what capitalism does to people in treating them more and more as things, with the result of all relationships being reduced to those of commodity production and exchange. The passion and depth with which these ideas are grasped and expounded is what gives the book its originality and force. They make it a stimulating and inspiring work in a period of much confusion, when Marxism seemed reduced almost wholly to the level of pragmatic politics and tactical considerations. But the very strength of the realisation of the key ideas involves oversimplifications which confuse as well as liberate.

Lukacs takes over Marx's idea that the dominant ideology in any class-society is that of the ruling-class, and applies it with the rigour derived from his notion of the proletariat. That is, he interprets it to mean that the whole of society is permeated and saturated by 'the ideological essence of a pure class-subject, which in turn is depicted as a pure reflection of the conditions of life and world-conditions of that class' (MCDONOUGH). However, the proletariat, because of its role and position, can achieve an ascribed or possible (*zugerechnet*) class-consciousness. This consciousness is objectively true, Marxist, revolutionary; it is objectively possible as the rational expression of the class's historical interests—the product of the historical development of the class, of its necessary activities and attitudes.

For Lukacs, in capitalism ideology can only be the direct emanation or manifestation of the exchange-system, of the way in which commodity-production tends to reduce all relations to relations between things. *Reification* (reduction to things) is the term he uses for this deadly dehumanisation and distortion of reality which is entirely determined by the economy in its workings. It is a direct ubiquitous reflection of those workings. But if this is so, we cannot even begin to show how ideology is transmitted through various sets of practices and institutions, each with its own specific nature and inner contradictions. The prevailing ideology is not a systematised representation of social relations embodied in actual practices and formations, and cannot be affected by the contradictions at work in the latter, by the complex class struggle which is in fact being waged all the time. So the arrival of a revolutionary consciousness in the proletariat can only be a spontaneous outburst brought about by the final clash of the contradictions inherent in the economic system, as if by a sort of universal electric shock. The workings of history do the whole thing; history becomes a teleological process with fated ends. (Such a system involves a circular reasoning. Marxism is identified with the theory of the proletariat, and the proletariat will take over and transform society because its theory is Marxism. And it is Marxism which tells us that the proletariat is the revolutionary class.)

Thus, Lukacs makes no effort to find the dialectical links between productive activity (involving both relationships and forces) and the social or cultural world in which the activity is carried out and which has complex dialectical links with the productive activity of past phases—these latter also having their rich social and cultural involvements and interactions. He ignores the fact that in a given society the conflicts and contradictions at work in the social and cultural fields will have their own inner dialectic as well as being organically linked with those in the economic sphere. Out of the total working-out of the conflicts and contradictions at the various levels there emerges the characteristic consciousness or worldview of a period or society, which is never at any two moments simply and flatly identical, but which reveals elements of continuity in change: a situation variously refracted in the consciousness of individuals.

In Lukac's historicism this sort of complexity in society and the individual disappears. Even the proletariat with its tremendous mission tends to lose its human character and become a fixed entity with permanent attributes. It is not a social force made up of individuals who attain a new and active cohesiveness, an evolving force with its own contradictions and uneven development, which, because it owns a determinate role in the structure and working-out of capitalism, develops the characteristics of opposition that in time can become revolutionary. It is seen as gaining its specific revolutionary nature rather by the sudden recognition of its position as the opposite of the capitalist class. At the same moment it realises what has been the role of reification in the capitalist world, and so reverses the situation, eliminating all the reifying tendencies and thus creating a new un-alienated society. (Lenin in 1920 had picked out Lukacs for his voluntarism and his use of Marxist phrases without proper attention to definite historical circumstances in the development of revolutionary struggle.)

But though it is necessary to make these comments on the limitations of *History and Class Consciousness*, it is not true that Lukacs is wholly unaware of them himself. He tries at one point to sketch out the stages in the self-consciousness of the proletariat and the confusions with which the class can be beset. He distinguishes between the actual situation at any given moment and the movement towards the revolutionary culmination. His subjective voluntarism, his looking to a spontaneous outburst, is tempered by moments when he looks to a Marxist party as the vanguard steadily seeking to learn through the experience of struggle. He keeps on relating real dialectical issues which he does not follow up. [2]

The one unrelieved error in the book lies in the treatment of subject/object, where idealist positions dominate. For idealism the subject is primary and there can be no object without a subject, while materialism holds that the objective forms of the natural world have existed, and continue to exist, prior to and independent of any subject. In social activity there is indeed always a subject-object relationship, though it is not at all a simple situation in which the human subject is acting on an object (another human being or some aspect of the material world) in a free and transformative way. The subjective element must not be abstracted as the intrinsically superior element. Rather, the relation of subject and object must be considered in a dialectical way involving the unity and conflict of opposites. (The notion of the subject as primary leads to the praxis-form of Marxism discussed above.)*

Thus Lukacs tends to treat subject in the way that Hegel does. For the latter Spirit or Absolute Idea breaks up, loses its unity, and thus brings about the existence of external nature. In nature it rediscovers itself and so achieves consciousness. It then goes on acting in this way through one level of incompletely subjective existence on to another, at each phase extending and deepening its consciousness, till at last all alienation from itself is ended and Absolute Spirit is regained by a return to a total self-consciousness. The original identity of subject and object is fully realised, with no more need of the subject to feel an objective world opposed to it and separated from it. Lukacs repeats this pattern, substituting Proletariat for Spirit. Humanity has been

---

* The dialectic which sees subject/object as fundamental opposites is anthropomorphic and ultimately idealist. Such terms must be discarded if we are to develop dialectics in a thoroughly materialist way.

34

alienated from true existence, with subject opposed to object, till at last the proletariat attains the self-consciousness represented by Marxism. By an act of cognition it ends the split between knowing subject and the separated or opposed object of knowledge. Thus it frees itself, frees humanity, from its alienated condition. The unity of subject-object (from this angle) is achieved by an act of self-knowledge, not by revolutionary struggle.

The idealist concept of subject/object is revealed in *History and Class-Consciousness* by another position taken over from Hegel. The objectifying process, in knowledge and productive activity, is equated with alienation; for the more that spirit or proletariat as subject finds itself confronted with the object, the more it feels itself separated-out and enclosed, alienated, in the object. To end alienation it is necessary to throw off objectivity, end the objectifying process, and absorb this false form of existence into the pure subject-object relationship, where the two sides or components are realised as identical, equal, unopposed. But in Marx's conception the objectifying process is the creative and productive process itself, by means of which human beings grapple with objective reality, realise it, and transform it. In so far as the realisation and the transformation are imperfect, elements of alienation, of distortion, will enter into the situation, into the comprehension of the activity and its relationships, into the social forms through which the objectification has been brought about. But to say that is in no sense to identify the objectifying and the alienating processes.

In his self-criticism of 1967 Lukacs admitted his error.

In the term alienation he [Hegel] includes every type of objectification. Thus 'alienation' when taken to its logical conclusion is identical with objectification. Therefore, when the identical subject-object transcends alienation, it must also transcend objectification at the same time . . . This fundamental and crude error has certainly contributed greatly to the success enjoyed by *History and Class Consciousness*. The unmasking of alienation by philosophy was in the air, and it soon became a central problem in the type of cultural criticism that undertook to scrutinise the condition of man in contemporary capitalism. In the philosophical cultural criticism of the bourgeoisie (and we need look no further than Heidigger), it was natural to sublimate a critique of society into a purely philosophical problem, i.e. to convert an essentially social alienation into an eternal 'condition humaine,' to use a term not coined until somewhat later. It is evident that *History and Class Consciousness* met such attitudes halfway, even though its intentions had been different and indeed opposed to them.

That is, he was so keen to show that the socialist revolution ended alienation that he took over uncritically the idealist terms which had the effect of making alienation an aspect of objectification. All that mattered was the ending of alienation, which would end also the enslaving aspect of objectification.

As the question of the relation of subject and object is of much importance we may glance at it further. First, there is the empiricist or mechanically materialist viewpoint, which puts all emphasis on the object. For it, knowledge is gained by the application of external criteria of logic to the object, so that the essential aspects of the latter are separated from the inessential and in effect become the object itself. Because of the mechanist relation of subject and object, the concept of the object and the object-itself become the same thing; the subject is merged with the abstraction of the object. Secondly, there is the idealist viewpoint in which these positions are inverted. Here the stress is put on the conceptual framework which the subject brings to the act of knowing, so that the reality is only that framework reflected and found in the object. In extreme idealism the spirit by its act actually created the object. For Marxism the relation of subject and object, both of them real, is a dialectical one, a discovery of kinships and differences which is brought about by the active connection, the dialectical unity and opposition in a moment of dynamic interconnection. To argue merely that Marxism proves itself in practice is to reduce it to the old empiricist-idealist positions (identical in obverse terms) and to lose the dialectical link of subject-object. (Althusser tries to evade the problem by making a distinction between the logical order and the 'real' order, natural, historical, or social; but this is merely to re-assert the old confusing split in terms of a structuralist system in which an abstract precision of terms is used to disguise the unsolved relationship.) What is implied by the dialectical relation of subject and object we shall consider further in dealing with science.[3]

Here it would be useful to look in more detail at Lukacs' use of the term reification, a use which was of great importance for the impact of the book and its after-effects. The term, *Verdinglichung*, is not found in Marx or in Hegel (as Marcuse asserts). It represents a rather rigid oversimplification of what Marx does say about alienation, especially in relation to the difference between use-value and exchange-value, in the *Grundrisse, Capital,* and *The Theory of Surplus Value.* Marx, in analysing the commodity as use-value, stresses that value is not one of its natural properties, but is born only when products are exchanged. It thus represents human labour in the abstract.

Labour capacity has appropriated for itself only the subjective conditions of necessary labour . . . separated from the conditions of its realisation—and it has posited these conditions themselves as things, values, which confront it in an alien, commanding personification.

In further analyses he describes one aspect or another of this situation: that the relation between men appears as a relation between things; that value appears to be a property of a commodity and so itself a thing; that the commodity gains a will or force of its own and is thus personified. The result is commodity-fetishism, in which the commodity is alienated from the activity of labour, from the product of labour. In the *Grundrisse* he had already stated the position that appears maturely in *Capital's* discussion of Commodity Fetishism:

> The social character of activity, as well as the social form of the product, and the share of individuals in production, here appears as something alien and objective . . . In exchange value, the social connection between persons is transformed into a social relation between things. [4]

In *Capital* he shows the importance he attaches to the nature of the commodity by opening his account with a long analysis of it. First he deals with use-value and exchange-value, then with 'the Mystery of the Fetishistic Character of Commodities'. He states that a definite social relation between men assumes 'the phantasmagoric form of a relation between things.' His term *phantasmagorische* has been usually translated as *fantastic*: which obscures his meaning. 'Phantasmagoric', first appearing in England in 1802, was used to describe optical illusions produced mainly by means of magic lanterns in London; then in 1822 for a shifting scene made up of many elements, and in 1824 for a series of phantasms or imaginary figures seen in a dream or fevered condition, or as conjured up by the imagination itself. *Phantasmagorische* is thus a stronger term than *fantastic*; it suggests an activity which transforms reality sensuously, intellectually, emotionally, in an alien way. Just what Marx meant by it is brought home by his development of the idea:

> In order, therefore, to find an analogy, we must have recourse to the mist-enveloped regions of the religious. In that world the productions of the human brain appear as independent beings endowed with life, and entering into relations both with one another and the human race. So it is with the world of commodities. [5]

Lukacs, despite his isolation of one aspect of alienation in reification, showed a remarkable understanding of Marx's thinking when he laid such emphasis on the alienating and fetishistic character of commodity-production. Later, the publication of the 1844 Manuscripts vindicated his general position in this matter. He opened up a vast new area of Marxist thought. In so doing he drew over to Marxism the many lines of anti-capitalist thought which had been seeking to deal with the issues of alienation but which felt forced into either total pessimism or utopianism.

These lines of thought had developed strongly in Germany with thinkers like Tönnies, the poet T. Storm, Weber, R. Michels, Thomas Mann, and many others. Lukacs' master Simmel, who merged elements from Kant, Hegel, Marx and Nietzsche, had especially affected him.* In working out his concept of form. Simmel saw man as a subject acting on the world so as to create structures which gained an autonomy independent of his will. He had no idea of the relation of this alienating process to the world of production, and saw the drives to resolve or overcome divisiveness as inherent in life and form (subject and object) and as begetting culture. For him the exchange form (with money as means of exchange) was merely the social form by which the subjective value in an object won an objective expression. But his critique of the 'culture of things' as dominating people had a strong effect on Lukacs.[6]

There is one more aspect of *History and Class-Consciousness* that must be considered. This is Lukacs' treatment of nature and science. He has been accused by Colletti, for instance, of taking as his focal theme 'the identification of capitalist reification with the "reification" engendered by science'. What Lukacs actually argues is that through reification human relationships take the form of laws of nature, the form of objectivity of the concepts of natural science. But his wording is not clear. He seems to be beginning a critique of science, in which he does link the methods and attitudes of post-Galilean science with capitalism.

It is anything but a mere chance that at the very beginning of the development of modern philosophy the ideal of knowledge took the form of universal mathematics; it was an attempt to establish a rational system of relations which comprehends the totality of the formal possibilities, proportions and relations of a rationalised existence with the aid of which every phenomenon—independently of its real and material distinctiveness—could be subjected to an exact calculus.

*Simmel was the first to sociologise Nietzsche and to merge the results with a generalised version of Marxism. He related his theories of form to ideas of commodity fetishism from *Capital*, though he rejected the labour-theory of value. He saw the division of labour as leading to debasement and a culture-of-things. (His idea that all social activity involved a creation of forms prevented him from differentiating worker, artist, scientist, or the owners of capital from the sellers of labour, though he tried to move towards such a distinction.) He ended unsure if money would make men more slaves to objects or enable inner private life to flourish afresh. He held that culture may resolve dualisms (life/form, subject/object), though that grew ever more unlikely in the modern world.

And he cites Tönnies: 'The supreme scientific concept which is no longer the name of anything real is like money, e.g. the concept of an atom, or of energy.' He argues that under capitalism all human relations, viewed as the objects of social activity, 'assume increasingly the objective forms of the abstract elements of the conceptual systems of natural science and of the abstract substrata of the laws of nature.' Though he does not elaborate the point, he insists that Engels'

deepest misunderstanding consists in his belief that the behaviour of industry and scientific experiment constitutes praxis in the dialectical, philosophical sense. In fact, scientific experiment is contemplation at its purest. The experimenter creates an artificial, abstract milieu in order to be able to *observe* undisturbed the untrammelled workings of the laws under examination, eliminating all irrational factors both of the subject and the object.*

It follows that natural science is not dialectical in its method and that its link with bourgeois society and its systems is very close. In this sense what Colletti says is quite correct; but we are left with the problem: Is scientific method necessarily mechanist? and if so, what is its relation to Marxism as a social science? Lukacs does not pursue the matter, but we shall consider its implications later. [7]

We must now turn to Lukacs' later development. He soon lost his 'messianic utopianism' (which in 1967 he saw as a passionate protest against mechanistic materialism). He moved to ideas of a union of all progressive forces against capitalism in its darkening state. The Blum Theses in which he set out these ideas were violently attacked by his fellow-communists, and he was forced to renounce them. However this recantation was in effect a lie; he maintained the essential position of the Theses for the rest of his life. Why did he deny the Theses? He wanted at all costs to remain inside the communist movement, where he felt that he could play a useful part in ways that he could not do from outside. He was affected by Hegel's idea of Reconciliation with Reality, which he saw as playing an essential part in enabling Hegel to complete his dialectic. So, finding no signs of effective revolt in the industrialised countries, he accepted the thesis of 'Socialism in One Country' as a necessary accommodation to the facts of the situation. To describe such steps as a surrender to Stalinism is nonsense. At the

---

* In 1967 he declared that it had been nonsense to write of experiment as pure contemplation, without interference from outside. Experiment always had a 'teleological' element as much as any act of economic production. (But these points do not touch the question whether bourgeois natural science is dialectical or not.) He also insisted that in his book nature often 'is a societal category', the dialectics that applies to society applies to it as well.

time Stalinism was in its first obscure stages; and if there were elements in the Soviet Union with which Lukacs felt dissatisfied, he saw no reason to doubt that the inner struggle there might lead in the right direction. In the 1930s, as things worsened, he felt that the primary need was to take part in the anti-fascist struggle. And this he continued until the end, though he tried to take advantage of any break in the situation, e.g. supporting Nagy in 1956.[8]

In the post-1926 situation, as he sought to reformulate his views he moved far from the positions of *History and Class-Consciousness*. Two important ideas were however carried on from that book: the centrality of the concept of totality in a dialectical viewpoint, and the need for the concept of mediations in order to avoid a mechanistic interpretation of the totality.

It is not the primacy of the economic motives in historical explanation that constitutes the decisive difference between Marxism and bourgeois science, but the point of view of totality . . . The primacy of the category of totality is the bearer of the revolutionary principle in action. . . .

The category of mediation is a lever with which to overcome the mere immediacy of the empirical world and as such it is not anything (subjective) that has been foisted on the objects from outside; it is no value judgement or 'Ought' as opposed to their 'Is.' It is rather the manifestation of their authentic objective structure.

That is, the mediations inside the totality represent the real inner connections in their full dynamic and dialectical pattern of interaction.

In his earlier work he had stressed the centrality of tragedy in the contemporary cultural situation. In early (Greek) epic he considered that the definition was concrete because every aspect of daily life was realised as owning a meaning and function in terms of the communal whole, so that essence and life were one. But the novel revealed the individual lost and crucified on his isolation in a situation where 'authentic life' was impossible. So Lukacs was attracted to the novel of crisis, above all to Dostoevsky, in whose work the non-authentic actuality was rejected in terms of a redeeming visionary hope. Now, in his effort to accept the socialist world born of 1917 and to help its culture, he took a diametrically opposite viewpoint: the problem was seen as one of stabilising and extending the culture of socialism. The wider political background was taken to be one in which the main issue was the creation of a popular or progressive front against reaction, against fascism. The hope of a new un-alienated culture, born overnight with the triumph of the proletariat, appeared quite utopian. So Lukacs took up what he felt to be the Leninist position in such a situation: the need for the new society to develop stably by taking over all that was valuable in past cultures, and incorporating it with the new elements derived from a socialist outlook. Socialist culture, then, did not begin at some abstract point, but like the revolution itself emerged out of the bourgeois situation, however much it needed to transform what it took over. The transformation would come about by leavening the elements carried over from the past with a Marxist consciousness, a new sense of the dialectical totality at work in history.

Lenin had been acutely aware in his last years of the extreme difficulty of creating the cultural basis in the Soviet Union that was necessary for a rapid movement into an all-round socialism. In his final tragic days, stricken down, he gave his thoughts mainly to this problem: 'For a start, we should be satisfied with real bourgeois culture: for a start, we should be glad to dispense with the cruder types of pre-bourgeois culture, i.e. bureaucratic culture or serf culture, etc. In matters of culture, haste and sweeping measures are most harmful.' Even this sort of programme was seen as a long-term project.

Lukacs then set himself to go deeper into bourgeois culture, especially into the great achievements of the bourgeois novelists, bringing to bear a Marxist sense of totality so as to make the works effectively assimilable by a socialist world. He expanded his notion of mediations so as to show how the various levels or moments of social activity were dialectically linked, interacting, according to their natures. Such a system was far superior to that of base and superstructure, but he never worked out in any specific way how the relative autonomy of the various spheres of social life operated. In his 1967 criticism of his early definition of totality he commented, 'I put the totality in the centre of the system, overriding the priority of economics.' However, in his analyses of the bourgeois novel, using his concepts of totality and mediations, he made many valuable Marxist advances in literary criticism. He accepted the term Socialist Realism to define the kind of novel which tackled the socialist situation with the same dialectical grasp of its totality as the great bourgeois novelists had had of their society; and in the earlier 1930s he analysed some of the best Soviet novels.

To call him a Stalinist for this reason is ridiculous. The Stalinist distortion of Socialist Realism lay in the direct mechanical relation of superstructure and base which we have already discussed; the socialist aspect was thus robbed of any genuine critical perspective and was seen as merely a stimulation of people to tackle the immediate problems of construction as laid down by State and Party. Lukacs later gave up discussing Soviet novels until the advent of Solzhenitsyn provided him with examples in which a serious effort was made to tackle and evaluate the political dimension of the setting.

His weakness, then, lay in the extent to which after the early 1930s he ceased to attempt to apply his criteria to the socialist scene. His analyses of bourgeois culture, for all their many virtues, thus tended to lose the dynamic virtue they would have possessed if linked with the attempts to found a valid socialist culture. This weak side of his work appeared in his controversy with Brecht and Benjamin, who were concerned with the immediate problems of validly linking the cultural and political struggles. Lukacs saw them as abandoning the effort to achieve in art the inclusive totality which he defined as the hallmark of creative virtue in the past: abandoning the effort to make socialist culture as broad and deep, and putting fragmented and limited issues in place of the full creative comprehension. In a way he was reacting against his own passionate acceptance of expressionist positions in his pre-1917 years. In early works such as *Soul and Form* he could now see only the limitations and derelictions. His denunciations of *Modernismus* had a certain force when directed against critics or artists who accepted the various movements at their subjective and idealist face value; but his remarks lacked point when he opposed Brecht, who was essentially saying that we must start from where people are, in all their complicated alienations, if we are to find ways of truly reaching and freeing them. That is, we must start from the bad new things, not the good old ones. Not that that meant we should end with the former.[9]

A complete Marxist aesthetic would embody the positions of both Brecht and Lukacs, defining their different points of reference, but also the way in which they finally meet and merge in the struggle against alienation, in the effort to reach a level where the new human integrations dominate. Brecht dealt with the problem of an effective fighting art in the post-1917 situation, Lukacs with the ways in which the movement to an integrated socialist culture could be helped by a deepened understanding of past creative expressions: the methods used by past writers to define in varying degrees the living inclusive totality of their societies. Lukacs did not mean that the study of past expressions could be academically put in place of the contemporary struggle. But he felt strongly that the breakdown of the inclusive totality in cultural expressions, in a capitalism which had lost its driving force, revealed what the class-world was doing to people with its increasing fragmentation and alienation: first through naturalism, escapism, decadence, art-for-art's sake, with ever sharper limitation of perspective and lack of interest in the wholeness of experience in the various modernisms, and so on. Just as the social revolution would reverse the alienating trends and overcome the deadening contradictions of capitalism in its imperialist phase, so Socialist Realism, if truly understood and worked out, would regain an inclusive totality of vision and richness of comprehension in terms of the new socialist perspective.

Such an argument had its strong element of truth. But once we try to apply it crudely and one-sidedly—without consideration for the specific moment of struggle, breakdown, alienation, aspiration, the specific level at which development must take place, the complex possibilities and restrictions that have come together in difficult entanglement—then, despite all our good intentions, we are in fact arresting the cultural process by the imposition of abstract criteria and preventing an organic breakthrough in the very direction that we most desire.

Lukacs was never unaware of the great importance of work, of concrete productive activity, in the Marxist view of culture (or politics). In his 1967 statement he claimed that in *History and Class-Consciousness* 'I recognised the way in which praxis had its origins and its roots in work,' but admits that he had failed to make the right applications of this recognition:

The purview of economics is narrowed down because its basic Marxist category, labour as the mediator of the metabolic interaction between society and nature, is missing. Given my basic approach, such a consequence is quite natural. It means that the most important real pillars of the Marxist view of the world disappear and the attempt to deduce the ultimate revolutionary implications of Marxism in as radical a fashion as possible is deprived of a genuinely economic foundation. It is self-evident that this means the disappearance of the ontological objectivity of nature upon which this process of change is based. But it also means the disappearance of the interaction between labour as seen from a genuinely materialist standpoint and the evolution of the men who labour.

Near the end of his life he tried to deal at philosophic length with the relation of culture to labour-process; but he had found it hard to incorporate such understandings into his method of social or literary analysis. Brecht put the case against him and others following the same line in a harsh form:

They are, to put it bluntly, enemies of production. Production makes them uncomfortable. You never know where you are with production. Production is the unforeseeable. You never know what's going to come out. And they themselves don't want to produce. They want to play the *apparatchik* and exercise control over other people. Every one of their criticisms contains a threat.

Productive activity changes the world, and so does creative expression. So Brecht can link his art-production with the struggles of the workers in a direct as well as an indirect way. He too has his Socialist Realism.

> We shall not speak of a realistic manner of writing only when for example we can smell, taste and feel 'everything'. When there is 'atmosphere' and when plots are so contrived that they lead to psychological analysis of character. Our concept of realism must be wide and political, sovereign over all conventions. Realistic means; discovering the causal complexes of society/unmasking the prevailing view of things as the view of those who rule it/writing from the standpoint of the class which offers the broadest solutions for the pressing difficulties in which human society is caught/emphasising the element of development/making possible the concrete, and making possible abstraction from it.

This attitude also has its limiting aspects that can make the definition of a work of art superficial, merely topical, and so on; but it does hold the necessary corrective to the elements in Lukacs which can become over-generalised, failing to bring out the way in which a true artwork is both 'production', embedded in a richly entangled and particular moment of change and struggle with its own specific potentialities, and a dialectical structure grasping past, present and future in a unified image.

It is instructive, too, to glance at the break between Bloch and Lukacs about the same time. 'Perhaps,' said Bloch, 'Lukacs' reality, that of the infinitely mediated totality, is not at all so objective.' Rather it is one-sidedly objectivistic, so that Lukacs reacts 'against every artistic attempt to bring about the dissolution of world-view (even should this world-view itself be capitalistic). Consequently he sees nothing but subjectivistic ruptures in an art which attempts to discover the new that already exists in the crevices. Consequently, he equates the experiment of dissolution with the state of decadence.' The argument was over the nature of Expressionism. For Bloch, that art both mirrored the dissolution of existing society and revealed a striving for a better world, a world that involved a radical rejection of the existing one and was subversive and potentially revolutionary. Artists may often not recognise the full scope and significance of the impulse that drives them, but their products can be decoded and the revolutionary elements brought up into full consciousness.[10]

In the light of these criticisms we must take a last look at Lukacs' concept of totality. It involves inner movement, tension, conflict, even if it refuses to deal with the sort of break, dissolution, new start, that Brecht and Bloch were concerned with. Lukacs has rejected his earlier tragic view that sees men as cut away from any possibility of fulfilment, as well as the utopian hope of a leap into completely unalienated community. Instead, a degree of reconciliation with reality, the existing state of things, occurs. Society is a product of human activity, human labour. People are a living part of it, however many forces of division and fragmentation impact upon them and thrive within them. To grasp this situation and to define it is the work of what Lukacs came to understand as Realism.*

In such a work the characters are typical. That does not mean that they simply reflect or refract some aspect of the totality. It implies rather a vital union of individual and social or historical characteristics. A person is simultaneously his separate self and all his social relations. He merges with the forces that have formed him and which keep acting on him, and yet he is more than their sum, more than their puppet. So the typical character is in no sense a mere allegory of social forces, a class-symbol, a photographic replica.[11]

Lukacs however does make a distinction between world-historical figures, who draw into themselves the main formative or revolutionary forces of their time, and the average figures, on whom those forces are playing with less powerful effect. In drama the large-scale historical figures claim a key-part; in the novel the characters reveal a more diffused and random response to the forces that the world-historical figures embody. Here the men and women will tend to react to different aspects of the situation, respond in a less coherent way, and so on. However, an active element will persist in all the affected characters, so that there is a dynamic relation of parts and whole. In the Naturalistic Novel, which mostly deals with the societies of advanced alienation where people seem the enclosed creatures of their circumstances, we meet the typical in its weak mechanistic form. The naturalist novelist looks in on a world which he thinks he understands; he tends to be a sort of overseeing god who manipulates his characters. He is thus himself the dupe of the forces that he thinks he so fully understands, putting an abstract or positivist conception in place of the dialectical grasp of the complex interactions and contradictions. The novel becomes a thesis, the characters illustrations of the thesis. The author imagines that he has an objective knowledge of the pattern he contemplates, a pattern which does not include the unpredictable and contradictory elements capable of suddenly upsetting the settled order of things.

---

* Lukacs' later developments are to some extent foreshadowed in *The Theory of the Novel*, 1914-5, where there is a movement from a metaphysical tension to an historical one: from the world in an abstract sense (external reality cut off from the subject) to society, which is itself changing and developing. So the hero turns from contemplation of something outside himself to the position of having to achieve an active relation to external reality. The movement is from Flaubert to Goethe and Tolstoy: Jameson 180-2

On the other hand if we take a true realist like Balzac we find that with him a character

is not typical of a fixed social element, such as class, but rather of the historical moment itself; and with this, the purely schematic and allegorical overtones of the notion of typicality disappear completely. The typical is not at this point a one-to-one correlation between individual characters in the work (Nucingen, Hulot) and fixed, stable components of the external world itself (finance, aristocracy, Napoleonic mobility), but rather an analogy between the whole plot, as a conflict of forces, and the total moment of history itself considered as process. (JAMESON)

Lukacs' totality is not, then, in any sense a static sphere in which the elements are merely interlinked in a rational system of mediations. It is dynamic, inseparable from process, a genuine dialectical fusion of individual and history. But there is a point at which Lukacs resists any further penetration into the entangled struggle, the point where the effective unity of the system seems threatened by the intrusion of all sorts of imbalances and disruptions. This is the revolutionary moment when the result can only be breakdown or the creation of a new centre of living, a new totality. It is the moment that interested Brecht and Bloch, each in his own way.

There is no need to go further into these problems. The essential thing to be brought out here is the way in which *History and Class-Consciousness* broke into the confused situation of the 1920s when the old formulations were increasingly losing the power to mobilise action and clarify the cultural and political struggle. By its massive philosophical force, originality and range, and despite distortions of Marxism—or in part because of them—it lifted the discussions on to a new level. It is on this level indeed that the argument has since proceeded, even when Lukacs' ideas have been hotly rejected. The issues included the nature of dialectics and its place in Marxist method; the relation of culture to the political and economic levels and the connection between a work of art with its living totality and the historical whole from which it arose and on which it impacted; the way in which people were affected by the alienating pressures of capitalist society and the manner in which these pressures could be defeated; and finally the nature of science and the question whether there was a gap between natural and social science.

We shall continue our analysis by first looking at Ernst Bloch—who is in many ways the antithesis of Lukacs—then at the Frankfurt School, especially Adorno, Horkheimer and Marcuse. After that we shall consider the impact of Structuralism in the postwar years, mainly in the work of Althusser, and the revival of anti-Hegelianism (the rejection or depreciation of dialectics) by men like della Volpe, Colletti, and so on. We shall then attempt a general evaluation of these developments in or around Marxism, and decide how well or badly the formulations set out in the first two chapters here stand up in the welter of differing interpretations of Marxism; how far they seem to answer the problems raised. [1] [2]

4   Ernst Bloch and the Principle of Hope

At first glance it is hard to see where Bloch fits into the Marxist tradition, even to describe him as a Marxist in any precise sense at all. Yet on a deeper view he is seen to deal with many questions that arise out of Marxism, important questions that are largely ignored by Marxists. What his work helps to illuminate is the nature of ideology, or rather of culture itself in both particular and general aspects, and it probes profoundly into certain psychological issues that we must understand if we are to make sense of the innermost content of social struggle, of revolutionary impulses and drives. His weakness lies in his inability to link his explorations of culture—his analysis of what it is in human beings that urges them towards new and more truly human goals—with the social and political world and its structures, its conflicts and contradictions, in an historically concrete way.

Born in 1885, he was at Heidelberg before the first world war and there began his contentious friendship with Lukacs. When the war came he moved to Switzerland, taking a pacifist position, and wrote his *Spirit of Utopia*. In the 1920s, in Germany, he defended the Russian Revolution and avant-garde art, especially Expressionism. Opponent of Fascism, he moved to Zurich, then to Paris, Vienna, Prague, and finally the U.S.A. He then wrote his main work *The Principle of Hope*. Returning to Germany in 1948, he was active in the GDR, where he was appointed director of the Philosophical Institute in Leipzig. His reputation rose high, but after the troubles of 1956 he was forced to retire and denied publication. In 1961 he was in West Germany. Offered a professorship at Tübingen, he participated in student protests against the Vietnam war, the Atom Bomb, and so on. He died in 1977.

Above all, Bloch repudiated all narrow or mechanist concepts of ideology—concepts which related expressions, emotions, attitudes directly to a socio-economic base and considered them then to be completely explained away. He was concerned to underline and understand the great positive element in our thoughts and emotions which, arising out of the present, drives into the future, creating goals,

49

aspirations, hopes and dissatisfactions with things as they are, in terms of a fuller human reality, a richer harmony and liberation of our energies. This vital element is to be found, not only in the obvious fields of forward-driving hope and revolt, but also, cored deeply in what has been superficially rejected as reactionary and false. As Habermas has put it, Bloch 'wants to save that which is true in false consciousness . . . Even the critique of religion is given a new-old interpretation. God is dead, but his locus has survived him. The place where mankind has imagined God and the gods, after the decay of these hypotheses, remains a hollow space. The measurement-in-depth of this vacuum, indeed atheism finally understood, sketches out the blueprint of a future kingdom of freedom.'[1]

That is to say, religion can be approached from two angles. It represents the alienation of human powers into an imaginary being, where they are cut off, lost, as Feuerbach long ago declared. Human beings vainly seek to reunite themselves with their own alienated powers by emotionally, intellectually, ritually uniting with God. But from another angle religion reveals a vast wealth of aspiration for harmony and happiness, the potentiality of endless sources of energy in people. What has been alienated and lost inside a false consciousness of life can be recognised in its human essence and brought back into earthly life, transforming it instead of merely feeding an abstraction (which through its alienated condition can stand oppressively over against life, supporting parasitic power-structures).

Marx, indeed, in 1843 set out in a letter to Ruge what in effect was a Blochian programme:

So our campaign slogan must be: reform of consciousness, not through dogma, but through the analysis of that mystical consciousness which has not yet become clear to itself. It will then turn out that the world has long dreamt of that of which it had only to have a clear idea to possess it really. It will turn out that it is not a question of any conceptual rupture between past and future, but rather of the *completion* of the thoughts of the past.

The same ideas are set out more fully in the discussion of religion in his *Critique of Hegel's Philosophy of Right*, 1844. Marxists have too often been content to ignore the rich complexity of the full statement and to cite the one completely negative point made against religion: that it is the opium of the people.

The criticism of religion is the presupposition of all criticism . . . Religion is the general theory of this world, its encyclopaedic compendium, its moral sanction, its solemn complement, its universal basis for consolation and justification. It is the imaginary realisation of the human essence . . . Religious suffering is at the same time an expression of real suffering and a protest against real suffering. Religion is the sigh of the oppressed creature, the feeling of a heartless world, and the soul of soulless circumstances. It is the opium of the people . . . Criticism has plucked the imaginary flowers from the chains not so that man may bear chains without any imagination or comfort, but so that he may throw away the chains and pluck living flowers. The criticism of religion disillusions man so that he may think, act, and fashion his own reality as a disillusioned man comes to his senses; so that he may revolve around himself as the real sun. Religion is only the illusory sun which revolves around man as long as he does not revolve around himself.

It is worth considering that passage, for it brings out how deeply Bloch's work is a contribution to Marxist tradition and method.

Bloch uses the term Hope for the unconquerable human element which reasserts itself even at the heart of defeat and confusion. He describes in *The Principles of Hope* the various forms and outlets it finds. He begins with 'small daydreams', then goes on to 'anticipatory consciousneess' and utopia. Next comes 'the reflection of wish-images' in display, fashion, fairytales, travels, films, plays, and so on; then 'the outline of a better world' in social utopias, technology, architecture, art (painting, opera, poetry), philosophy, leisure. He ends with the 'wish images of the fulfilled moment', dealing with ethics, music, death, religion, nature, the highest good. Even this brief sketch of the contents will bring out how little systematised is the account. Bloch rambles on from the way Hope appears and operates at all levels of experience, in all the connections of man with reality:

from the ontological itself, in the central and crucial analysis of human time, fanning out to touch upon existential psychology (the meaning of such phenomena as anxiety and disappointment); ethics (the study of hope institutionalised in traditional ideals and values); logic (the conceptual categories of the possible); political science, both of a conventional type, in the studies of the various theories of the state and of social organisation, and of a Marxist character, in the analysis of revolutionary strategy; the social planning inherent in the conception of Utopias of all kinds; *Technik*, not only in the sense of the scientific achievements of the world of the future, but also in terms of the way in which it alters our relationship to the objects around us; sociology, in the form of the analysis of the wish-fulfilments of advertising and popular culture, ideological and literary criticism, finally, in all an all-embracing account of the archetypes of Utopia in art, myth, and religion. (JAMESON)[2]

The impact of Hope on a person is manifested in Astonishment, which is the correlative of the subjective side of the objective world and thus expresses the active relation that is set up. It registers the response of the self and reveals that what is found is not something already known, calculated, measured or understood. It lives in a dialectical union with its opposite, 'the darkness of the lived moment'. Astonishment and this Darkness represent two poles. The Darkness may also be termed the anticipatory disposition of the world. The Darkness and Astonishment tug at one another all the time. One implies the other; Astonishment, says Bloch,

is the very source or origin of the world itself, ever at work and ever hidden away within the darkness of the lived instant, a source which becomes aware of itself for the first time in the signature of its own estuaries as it resolves itself into them.[3]

Bloch often uses a portentous and overwrought style, e.g. 'The symbolic intentions of the Supreme and the Omega imply the darkness of the Alpha or of closest proximity'. The terms often seem to suggest that psychic moments like Astonishment are forces existing as pure agents in their own right. But at the same time his style does conjure up the exciting and deep-going nature of the experiences described and generalised. Bloch wants to make us realise the indescribable nature of the experience as the new is truly born: the merging of the luminous Hope with the Darkness, the confusion and not-yet-organised elements of experience in its immediacy.

In the moment of Astonishment something new is born, a new unity of the self and the world in however unstable a form. There, time is something different from clock-time. Bloch is thinking of Bergson, who first stressed the essential spatiality of logical concepts (of any form of relationship between elements already known, assimilated) as opposed to the specific character, the uniqueness, of lived-time, *durée*. Bergson however failed to define the lived-time except in an abstract way as process or change, and so succumbed at the crucial point to the very system he was criticising. Bloch points out that for him time is seen 'merely as the abstract opposite of repetition, indeed very often as the mere reverse of mechanical uniformity'. [4] (Marx in 1844, had, however, anticipated Bergson, without falling into his idealism; he noted how the alienating forces made time into clock-time, that is into mere mechanist repetition. In the world of capitalist exploitation, 'Time is everything; man is nothing; he is at the most time's carcass. Quality no longer matters. Quantity alone decides everything'.) The moment of Astonishment makes time fully concrete and restores quality to experience.

But the moment does not automatically have this positive effect. If it does, it produces 'expectation-effects'. But if it fails to achieve a breakthrough, a new concrete unity of the self and the outer world, it begets 'filled effects or emotions'. In these the self indeed looks to the future, but in a one-sided way, dominated by egoist emotions such as greed or envy. Here the future, says Bloch, is inauthentic. The fulfilment which is sought has no wish to change the world; it aims only at some particular object, which it has so far lacked. It is uninterested in the rich complexity of relationships and interdependencies in the real world. Very different is the nature of the expectation-effects and the way they work. They are not concerned with some isolated source of satisfaction. They are absorbed in the living richness and patterning of the world, and out of them will emerge a fuller self, strengthened through the union with otherness. In the darkness of the lived-moment the self discards its defences, its hardened armatures, and is oriented towards the future, towards what is not yet existent. Hope is the archetype of the forward-looking emotions; it reveals their typical structure and is their clearest and most effective manifestation.

But what impedes and distorts the release of Hope? Bloch introduces here the concept of the *Sperre* or Block. The Block is everything in the human system that resists the *Novum*, the liberating movement into the future: for example the static logic and mechanistic attitudes which cannot conceive of a dialectical movement into new centres, on to new levels. The Block finds its plainest expression in what Bloch calls the myth of the absolute presence. This myth argues that something like a plenitude of beings already exists, so that the movement of Hope into the future is unnecessary, meaningless. Where the myth rules, time is arrested. But in its working-out the myth slides away from the present and looks back into the past in which somehow resides the lost source of plenitude, a source that exists before birth. An example is the Platonic doctrine of pure Forms, which were known to the soul before birth and which are sought again through memory. Another is the Christian creed of a lost Paradise. Freud's system too is oriented towards the past, where the controlling patterns of experience are thought to lie buried; the unconscious is that which has ceased to be conscious. Bloch uses the term Anamnesis for the backward-turning of Hope (he sees the detective story as a quest back in time for the solution of something that has gone wrong: a rationalisation of the myths of the primal sin or error).

Nihilism or lack of all faith is also a Block. It is the complete reverse-of-negative of Hope in its structure, whereas Anamnesis is the obverse. Neither Nihilism or Anamnesis are simply negative and destructive. They both hold the truth in distorted ways and so can play important roles in deepening the awareness of reality. Anxiety cannot be intellectually refuted, but it can be transformed into the positive anticipation that is its opposite and correlative. The negative implies a positive which is ontologically prior to it.[5]

Bloch seeks to analyse the structure of the moment when the new potentialities assert and express themselves in a given situation. He distinguishes three dialectical categories: Front, Novum, Matter. Front is the particular section of time that is coming up with the next set of problems, the next phase of struggle. It is the situation that confronts people. Novum is the real possibilities in that situation, the element of not-yet; it has to be tackled and grasped. What people feel at this moment is the movement out of the existing pressures into a new dimension, into the reality of freedom, into an enhanced humanity. Matter is the situation itself: matter in the Aristotelian sense of activity with a substratum of possibilities. Bloch says: 'Precisely as being in movement, matter is being that is not yet manifest; it is the ground and substance in which our future, its own future too, is carried out.' The Novum emerges as the new social self, which is equated with revolutionary change involving a breakthrough of the new, a rupture with the past, an advent of the qualitatively new: the dialectical leap on to a new level of life. Marxism is the consciousness that directs the Novum with full force into activities seeking the end of the old divisions, the achievement of communism. (Before 1917 the Novum showed itself in periodic outbreaks, revolts, discontents. After 1917 it holds a perspective of successful change, of a definite break with the old divisions.)

A central function of art is the making-sense, the clarification, of the lived-moment. Bloch here differentiates allegory and symbolism. In the first the self opens out on to otherness, all that is not self; in the second it folds all things back into unity. The symbol involves a determination of the goal; allegory is a determination of the way. The two merge in providing and making possible the goal, a unifying meaning and purpose; they also provide the impetus and system whereby the self finds its way forwards to the goal and is saved from being distracted and lost.[6]

Bloch also uses other terms in his attempts to define how it is that the utopian impulse finds its true way forward and yet breaks down. He writes of the Tendency and Latency in things. The first represents the vital possibilities of development present in a given moment; the second refers to the more purely aesthetic or perceptual potentialities in the same situation or objects. The two aspects are linked with dramatic and lyrical ways of presenting a situation in its not-yet-being. Tendency has affinities with the allegorical, Latency with the symbolic. They combine to express the forward movement of the whole self in all its richness.

If Bloch stresses the great possibilities in ever-recurrent Hope, he deals equally with the blocks and miscarriages. In the darkness of lived-time there is no effective plenitude of being. Instead there is a sort of emptiness, an inadequacy: only figures of a hope, a desire, that has not yet fully revealed or realised itself. Hope is thus frustrated always by its own nature. What comes out of its impact, its drive into life, is something not expected, not calculated for. That is why the negative aspect is so important, setting us the problem of transforming it into the positive. The experience of the struggle to transform it is one of both anguish and joy, a crucifixion ending in a resurrection. There is no rebirth without the previous death:

Insofar as precisely that closest, most genuine, continuing being-present to the world is really nothing of the sort, no human being has ever really lived, at least not in that sense.

In the sense of full integration with the lived-moment.[7]

Yet it is this gap, this failure, this block, which provides the deepest dynamic, driving people forward and turning contingent desire into a figure, a symbol, a foretaste of the ultimate presence of utopia, of unbroken integration of individual and collective inside the new unity of participation. In one sense the utopian moment can only be regarded as the unimaginable. To bridge this gap a sort of allegorical structure is built into the surging utopian impulse, a structure however which cannot define or hold that impulse in its real and complete force and direction. Art and religion with their allegorical and symbolic constructions are called in to build on the impulse with its power to stir the depths of human reality. So the plenitude of the final utopian moment is not altogether lost, an anticipation of it is sustained, most clearly in the mystical union with deity and in the way that music (both in form and content) can carry the bearer away into its vital dimension.

The images of art, like little islands before us, are as paintings on glass which have only just begun to glow, stimulating our attention, and which people indicate, explicate, and then again abandon. And this is indeed the criterion of a purely *aesthetic* illumination, viewed from the point of view of its ultimate categories: *how may the things of this world be completed, without their ceasing, apocalyptically, to exist . . .*

What the sonata form completes in time, the dome, for example, completes in space.[8]

Bloch's style, it will be seen, abounds in paradox, in extreme statements which are then modified or contradicted. By these means he strives to bring his concepts vividly home, to make each moment of the described experiences felt with all possible force. The modifications or contradictions he then introduces are felt as emerging out of the actual struggle to control the absolute statements, to see them in a fuller system of relationships: not as logical sections of a comprehended system, but as dialectical aspects of the total experience as it is painfully and rapturously grasped. The method has its severe limitations, but also its triumphs.

The struggle is to drive through all blocks and arrive at the not-yet-conscious. The unconscious is thus seen as lying ahead, an obstacle to the drive which seeks new unions with the world, an intensified fullness of being. What keeps on pressing forward and unfolding itself is not an a-historical human essence. It is always linked with the stage reached by people in their 'co-productivity with nature'—that stage in turn being linked with the social, economic, political formations in which the struggle is waged.[9]

But what interests Bloch are the signs and expressions of the not-yet. He probes cultural and psychological experience, past and present, for them, for everything that reaches out from the present into the future: the daydreams and desires of youth, the new forms of living that are confusedly thrown up in times of rapid change, the creative processes that strive to give intelligible form to ideas and impulses that resist clarification. He sees daydream and fantasy as essential elements of human personality, of human development. In them we may find the key to the understanding of both oppression and liberation. However strong the repressive forces may be, human wishes and hopes break through, giving voice to what has been repressed, to the need to destroy repression, to the quest for freedom. Dreams are 'the first step to art' and the source of the social utopia. They play an important part in the radicalisation of intellectuals.[10]

It is of interest to note how close in some ways is Lenin's account of the omnipresent role of fantasy, though of course he does not mean to allot to it anything like the wide range of powers that Bloch does:

The approach of the (human) mind to a particular thing, the taking of a copy(= a concept) of it *is not* a simple, immediate act, a dead mirroring, but one which is complex, split into two, zigzaglike, which *includes in it* the possibility of the flight of fantasy from life; more than that: the possibility of the *transformation* (moreover, an unnoticeable transformation, of which man is unaware) of the abstract concept, idea, into a *fantasy* (in letzter Instanz = God). For even in the simplest generalisation, in the most elementary general idea ('table' in general), *there is* a certain bit of fantasy. (Vice versa: it would be stupid to deny the role of fantasy, even in the strictest science: cf. Pisarev on useful dreaming, as an impulse *to* work, and on empty day-dreaming.)[11]

We may note, too, how Bloch's thought shows a strong impact from Nietzsche, taking over the stress on ceaseless becoming, with a goal somewhere in the future. Zarathustra cries: 'Man is great in that he is a bridge and not a goal: man can be loved in that he is a transition and a perishing . . . It is time for Man to mark his goal. It is time for Man to sow the seed of his highest hope.' The goal is the *Uebermensch*, the Beyondman in whom the rending contradictions of existent Man are overcome. (The translation 'Superman', helped by Bernard Shaw, hopelessly vulgarises the concept.) Though Nietzsche is thinking in existentialist, not in historical terms, the not-yet in his thought leads on to Bloch, who however gives it a quite different social basis.

Bloch, we noted, is throughout protesting against oversimplified and mechanist versions of Marxism, which undervalue or ignore theory and the complexity of the human situation. But how far does he himself give us any valid clues as to the application of his theory and as to the relation of the impulses of Hope to political action? First, he certainly does stress the need for a struggle. Marx is guided, he says, simultaneously 'by Jesus with a whip and the Jesus of brotherly love.' Sometimes evil can be conquered by the kiss of love, 'Yet the rule is still that the soul must accept guilt in order to destroy existing evil, lest it incur the greater guilt of idyllic withdrawal, of seeming to be good at putting up with wrong. Domination, or power in itself, is evil; but it takes power to counter it.'[12] But he keeps falling back upon generalised concepts, not related to any specific historical developments, to explain the drives on which his philosophy depends.

The not is the lack of something and the flight from this lack; hence it drives toward that which is lacking. With the not drives are modelled in the living being: as drive, need, striving , and primarily as hunger.

The use of the idea of hunger seems to give a material basis to his argument, but in fact he merges hunger with dissatisfaction or urges or any kind:

All other drives are derived from hunger; and henceforth every longing turns upon the desire to find satisfaction in the what and somewhat that accord with it and are outside it. This means that all lives must tend towards something, or must move and be on its way towards something; and that in its restlessness the void satisfies beyond itself the need that comes from itself. This kind of want is soon answered, as if there had been no question, no problem. But satisfaction is always transitory; need makes itself felt again, and must be considered in advance, above all to ensure its disappearance not merely as hunger and deficiency, but as lack of what is most necessary.[13]

Equally unsatisfactory is his recourse to Aristotle's definition of matter as both activity and potentiality. We may take this definition to imply a logical priority of potentiality over actuality and necessity (over mechanistic fixed systems). Then inherent in all process is the drive to the realisation of the potentiality in the situation, a drive that provides both *telos* and *entelecheia*, the goal or end and the conditions under which a potentiality becomes an actuality.[14]

There is in such positions a pseudo-materialism in which logical devices simply attribute to matter the structures and movements for which one needs to find a specifically human explanation. Bloch does not link his drives in any clear way with the socio-economic situation, and though he makes abundant analysis of a large number of cultural and psychological factors he makes only slight connections, if any at all, with the class-struggle and with historical development. It is not enough to assert:

Bloch has a unique concept of the specific mode of experience of the masses; imagination, the banal superstitious content of the consciousness of the common people—all this is a constitutive element of the materialist understanding of science, which can no more be separated from the mode of experience of the masses than it can from the 'coproductivity of nature' . . . (NEGT)[15]

Bloch himself insists that the revolutionary goal is the linking of the workers' consciousness with the reality of their situation. While the gap continues, the potentialities there cannot be understood and actualised. As usual he clouds his meaning somewhat with abstract formulations:

The lack of mediation with the material continues to be common to both bourgeois economy and technique. Crisis as well as accident form for both these abstractions unsurmountable barriers, for both are contemplative, both are realistic. Both are characterised by the pure indifference of form to content. And this does not occur just in crimes but in technological catastrophes as well. Here and everywhere the lack of mediation of the bourgeois *homo faber* with the material of his work avenges itself, especially at the moments of incomplete productivity, with the tendency and latency in the material of nature itself. And only when the subject of history, the working human being, understands him or herself as the producer of history . . . can he or she move closer to the seat of production in the world of nature . . . Natural energy as friend, technology of the release and delivery of the creations slumbering in the womb of nature, all this is part of the most concrete of concrete utopia.[16]

Bloch is stressing the active relation to nature involved in productive activity; people discover themselves in nature as well as using and transforming it. In the bourgeois world they are at best only imperfectly and sporadically conscious of this relation. Technology becomes a thing in itself, acting and developing solely by its own inner laws and systems. This more-than-imperfect consciousness of the true human relation to nature is at all points linked with the distorting elements of class ideology that pervade the minds of people, the degree to which they are treated as things, and so on. (Bloch uses the term 'lack of mediation with the material' to express the lack of any true unconsciousness merging people with the nature they transform.)

To become aware of the truth of social relations is to become aware of one's real living relations with nature. An intuition of the reality continually asserts itself in the emotions and ideas that Bloch gathers under the heading of Hope. The function of Marxism, as he sees it, is to strengthen and develop all the elements of Hope until they are effectively united with our conscious processes, our ways of organising society and production. Then and then only our consciousness will achieve a dialectical union of past, present, and future, and we shall be able at last truly to mate with the earth while building an harmonious society in which creative energy is given a maximum of chances to liberate itself.

In these positions we can recognise the sketch of a system that would concretely link Hope with both the class-struggle and productive activity, and thus give each of its manifestations a definite historical basis. In such a system the Block would be more than the resistance of static logic, of all the mechanistic attitudes and forms that have been built into people and all around them; it would incorporate all the socio-economic elements, all the political formations, of a class-world.

But as things are, Bloch says, we are ultimately 'still in a state of non-being.' The problem is to break through the fettering limits of this level. Somehow or other Marxism can provide us with the means of this breakthrough. 'Marxist philosophy is that philosophy which ultimately relates itself adequately to becoming and to what is still approaching . . . Marxist philosophy is a philosophy of the future.' That is, a philosophy of living process, of becoming, cannot be satisfied with analyses of the past or with analyses of the present that by their nature are abstractions or schematisations derived from (inevitably incomplete) examinations of the past (even the recent past). To press into the present in its fullness we need a more complex, and at the same time a more unitary, comprehension of the life of men and women.[17] Bloch thus continually presents a challenge for the extension and deepening of Marxist perspectives. We need to realise indeed that the human being is incomplete, is continually both torn and impelled forward by unsatisfied needs and unrealised potentialities. Herein lies a deep and constant human element which cannot be separated from all the various activities by which people develop. In particular art, philosophy, religion are reservoirs of the needs and potences that keep on struggling for fuller release, for total integration with nature as well as for social harmony. Bloch argued for the 'ontological identity' of aesthetic and material production in a substratum of nature. In such ideas he gave us signposts to the more effective development of Marxism, even if he himself could not go far along the lines he opened up.[18]

We must begin by asking, if indeed the impulses and ideas gathered under the term Hope do exist, how and why do they come into existence. A clue is to be found in the correlation Bloch makes with art and religion. His Hope is a product of the collective nature of all human systems, of the coming-together of people in work, in productive activity. A deep supply of surplus energy is set up and released: that is, energy vitally connected with productive activity but not absorbed into it. The individual is in continual tension with the collective, which enhances his energy, finds outlets for it, and yet leaves a surplus not directly employed. The energies stirred and brought together in work are raised to a new power, partly dispersed, partly concentrated afresh. Part of them brim over in the play of sense and mind which issue in art, in the ceaseless release of fantasy to which Lenin drew attention and which Bloch analysed at length, fantasy arising out of work, personal relations, sensuous experience, and so on. This fantasy plays around everything connected with the individual, from the smallest and most trivial matters to the most important and crucial events, acts, experiences and relationships.

In a divided society the play of fantasy grows more complex and takes as one of its directions the overcoming of the obstructions and limitations created by the divisions and affecting the individual at every point. The analysis of art and religion reveals the struggle between the uniting and dividing factors in all concepts and depictions of human existence. This struggle can take an infinite number of forms according to individual experience and the social whole in which it occurs; it is pervasively present. In the same way the sense of the collective, of the liberations and frustrations in the productive sphere, in all the spheres of life, begets both the Hope and the Block in Bloch's sense of the terms. Sometimes the Block prevails; sometimes the Hope dominates. We thus get social passivity or revolt, and so on. The Hope and Block are to be found at all levels of experience, at every moment of human life, sometimes confused and limited in their operations, sometimes attaining great strength and concentration, but always present in some shape or other, some degree or other. We can connect them, directly and indirectly, with the class-system, the class struggle.[19]

Along some such lines as are here sketched-out we can make Bloch's ideas a vital part of Marxism. They bring into a dialectical unity the forces that have flowed into art, religion, revolt; they explain the vision of the future which one way or another underlies all struggles to advance the human condition and to actualise in small or large ways the ideas of justice, equality, fraternity.

Furthermore, we can use Bloch's work in meeting the reproach made by Timpanaro that Marxism has had little to say about individuality, its nature and role, about sensuous existence with all its joys and frustrations, about sex and love, about all the disasters that can and do beset the individual, including illness and finally death. The substance and texture of individual life are indeed to be found expressed in their fullness and complexity in the various forms of art. Here then is an important point where we can bring together Bloch's concept of Hope and our analysis of art expressions, linking it dialectically with our analysis of society but not submerging it in that analysis. For political economy, for historical materialism in general, the individual is a mere unit who disappears in the discussion of the structures and systems of the mode of production. But to subsume the whole body of actual experience in a socio-economic analysis, however necessary for the elucidation of a key aspect of human development, cannot be satisfactory in a full presentation of a materialist view of life. With the aid Bloch's positions and an adequate comprehension of the nature and role of art, dialectically linked with the larger historical patterns, the full presentation can be achieved.

Bloch continued all his life to look for the Novum in the upheavals going on around him. He made a whole-hearted response to the 1917 revolution; then in the 1930s he was primarily concerned, like Lukacs, with the anti-fascist struggle, so that it was all the easier to see only the positive side of what was going on in the Soviet Union. Not that he was ever a capable or penetrating critic of the contemporary situation. What stirred him was the sense of deep changes bursting out all round him, which, despite checks or confusions, could not fail in the end to make utopia concrete. Here indeed we see the limitations of his virtues; but it is nonsense to describe many of his comments (as Kalokowski does) as 'like a downright parody of Stalinist propaganda'. He inevitably saw points of realised Hope rather than Blocks. However, in speeches after 1961 he took up a position in favour of democratic socialism and declared that Marxism needed to be renewed, related to changing circumstances. In 1974 he remarked that commodity-production and all that it implied was not withering away in the Soviet Union, 'That's not at all what is happening in the USSR, where the State is growing stronger and stronger—that's not the Marxist way; something isn't quite right there.' But as he felt sure that the impulse of Hope was alive among the people of the class-world, so he felt it at work also in the socialist societies, making people there satisfied with nothing less than full liberation. His expulsion from the GDR came as a tragic climax to his life.[20]

5 Adorno and the Frankfurt School

The Frankfurt Institute of Social Research was set up in 1923. Its aim was to deal more adequately than the existent academic bodies with the changes in national life since round 1880, with what was seen as a crisis in culture. The changes were based in the rapid growth of German capitalism and the new world-role of Germany. Marxism played an important part in the views of the leading thinkers of the Institute, but they always kept it to some extent at arm's length. By the early 1930s the Institute dropped any direct relation to working-class movements and concentrated on matters of culture and social authority. Among its leading members were Theodor W. Adorno, Max Horkheimer, Herbert Marcuse and the economist F. Pollock. Others were connected with it for a while, e.g. Erich Fromm. When the Nazis came to power the leaders moved to France, then to the United States. After the war Adorno and Horkheimer returned to Europe and tried to carry on with their critique of German society: Adorno turned more and more to aesthetic issues.

Strong influences on him were Nietzsche, Simmel and Lukacs, and Marx (in some selected points). Nietzsche influenced him far more fundamentally than he did Bloch. Again it was the concept of Becoming, *Werden*, that had the deep effect. All previous philosophers were seen as falsifying their views of life by refusing to recognise that it was always in a state of continuous and dynamic process or change, and that to make any absolute or definite statements or analyses of it was to arrest it and to impose a judgment or value from outside. Adorno took over from Nietzsche the position that because of the systematic falsification of reality that had been carried on there was need for a Transvaluation of All Values. It was necessary to realise all the while that the apparent fixity of the world and of values was derived from ignoring or distorting the dynamic essence of reality, 'that restlessness, that inward shudder, which Hegel called Becoming.' Philosophic systems must be rejected on the grounds that 'the totality of the world is not appropriate to our forms of consciousness.' The will-to-power constituted the world and our modes of thought at all times.[1]

Adorno developed these positions in a thorough-going attack on the Enlightenment, in which rationality was used with particular force and consistency to impose its domination on the refractory universe of process. In the Enlightenment reason and domination were completely fused. Adorno paid many tributes to Nietzsche for his liberating effect. He was 'the dynamic thinker par excellence'; as 'the irreconcilable adversary of our theological inheritance in metaphysics' he rejected 'the speculative concept, the hypostasis of the mind.' He cites his statement: 'Nothing occurs in reality which strictly corresponds to logic', and declares:

Nietzsche's liberating act, a true turning-point of Western thought and merely usurped by others, was to put such systems into words. A mind that discards rationalisation—its own spell—ceases by its self-reflection to be the radical evil that irks it in others.

To the positions drawn from Nietzsche Adorno added others from Simmel and from Lukacs' *History and Class-Consciousness:* Simmel's view of the social world as a world of external objects that seem to live a life of their own, alien forces oppressing the individual, who, though he had created them, is less and less able to assimilate them; and Lukacs' thesis of a universal reification afflicting people of all classes in developed capitalism. Finally he added ideas drawn from Marx's thesis of commodity fetishism.[2]

How, then, is Adorno to work out a philosophic system? Behind all past systems he detects the will to dominate, to control the world by steadily identifying it with the concepts of the systems. Nothing must escape, 'There is a will to identity in every synthesis'. Philosophies have worked thus with 'a paranoid zeal', seeking to devour everything different (inferior)—'The system is the belly turned mind.' The kind of thought that functions only by constructing and controlling nature (the world, society) is the 'pragmatic' mode of identifying; its coercive mechanism is seen as formation. 'What men seek to learn from nature is how to use it in order wholly to dominate it and men. Enlightenment behaves towards things as a dictator towards men. He knows them in so far as he can manipulate them.' To counter such systems Adorno sets himself to develop a method he calls the Critical Theory. It seeks at every moment to put the reader on guard against a use of logic that sees things in fixed categories and introduces a metaphysical rigidity into its judgements, turning the living elements of Becoming into separate things.

His main term for the falsifying thought-systems is Identity Thinking. Such thinking arrests reality by seeing unlike things as like. It holds that a concept fully and truly covers an object when in fact it does not. It thus incorrectly makes the object the equivalent of its concept, and in fact goes round in circles. Take the idealist dialectic of Hegel: 'By its return to the starting-point of the motion, the result was fatally annulled; this was supposed to bring about a continuous identity of subject and object.' (The term identity-thinking comes from Hegel, who used it to define the way that understanding, which includes the conventional modes of scientific thought, unfolds things in their abstract undifferentiated identity. 'Modern philosophy . . . reduces everything to identity. Hence its nickname, the Philosophy of Identity.')[3]

Critical Theory then must at every moment find ways of making the reader aware of the traps and gaps in identity-thinking, all the ruses of reason. It starts with a view of reality as divided, rent with antagonisms; something too complex and elusive to be represented by any system that sets as its goal or criterion unity, simplicity, clarity. It drops any idea of setting out first principles, which by their nature oversimplify or distort a reality made up of contradictions and unforeseeable changes. It refuses to define its concepts, since to do so is to make them identity-instruments. 'Disenchantment of the concept is the antidote of philosophy.' Even to define terms is to fall into a trap. So Adorno uses the same term in many different senses, hoping to stir the reader into actively grappling with the problems raised, into recognising the contradictions and conflicts inherent in the aspect of reality under consideration. No attempt to come to grips with reality, he asserts, can ever be fully satisfactory. We have to use words, and we cannot eliminate the 'mythical remainder', the deep impress left on and in them by the endless past efforts to use them in the struggle to understand and control the world. Any attempt to purify language, as if some sort of pristine meaning can be obtained, is to create a different kind of myth, a worse one. It results, not in an objective scientific style, but in new distortions, lacks of correspondence between the words and the reality they are supposed to reveal and explain. But, whatever the difficulties, we cannot evade the problems of the way that words veil or reveal reality; and so the words used in any systems, philosophical, sociological, artistic, are of primary importance. The problem is to get inside them and strive to clarify what is their relation at any given moment to the reality with which they deal. 'The semblance and the truth of thought entwines'; and so, in philosophy or sociology, 'nothing is meant in a completely literal manner, neither statement of fact nor pure validity.'[4]

To bring out what is the semblance of thought and what is its truth, Adorno resorts to all sorts of tricks with words, breaking up a formulation or approaching it from several different angles. Irony is a favourite device of his: irony as the use of words to convey the opposite of their customary meaning, or irony as some apparent perversity of fate or circumstances. He takes familiar phrases or ideas, even well-known book-titles, and changes a word or two; he then expounds them as if they had to be taken seriously and literally. He thus at times throws new light on the original idea through the new angle of approach; or he gives the effect that social attitudes and ideas have got out of control, gone a bit mad or topsyturvy. But once again the literal interpretation must be rejected. What is aimed at is the effect of a particular discrepancy between words and reality, which hints at what the reality is. Irony advances 'by way of extremes', as does the dialectic. It represents or suggests 'the difference between ideology and reality'—though Adorno proceeds to complicate the situation by remarking that that difference has in fact faded out, with the result that it is impossible to separate ideology and reality. So the trick of using irony without comment, presenting an object as what it claims to be but in fact is not, fails to work. The standard for measuring discrepancies is itself 'a lie'. But even this statement is not to be taken literally; it is meant only as yet another jolt. For if all standards were lies, Adorno's whole work would be pointless. He is in fact still using irony in the way he stigmatises as no longer possible. [5]

Irony with its devious inversions can indeed drop its tricks and give way to a direct form of inversion. The concept of Critical Theory

is formed by the inversion of the concepts which govern the economy into their opposites: fair exchange into widening of social injustice, the free economy into the domination of monopoly, productive labour into the consolidation of relations which restrict production, the maintenance of the life of society into the immiseration of the people.

Not that irony is the only shock-tactic. Adorno uses fantasy, any kind of exaggeration or provocative formulation. He sets out an idea without enlarging on it, then later re-states it with different emphases (parallaxes). Though an object cannot be defined, a series of phrases may approximate to it. He calls this method a constellation, and uses the terms paratactic, concentric, 'like a spider's web'. Further he makes much use of chiasmus, a figure of speech in which the order of words in one clause is inverted in another: 'History is nature, nature is history'. At times the whole structure of a piece may be based on this system. [6]

Marcuse in his later days summed up Adorno's position:

It was that ordinary language, ordinary prose, even a sophisticated one, has been so much permeated by the Establishment, expresses so much the control and manipulation of the individual by the power structure, that in order to counteract this process you have to indicate already in the language you use the necessary rupture with conformity. Hence the attempt to convey the rupture in the syntax, the grammar, the vocabulary, even the punctuation. Now whether this is acceptable or not I don't know. The only thing I would say is that there lies an equally great danger in any premature popularisation of the terribly complex problems we face today.

Probably in part through Marcuse, in part through a spontaneous reaction to the situation, ideas close to those of the Frankfurt School appeared among rebellious American Youth-groups in the later 1960s.

Revolution must break with the past, and derive all its poetry from the future (International Situationists). Our programme is cultural revolution through a total assault on culture, which makes use of every tool, every energy and every media we can get our collective hands on . . . our culture, our art, the music, newspapers, books, posters, our clothing, our homes, the way we walk and talk, the way we smoke dope and fuck and eat and sleep—it's all one message—and the message is FREEDOM (White Panthers). The division between left-right is false . . . the division is between life and death. Hip-life consciousness must replace political death consciousness and tribal social consciousness must replace left wing party consciousness and revolutionary hope . . . Western civilisation must be destroyed . . . and new life-forms created . . . the struggle is as total as life itself (Sun Eagle, Summer Solstice, New Mexico).[7]

I myself wrote in the early 1970s: 'One aspect of this new line of thought was the belief that if a work of art itself exposed the system of construction and had "nothing to hide", it was in effect exposing the way in which capitalism needed a respectable or decorative facade behind which to carry on with its dirty work. Art that attempted to depict reality in any integrated way was accused of willy-nilly making a contrived or unconscious apology for the claim that bourgeois society itself was integrated in an harmonious and laudable way.'

Adorno (again influenced by Nietzsche) himself felt driven to prefer short unrelated sections, essays, aphorisms, finally scraps or snatches of thought, *Prisms, Minima Moralia, Philosophical Fragments.* 'From my theorem that there are no philosophical first principles, it follows that one cannot construct a continuous argument with the usual stages, but one must assemble the whole from a series of partial complexes . . . whose constellation not [logical] sequence produces the idea.' In an essay *On the Nature and Form of the Essay* he championed the short form: it 'thinks in breaks because reality is brittle and finds its unity through the breaks, not by smoothing things over.' It has the features of an anti-system.

As an example of his essays we may take that on Society. Any idea we have of society, he says, is inevitably incomplete, partial, inadequate, and full of contradictions. But by analysing the terms we use in describing our understanding of the concept, we gain glimpses of what is indeed the concrete reality of social life at any given moment. Society is not an empirical object that we can select, take up, study directly from our own experience. From this angle we find correctness in the neo-positivist position which looks on the very idea of society as an abstract construct or a mere methodological hypothesis, but with no other kind of existence. And yet all the while society, precisely in the rejected supra-personal forms, is present with us, affecting and constraining us at every moment. It is not-there, invisible, breaking through all definitions, an impossible concept, yet all the while the most concrete of all the realities in our lives.

While the notion of society may not be deduced from any individual facts, nor on the other hand be apprehended as an individual fact itself, there is nonetheless no social fact which is not determined by society as a whole.[8]

In this way, by detecting and laying bare the contradictions in our thinking, we find that they reflect or express the contradictions of their object. Just as the initial contradictions in the concept seem to deny us any possible access to the real objects to which they are supposed to correspond, we gain the denied knowledge, or at least some aspects of it.

However, in seeking to justify and give substance to his negative or critical method as having a fundamental virtue apart from its necessary use against the rationalising intellect, Adorno claims that 'Thought, as such, before all particular contents, is an act of negation, of resistance to that which is forced upon it; this is what thought has inherited from its archetype, the relation between labour and material.' That is, he sees at the heart of labour, the productive process, not the positive aspect of the worker uniting with nature, but the difficulties and resistances encountered in the act. The worker has the act 'forced' on him. Adorno is thus transferring to the productive or creative act, at all times and stages, the element of enslavement that comes to the fore under capitalism. He is admitting that that element so obsesses him he puts it at the core of all his thinking.

What part then does dialectics play in his work? Why does he need a special negative theory if dialectics is doing its proper job? He replies that dialectics has degenerated into a dogma and has worked out as impoverishing experience. He does not elaborate these charges, but we know from the body of his work that he refuses to accept the way that Marx works out his thesis of surplus value, that he considers the proletariat to have lost its revolutionary role (if it ever had one), and sees no force or class capable of transforming the situation of monopoly-capitalism. From his viewpoint, then, Marxism has shown itself to be full of illusions and to have miscarried as a guide to action.

So it must be full of errors and forms of identity-thinking that have falsified its systems. He says: 'Dialectical knowledge is taken too literally by its opponents.' He should add, 'and by its advocates'. Since the literal meaning has proved false or insufficient, it must be revised, taken to pieces, then put together again in the light of critical or negative theory: 'The dialectic advances by way of extremes, driving thoughts to the point where they turn back on themselves, instead of qualifying them.' The dialectic here is that of critical theory, which realises when a formulation has reached the end of its relevance, and which then drives on to a point of break.

Dialectics is the self-consciousness of the objective context of delusion; it does not mean to have escaped from that context. The objective goal is the break out of the context from within . . .

It means a double mode of content: an inner one, the immanent process which is the properly dialectical one, and a free unbound one like a stepping out of dialectics. Yet the two are not merely disparate . . . Both attitudes of consciousness are linked by criticising one another, not by compromising . . .

Dialectics is the consistent sense of non-identity. It does not begin by taking a standpoint. My thought is drawn to it by its own inevitable insufficiency, by my guilt of what I am thinking.

In a sense, dialectical logic is more positivistic than the positivism that outlaws it. As thinking, dialectical logic respects that which is to be thought—the object—even where the object does not heed the rules of thinking. The analysis of the object is tangential to the rules of thinking. Thought need not be content with its own legality; without abandoning it, we can think against our thought, and if it were possible to define dialectics, this would be a definition worth suggesting.[9]

The wielder of negative dialectics insists that he cannot be criticised from either the logical or the factual viewpoint, as he has declared that such criteria are irrelevant to him. Indeed, he says, his intellectual and moral superiority is based on the fact that he disregards such criteria. This disregard is the essential point of negative dialectics. A difficulty however in Adorno's statements lies in the fact that he does not clearly differentiate in his terms between pre-Adorno dialectics, his own negative dialectics, and the interaction of the two. The reason perhaps is that he wants to shake us up and make us think out the issues for ourselves, so that we will be able to make our own differentiations. We may sum up as follows.

Rationalising or reifying thought is identity-thinking. It identifies concept and object because the mind seeks to grasp and dominate all things, and so needs systems that arrest reality, take it to pieces and put it together again. Non-identity thinking is the method of the negative dialectic. It exposes wherever possible the attempts of identity-thinking to arrest and falsify reality. It criticises society. Its criticism is positive and determinate in that it seeks to unveil and set out the truth of society as far as is possible; but it is not positive in that it refuses to confirm or sanction what it criticises. On the contrary it seeks always to bring out the unrealised or hidden contradictions between thought and reality. (It is one of the inevitable gaps in Adorno's system that he cannot explain how non-identity thinking arises. He asserts that theory is possible and necessary, and that we must be guided by reason. Yet his whole position assumes that reason cannot make the first step without at once falling into reification. So there is no starting-point, and indeed the recognition of this baffling fact is announced as the supreme achievement of non-identity thinking. Not that even here Adorno makes a perfectly clear formulation. It would be against his principles to do so.[10])

Non-identity thinking might be called true dialectics, or at least a necessary aspect of its method. Adorno's fear that any definite system will become tyrannical and impose a set pattern on to process makes him averse from clearly elevating dialectics as a method or defining exactly what he means by it. He appears to accept the Hegelian system and its terms in the way they were criticised, reoriented, re-employed in a materialist world-view by Marx; but he is never precise in such matters. The stress on non-identity thinking implies that in some radical way dialectics or Marxism is being revalued, reorganised, made more adequate to deal with all the tricks of the abstracting intellect. But how Marxism goes on, after the exposure of the reifying tendencies, to develop new positive positions for understanding and transforming reality is not clarified, is indeed hardly touched on. For to raise this question would have meant an attempt to reapply and develop the Marxist concept of the unity of theory and action, and that in turn would have led into the field of politics and the struggle to bring about a free (unreified) society. But that was something that Adorno was totally unwilling to do.*

Where he does attempt a positive statement he can only set out his hope in a semi-mystical form. Thus he comments that 'the overwhelming objectivity of the historical movement in its present phase consists so far only in the dissolution of the subject, without giving rise to a new one.' What can dialectics do in such a situation? He replies, 'Its truth or untruth, therefore, is not inherent in the method itself, but in the intention of the historical process', which must be to integrate freedom and happiness. 'The only philosophy which can be responsibly practised in the face of despair is the attempt to contemplate all things as they would present themselves from the standpoint of redemption. But beside the demand thus placed on thought, the question of the reality or unreality of redemption itself

70

hardly matters' (*Minima Moralia*).

Yet he did try to link his positions, which united key elements from Nietzsche and Lukacs, with certain fundamental ideas drawn from Marx. With his rejection of all first principles he could not claim that Marx's attitudes definitely established anything about life; so he called his Theory of Value the *Urphänomen* (the original phenomenon), the *Urgeschichte* (the prehistory or early history), the *Urmodell* (the primary model) of reification; and he identified the mechanism of identity-thinking with commodity-exchange under capitalism.[11]

The exchange principle, the reduction of human labour to its abstract universal concept of average labour-time, has the same origin as the principles of identification. It has its social model in exchange and exchange would be nothing without identification.

The equalisation of commodities to a monetary value in price made unlike things like. Values seem to people to be a natural property of commodites, though in fact only use-values are their properties. 'As values,' says Marx, 'commodities are social magnitudes, that is to say something absolutely different from their properties as things.' He holds that in commodity-fetishism 'a definite social relation between men . . . assumed the phantasmagoric form of a relation between things'. Adorno was not much concerned about this point. What mattered to him was the way in which Marx's ideas could be linked with the problem of knowledge in a world of reifications. So he seized on the formulations that value appears to be a property of a commodity and that the object is thought to fulfil its concept when in fact only use-values are properties. Marx says that exchange value is 'the only *form* in which the value of a commodity can manifest itself or be expressed'. Adorno carries this ideal over in his theory of reification by holding that a relationship between men appears in the

* Horkheimer began by trying to link Critical Theory as a mode of cognition with the proletariat (following Lukacs). The theoretician and the oppressed class make up 'a dynamic unity,' his 'representation of the social contradictions appears not just an expression of the concrete historical situation, but rather as a stimulating, transforming factor in it.' He then links the theoretician with 'the advanced parts of the class.'

The conflict between the advanced parts plus theoretician with the rest of the class is to be seen 'as a process of mutual interaction in which consciousness unfolds with its liberating and propulsive, disciplinary and aggressive powers' (5) ii 164. (Shortly before he equates the advanced part with a 'a party or its leadership.' Note that he does not see the theoretician as linked with the proletariat as a whole.) Only once again (ii 166) he refers to organised struggle. 'The overpoliticisation of theory leads logically to the substitute of the theory as a surrogate for politics,' Therborn, 91.

form of a property of a thing. What is truly the property of a thing is non-reified: it is, one may say, its own use-value. The problem of critical theory is, then, to derive the non-reified concepts from the reified form in which they necessarily appear in capitalist society.[12]

In thus taking over elements of Marx's theory of value, Adorno quite ignores the distinction of abstract and concrete labour, and the whole question of the extraction of surplus-value. He wants to unite philosophy and sociology, but along certain narrow lines that keep clear of all political issues. As we saw, he denied that he was without hope, but he provided little theoretical basis in his work for any possibility of revolutionary change. That basis could only have been introduced if he had linked his concepts of non-identity thinking with the class-struggle. However there was one aspect of those concepts that did suggest the possibility of a non-reified society. Non-identity thinking realises that the object is not really captured by reified or identity-thinking; it thus looks beyond the limited and arrested situation into a deeper reality. Adorno calls this glimpse-beyond the seeing of Utopia. Further, identity-thinking appears when we use a concept paradigmatically to collect the particulars it denotes; but concepts also refer to their objects. That is, in Adorno's terms, they also refer to the conditions of their ideal existence, the conditions that would make them fully and concretely possible. They would then truly cover their objects. Freedom for example would then be truly freedom. Thus the glimpse of Utopia again appears in the reference to the conditions and ideal existence enclosed in concepts. Here is a thin gleam of the complex of forces gathered in Bloch's Hope. But the gleam would only become active and meaningful if Adorno made the step to link non-identity thinking with political struggle.[13]

So he is left with a society of increasing reification, in which there are no inner forces making for renewal. As usual there is a contradiction in his position. At times he speaks of society as 'completely reified'. The exchange system dominates it so thoroughly that it in effect controls all class-formations, institutions, organisations, as well as the behaviour and inner life of all persons. There are no interstices or antagonistic groupings that could beget or stimulate a critical consciousness, an outlook independent of the reifying forces that reduce everyone to a common denominator. The victims accept the appearances of society as they have no awareness of the way they are manipulated. The utopian possibilities that we discussed above are in such a situation forever blocked and banished. Yet with his paradoxical method Adorno at times argues that non-identity thinking can be born out of the midst of identity-thinking, 'No matter to what extent the mind is a product of that (reified) type, it implies at the same time the objective possibility of overcoming it.' This admission is, however, thrown in as a mere logical possibility. The contrary force or intuition is not linked with any social grouping or movement. 'Everything is one . . . Today the forces of production and the relations of production are one . . . Material production, distribution, consumption are ruled together.' There is no class-analysis of the dominating political forces that reflect the situation where 'exchange-value has deceptively taken over the function of use-value'. They merely carry on in an autonomous way: 'Universal history must be construed and denied.' Construed, or there is no way of grasping the historical processes that have issued in the impasse; denied, because there can be no history if the impasse continues, depriving people of any human goal in a capitalist society that automatically throws up new forms and extensions of dehumanisation, reification. There is a strong tendency to see technological developments, linked with identity-thinking, as the sufficient motive force of history under monopoly-capitalism. 'Formalisation of reason is only the intellectual expression of mechanised production.'[14]

On this basis Adorno, and Horkheimer with him, develop their picture of a society without any inner forces of revolt, any elements making for renewal. Cultural production in such a world becomes the culture industry, linked at all points to the flattening and falsifying forces of social exchange and identity-thinking (The exchange system is not defined as determining the reifications; rather we are presented with two systems owning the same internal structure.) Adorno makes no analysis of the full relations of an art-product to its historical moment. Rather he works from the viewpoint of its form. What has been realised in the form gives the best key to the content, to the possibilities of the determinate moment from the which work sprang. So we arrive at the historical moment by analysing the nature of the form, its structure, contradictions, and resolutions. We do not work from the social moment, the historical situation, to the art-product.

Rather, that is Adorno's aim, but the comprehension of the social moment thus arrived at is not in any way historically precise.

The unsolved antagonisms of reality recur in the work of art as the immanent problems of the form. This, not the entry of objective moments, defines the relations of art to society.

All very well, if by this kind of analysis we do in the end arrive at the 'objective moments', the actual social situation in all its specific possibilities and resistances, and understand better the particular way in which they are refracted in the work of art. But Adorno in fact takes a very restricted view of what he calls the antagonisms of reality, because of his limitations of Marxist theory to the matter of exchange. He wrote to Krenek in September 1932:

The commodity character of music is not determined by its being exchanged, but by its being *abstractly* exchanged, in the way in which Marx explained the commodity form: hence not an immediate but a 'reified' exchange relation occurs. When you explain the way 'art has become autonomous' as the decisive change, that is exactly what I mean by its commodity character. Only it is the same phenomenon described not from the side of the *relations* of production, but from the side of the *forces* of production . . . If by capitalism one understands more than mere 'for money', namely, the *totality* of the social process defined as a unity of exchange by abstract labour time, then, in an exact sense, capitalism has made art into a commodity *together with* men. The commodity character of art as the objective side, and the destruction of 'human dignity' as the subjective side are equivalent and cannot be torn apart from each other.[15]

What interests him is not the historical moment in all its complexity of struggle, defeat, resolution, possibility, but the system of economic production, exchange, reproduction and consumption that is involved. So he discusses the social or historical situation almost wholly in terms of the forces and relations of production. He distinguishes them so that exchange and reproduction fall on both sides of the distinction instead of being allotted to one side or the other. He sees however a basic conflict or contradiction between forces and relations as far as culture is concerned. So in dealing with modern music he does not consider the social situations in their fulness; he is interested only in the economic abstractions. He starts with the commodity character of the music and the fact that the way in which it is exchanged gives rise to fetishism. The ever-more extended systems of mechanical reproduction swell the volume of exchange of cultural products and thus beget new forms of art without altering in the least the essential commodity-character of what is turned out.

The idea of music as a form of production is valuable, but the way in which music is related abstractly only to the forces of production robs the idea of its vital possibilities.

Innovation in [artistic and musical] production is judged in terms of the significance accorded to the dominant relations of production, and the designation 'forces of production' is really reserved for what resists those relations and not for new techniques or for new technology as such. Composition is not, however, a relational term in the way work or 'labour-power' are for Marx. In the realm of consumption, the 'culture industry' is a force of production in the sense that it constitutes a changed form of social domination and control, while considered under the relations of production, it is responsible for new kinds of social behaviour which Adorno examined by using Freudian categories. (ROSE)[16]

In this kind of way Adorno tries to develop his sociology of music and literature by examining genres or particular works of art in the light of his idea that a contradiction has intruded between the forces and the relations of production. 'The forces of production,' he argues, 'are displaced into high, quasi-privileged spheres, isolated, and therefore, even when they incorporate true consciousness, are also partly false. The lower spheres obey the predominant relations of production.'[17]

But when we ask what he really means by the forces of production we find that he merely refers to musical skill in composition (for the market or not) and the techniques and technology that determine the composition and are its tools or means. He does not even refer to the general preconditions of buying and selling labour-power, or the labour-process itself. By the relations of production he does not mean the class-positions or roles of everyone involved in the productive process, but the particular tastes and attitudes, social and personal, which in general determine the reception and consumption of the products. (In any event, for him, the relations of production are created and controlled by the reifications and dominations arising out of the exchange-system.)

His position that art is at once an autonomous form and a social fact, with no real links apart from the forces and relations of production in his very restricted sense of those terms, explain why there is no movement into political action. Indeed, in such a world political action can have no real significance. What he has done is to supplant the analysis of the historical movement in its fullness, which includes political and social struggles of all kinds and at all levels, with a consideration of the relations of Subject and Object in their various possibilities. So his notion of an effective coming-together of the subjective and objective worlds—what he calls Reconciliation —remains a mere logical possibility, a form of abstract utopianism.

A Blochian element indeed comes in when he tries to link a dialectical concept of historical change (in which the various moments are integrated in terms of the possible relations of subject and object) and the hypothesis of a moment of plenitude, of total reconciliation. Such viewpoints are liable to be linked with a looking-back to some paradisiac state or a dream of some utopian future. But in cultural analysis, where the dialectical opposition of form and content takes over from that of subject and object, the position has more virtues and possibilities:

For if we are in no position to judge the concreteness of life at any given moment of the past, at least we can evaluate the adequacy of form to content in its cultural monuments, and are able to measure the reconcilation of

75

intention and medium and the degree to which all visible matter is form, and all meaning or expression concrete embodiment. (JAMESON)[18]

Adorno finds in Beethoven the fullest achievement of this kind of reconciliation, a precarious and yet sustained balance 'between melody and development, between a new and richer thematic expression of subjective feeling and its objective working through in the form itself.'

In such areas his work is full of suggestive virtues. But the method breaks down when he comes to the present, since any idea of reconcilation with a world of total reification can only lead to disaster, to extreme dehumanisation. Here Adorno makes an invalid equation between the aesthetic integration of the possibilities of a situation and the acceptance of the prevailing social powers. Beethoven in a sense accepts the historical epoch in which he finds himself, but only insofar as he enters at the same time into its deepest conflicts and expresses its human potentialities. For Adorno such a relationship is impossible in our world, since any coherent statement, whatever its content, is seen as damned by its form as a reconciliation with evil. Here the weakness of his notion of form, with its severe limitations as to what constitutes content, takes over.

It is argued that in a world of total reification any musician using accepted tonalities or structures is simply a conformist, accepting and aiding the ruling powers with their fetishistic identity-thinking. Adorno brings out this point by his comparison of Schoenberg with Stravinsky. The former in his early work rejected all accepted tonality, yet had no system of his own: he negated the existing systems. His atonal music is

no longer the mimesis of passions, but rather the undisguised registration through the musical medium of bodily impulses from the unconscious, of shocks and traumas which assault the taboos of form inasmuch as the latter attempt to impose their censorship on such impulses, to rationalise them and to transpose them into images. Thus Schoenberg's formal innovations were innately related to the changes in the things expressed, and helped the new reality of the latter to break through to consciousness. The first atonal works are transcripts, in the sense of the dream transcripts of psychoanalysis.

Adorno thus identifies aesthetic rules with the prevailing forms of social domination, while the impulses or drives coming up from the Freudian unconscious are seen as deep spontaneous revolts against those forms. The repressed impulses or desires are identified with the baffled forces of renewal. The release of the latter, the 'return of the repressed,' can come about only through a 'shattering of the social contract with reality.'[19]

Stravinsky uses recognisable forms and so is rooted in the

acceptance of domination. His work is a demagoguery that can be compared with Fascism. Adorno thus totally rejects any form of realism, any expression that deals directly with social reality. Politically that expression may be revolutionary and opposed to all bourgeois ideas and ideals; but if it is intelligible in any fully worked-out sense, it has succumbed to the systems of rationality which Adorno identifies with capitalist domination. Any discussion on art—'Where is it going to lead?'—is at once 'a mutilated form of social control'. To talk of the necessity of art 'terribly prolongs the exchange principle'. The possibilities of art today cannot be settled in any connection with productive relations; 'the decision depends only on the productive forces.' Adorno thus attacked Benjamin's ideas about the revolutionary potentiality of new cultural forms (genres), such as cinema, radio, and so on, as a capitulation to 'Brechtian motifs'—above all:

the appeal to the immediacy of interconnected aesthetic effects, however fashioned, and to the actual consciousness of actual workers, who have absolutely no advantage over the bourgeois except their interest in revolution, but otherwise bear all the marks of mutilation of the typical bourgeois.

Adorno considered that Brecht's continued adherence to Communism was a proof of the 'bad faith' of his work.[20]

Adorno's concept of Form, we saw, was supposed to provide a method of deep analysis which brought out the way in which an art-work reproduced in its own system the structure and contradictions of reality; but he failed to go further and link the new comprehension of form with an enriched vision of the full human reality that had gone to make the form-content unity. If he had done so, he would have shown the complex relationship between the manifest content (the artist's intentions and conscious perceptions) and the far deeper and more extended content revealed in the form, in its tensions and integrations, its dynamic structure as it operated at different levels of conflict and resolution.[21] But he could not thus realise the dialectical unity of form and content, the way in which in the last degree the form was the resolution of the conflicts comprehended in the content in its totality. He was interested only in the relation of the artwork to the exchange-system, the concept of fetishism, which he has isolated in Marxism and taken over as if it alone concentrated and expressed all the possible conflicts and contradictions in bourgeois society.*

---

* We may compare Goldmann's positions. He too saw reification as pervasive under advanced capitalism, ending any revolutionary role for the workers. So he turned away from Socialist Realism to works that reflected the ultimate alienations of our world. Thus, he admired

He saw the only hope in a total rupture with existing relationships, though under capitalism attempts at such a rupture lead to various impasses, to an art more and more passively reflecting alienation as a state of being.

It is surprising enough and paradoxical that Adorno is content to oppose to empirical reality a fictive ideal reality into which he moves by 'transcendence,' that he breaks the dialectic of the relations of production and the forces of production, turning to one to condemn the hardness of capitalist society and to the other to imagine a future liberated society. (JIMENEZ)[2 2]

We are left, then, with the culture-industry as the overwhelming fact of existence under monopoly-capitalism. In 1932-3 Horkheimer had seen the breakdown of the family as leading to the premature socialisation of the ego through a whole system of extra-familial agents and agencies. The result was a manipulated and controlled consciousness. 'The experts of the mass media transmit the required values; they offer the perfect training in efficiency, toughness, personality, dream and romance.' The modern man finds himself merged with all his fellows by 'the overpowering machine of education and entertainment,' through which all detrimental ideas are eliminated and he himself is in a state of anaesthesia. Only the avant garde in art protest 'against the infamy of existence', for art, 'since it became autonomous, has preserved the utopia that evaporated from religion'.

By the time of *The Dialectic of Enlightenment* things have grown much worse. Art, with its autonomy renounced, has taken its place among consumption-goods. With leisure 'a forced activity', culture, the creature of the market, disseminates among everyone 'obedience to the social hierarchy.'

The universal reduction of all specific energies to a single, equal and abstract form of labour, from the battlefield to the film-studio. But the transition to a more human situation cannot take place, because the same thing happens to the good as to the bad.

Adorno and Horkheimer succumb to élitist values; they feel only contempt for the masses. All popular art is aimed at reconciling and enslaving audiences to the capitalist situation. Conformity replaces consciousness. There is no hope whatever in the working-class as an independent force, culturally or politically.

Robbe-Grillet's *Les Gommes* as reflecting the self-regulating mechanisms of capitalist society, his *La Jalousie* as reflecting reification. He wants works that 'correspond' to the dominant social phenomena.

Marcuse developed these positions even more strongly in works like *One Dimensional Man:*

A comfortable, smooth, reasonable, democratic unfreedom prevails in advanced industrial civilisation, a token of technical progress . . . That this technological order also involves a political and intellectual coordination may be a regrettable and yet promising development . . .

The apparatus imposes its economic and political requirements for defence and expansion on labour time and free time, on the material and intellectual culture. By virtue of the way it has organised its technological base, contemporary society tends to be totalitarian. For 'totalitarianism' is not only a terroristic political coordination of society, but also a non-terroristic economic-technical coordination which operates through the manipulation of needs by vested interests. [23]

The emphasis here grows more and more on technology and science as the forces producing a mechanised and subservient society (this point will be discussed later on). As with Adorno and Horkheimer, Marcuse has many things to say of modern society that are both deadly and true; but he, too, in the long run oversimplifies and is unable to see the elements that are positive and capable of transforming the situation. However, he was not so bleakly dogmatic as Adorno about the impossibility of any form of protest in literature. He praised Brecht's dramas with their attempts to create an objectifying sense in the audience (the so-called estrangement effect). Here as in other avant garde protests he saw 'literature's own answer to the threat of behaviourism, the attempt to rescue the rationality of the negative'. After the youth-revolts of 1968 he was yet more optimistic about various avant garde developments:

These are not merely new modes of perception reorienting and intensifying the old ones; they rather dissolve the very structure of perception, in order to make room for what? The new object of art is not yet given, but the familiar object has become impossible, false. From illusion, imitation, harmony to reality—but the reality is not yet 'given'.

The idiom is still much the same as that used by Adorno in dealing with Schoenberg, but there is something more hopeful in the tone. Marcuse still looks for the spontaneous breakthrough or rupture. He has no faith in the working-class and looks for the rebels in off-beat nonconformities, 'catalyst groups'; but the horizon has somehow widened. [24]

What positive achievement can we then put to the credit of Adorno and his colleagues? In their attack on the culture-industry they said many true and important things about the tendencies in bourgeois society. But in all their analyses and formulations they saw such tendencies as absolute, without any significant internal conflict. By abandoning the idea of class struggle they left the field hopelessly open to the dehumanising forces, which they variously termed reifying, fetishistic, mechanistic. They were unable to explore the situation for counter-forces, different potentialities.

Despite all that, Adorno's account of the rationalising and arresting intellect is useful as a reminder that the dialectic has its limitations and weaknesses. Like any system it needs continual reconsiderations: criticism that seeks for its weak points. There is nothing sacred in the Hegelian terms that Marx took over and reoriented. They provided a starting-point, but are clearly no more than simplified formulas, extremely broad and generalised laws that enable us to take the first steps in grasping how development occurs. So Adorno's systems of identity-thinking and non-identity thinking, whatever the limitations of the manner in which he defined and applied them, are important in pointing to ways in which the dialectic can keep on criticising and renewing itself. In the continual intrusion of non-identity tricks into his discourse he reminds us that the dialectic is not something to be reserved for special occasions; it should become inseparable from all our responses to life.

Adorno's concept of Form in an artwork again opens up valuable new lines of approach, even if once more a one-sided attitude ends by emptying his method of analysis on any vital social content. The concept needs to be worked out in a fuller and more truly dialectical way.

Finally, though he had no clear idea of the relationship of culture to the socio-economic or political levels, yet by insisting on its autonomy and by devoting a great deal of his work to the question of culture, its nature and function, he did much to broaden Marxism in necessary ways.*

* Horkheimer's decline. In 1950 came *The Authoritarian Personality*, with Adorno as senior author, Horkheimer as director of the research project behind it. All stress is put on personal and psychological factors, with the aim of personal re-education to root out fascism. Horkheimer ended by writing of the 'menace of the yellow race' and the virtues of competition: Therborn 106-110.

6   Structuralist Marxism: Althusser

Language is the most vital element in human life and consciousness. Without it human thought in all its variety and extension, its integral connection with every form of activity, inner and outer, could not exist. Without it there would be no human society at all; it enters organically into every sphere of our existence. Yet the science of language, linguistics, is the most abstract of all intellectual disciplines, outside of mathematics and the like, and is quite unconcerned with language's dynamic and ubiquitous role. Ferdinand de Saussure founded the modern system with a book published in 1916, three years after his death, though his first work went back to 1879. He insisted that language as a total system was complete at any given moment, 'To the degree that something is meaningful, it will be found to be synchronic.' A synchronic system is one that embraces all its elements at a given moment, while diachrony deals with those elements and their changes over a length of time. We have here an opposition that is not dialectical, since the two concepts are based on quite different approaches, different aspects of the reality in question. The first exists in the immediate lived experience of a speaker; the second is an intellectual construction derived from comparisons between one moment and another by someone standing outside the system. History with its complex fulness has been thrown out and we deal only with an abstracted system of signs. The diachrony of linguistics is concerned with explaining phonetic changes and the like, not with the body of social experiences and developments that underlies the construction and extension of language in its vital use. At root linguistics is based on a synchronic outlook, concerned with the system as it exists at a given moment; it cannot absorb a concept of change in any true historical sense.[1]

Inside the system there is an opposition between *langue*, language—the synchronic totality of possibilities—and *parole*, speech—the individual act of speaking, which actualises something of the possibilities. Language is a system of signs, which are quite arbitrary, with their meanings based in social convention. 'The linguistics sign unites,' says Saussure, 'not a thing and a name, but a concept and an acoustic image.' These terms were replaced by a new pair: the signifier and the signified. What is signified is a concept, what signifies is the acoustic image. The power to speak is re-phrased as the power to create and use signs.

Once we thus convert the endlessly protean body of linguistic activities into a matter of signs, the ground is prepared for the abstraction of those activities in a self-sufficient synchronic system unrelated to the tensions, conflicts, and transformations of meaning that make up life. The question of the referents of the sign disappears. The signified, isolated for study, turns into a sign system in its own right: the system is essentially circular. 'Only the relationship of one signifier to another engenders the relation of signifier to signified'(LACAN).

The lines of flight of his [Saussure's] system are lateral, from one sign to another, rather than frontal, from word to thing, a movement already interiorised in the sign itself as a movement from the signifier to the signified. Thus, implicitly, the terminology of the sign tends to affirm the internal coherence and comprehensibility, the autonomy, of the system of signs itself, rather than the constant movement outside the symbol-system towards the things symbolised . . . (JAMESON)[2]

Since the system is now self-contained, self-sufficient, the only way of keeping some conviction of connection with life is to assume that the totality of systematic language is analogous to the organised structures of the real world. Thus Lévi-Strauss assumes some pre-established harmony between the structure of the mind (ultimately of the brain) and the order of the outer world. The sign-system as a whole somehow corresponds to the total structure of reality without a one-to-one linkage of individual units on either side of the dividing line. A relation to life is thus devised by an idealist interpretation of the situation. In language the notions of difference, distinction, opposition, which in other spheres of thought do not always imply one another, are here all one and the same. For Saussure:

Language is not an object, not a substance, but rather a value; thus language is a perception of identity. But in language the perception of identity is the same as the perception of difference. Thus every linguistic perception holds in its mind at the same time an awareness of its own opposite.[3]

We are reminded of Adorno's identity-thinking, which in the critical mind begets its opposite; but what there was dynamic has become flat, passive. Non-identity thinking is absorbed in identity-thinking; the possibility of dialectics is lost. The main expression of the linguistic system of identity-difference, with its phantom or parody of dialectical contradiction, is the combination of the distinctive features in a series of binary oppositions: a tension between presence and absence, between positive and negative (zero) signs. One of the two terms is conceived as positively owning a certain feature, while the other is seen as deprived of that feature.*

We see, then, why structuralism as developed by linguistics was seized on by the immanent school of literary criticism (concerned with the inherent qualities of a work which is treated in isolated self-sufficiency). This school refused to look outside the text or set of texts under consideration in the search for the explication of its structure.We are near the world of pure semiotics: everything stands for something else. 'As soon as there is society,' writes Barthes, 'every usage is converted into a sign of itself.' Such a position has its value insofar as it attacks the empiricist notion of facts as things speaking for themselves, and points out that things have meanings for people and that the world of interpretations must be taken into account, together with its relation to the world of structures and matter. But in practice it tends all the while to reduce social life to a sign system and to ignore social structures and history. Signs are seen as determining physical behaviour and its controlling ideas, turning it into social practice. 'Semiology' writes Barthes' 'is the science of forms, since it studies significations apart from their content'. Marx long ago demolished such positions, remarking that those who separate form and content grow bemused and confused at the problems they've created, and so ascribe the origin of the form to conventions, to the 'so-called universal consent of mankind'. In his phrase language becomes an 'arbitrary function.'[4] The codes thus built up can be manipulated as if they were self-sufficient things. Barthes in *Mythologies* tries to show that the structure of a discourse is a coded ideological language and the ruling class produce and disseminate their ideology as a code that the masses passively accept and use:

Barthes creates a world of abstracted, logical systems of signification. The world has lost its social and historical roots. Yet these very roots, as they are sedimented and filtered in the experience of the semiologist, must determine the meanings he gives to the message. Only by granting the messages under examination a definite meaning can their internal logic be abstracted. Thus,

---

* 'Levi-Strauss likes to claim that he has shown "wonderful symmetries", "perfect homologies," or "complete inversions" in myths, but it would be fairer to say that if his descriptions of them are often "wonderful", the relations he describes are not. "Perfect symmetries" are truly achieved only by ignoring some of the data and by re-describing the rest in terms of carefully selected abstract synecdoches,' Sperber, 40. See also Weimann (1) ch. iv.

to supersede semiology as a research method must be to return forms of significance to the practical contexts in society and history which generate them and enable us to read them . . . Semiology is geared neither to the description of modes of interpreting signs nor to the discovery of the social character of those signs. (SUMNER)[5]

Any attempt to link signs with their practical context is denounced as a surrender to empiricism. As a result structuralists cannot explain how a structure changes and develops, or how it came into being in the first place.

The essential moment of the linguistic work is, therefore, that of the immanent analysis of language, in the course of which one considers only the interior relations of the system, by excluding all that have to do with the relations of the system with men, culture, society. In short, with the outer world, where one makes efforts to establish a 'code' only by any other considerations whether it be physiologic, psychologic, sociologic, or historic. (BURGELIN)

We may then justly sum up structuralism in Sumner's words:

Structuralism has taken the blood and fight out of history. Indeed structuralism could be said to have taken the history out of history, and left it with the rotting skeletons of form which act as signposts or monuments to an elusive, never-present reality . . . Structuralism has not just neglected the social context of the cultural message in its attempt to discover universals . . . its basic concepts and consequent techniques logically exclude any concrete analysis of the social nature, movement and function of ideologies.[6]

Neo-structuralism in France during the 1960s and 1970s, as in the *Tel Quel* group, loosened up the rigidities, without making any essential change. Barthes had argued in 1971 that there is no general semiological system; each text has its own. That is to say, each text must be viewed in its 'difference', as the accomplishment of many codes. Reading should focus on the difference between texts, the relations of proximity and distance, of citation, negation, irony, parody. Such relations can be argued about indefinitely and thus defer any final meaning. So neo-structuralism leads only to an increased subjectivism, indeed an anarchic state of ceaseless questioning, without transcending the limitations of the older structuralism.

At every moment in its development semiotics must theorise its object, its own method and the relationship between them; it therefore theorises itself and becomes, by thus turning back on itself, the theory of its own scientific practice. (KRISTEVA)[7]

As usual we meet a circular process which can never find an effective relation to reality, but must return to ceaseless variations of its dogmatic formulations. The neo-structuralists are concerned with the mechanism of the production of significant systems: that is, their mode of production. But they can only approach the mechanism from within. They seek to systematise the system, not to view it in perspectives that would truly relate it to the world of process.

An example is Derrida, with his idea of de-constructing philosophical or other writings in order to bring out the inner contradictions of what seems a coherent and harmonious system of thought.[8] His de-constructions have been seen as undermining the accepted notions of authorship, identity, selfhood, since they demonstrate that where language is used most consciously it reveals powers that we cannot control. Self-contradictions cannot be avoided, says Derrida. The lines of argument in the analysed texts call their premises into question, and so on. Meaning is explained in terms of an underlying system of differences. (Structuralism, says Burgelin, is a 'pure system of differences'.) The same sort of point is made by Barthes: the emergence of contradictions in thought seem to deny the existence in us of some 'consistent essence of which our public behaviour is the unique expression'—or by Foucauld: the free play of desire which power or the superego keeps on repressing.[8] Continually these thinkers turn to Freud for terms or explanations as through their structuralist analysis elements emerge from a text which were not intended by the author or which he was not aware of. The terms *presence* or *absence* are much used. Social links are ignored or denied. Thus Derrida and Kristeva hold that 'meaning can only be constituted by semiotic systems, a view that denies the ability of social relations to constitute the form of things-to-be-signified, and to necessitate particular relations of signification' (SUMNER).*

But before we go further we may glance at a structuralist whose thought has little to do with linguistics: Lucien Goldmann. His main work, *The Hidden God* (1955), examined Pascal, Racine, and the Jansenists, and sought to link structures of consciousness with specific situations of social classes. Humanistic science, he held, could solve the traditional opposition (stressed by neo-Kantians) between understanding and explanation, as well as the break between facts and values, and could unite the historical and genetic perspective with the structuralist. He saw cultural activity as essentially the work of social

---

* We do not need structuralism to tell us that language is a wide and powerful reservoir of social thought and emotion, and that, when it is used with great concentration, it will bring in elements that lie outside the conscious range of the writer. The grasp of a writer of any deep significance is sure to be much more complex than he realises. It is not language as a thing-in-itself that has this effect; it is the social content of language, stirred ever more widely and deeply by the creative struggle of comprehension.

groups (especially of classes as historically privileged communities), not of individuals. He took from Lukacs (1923) the idea of the difference between actual and potential class-consciousness. The latter was found by our relating the empirical or actual consciousness of a class to the totality of the historical process in which it existed. We thus uncovered what the class would think, feel, desire, if it fully and truly understood its position. (Potential consciousness is a theoretical construction, of little use except in helping the inquirer to find the expressions in a given situation which most clearly and fully integrate the ideas, emotions and aims of a class. For the proletariat it signifies the advent of an effective revolutionary consciousness, as with Lukacs; but Goldmann in fact held the pessimistic view of the proletariat that we found in the Frankfurt school.)[10]

The structuralism of the anthropologist Lévi-Strauss is concerned with the construction of internally connected wholes; genetic structuralism of the Freudian type is concerned with the psychological origins of the meanings under consideration. Goldmann saw his genetic structuralism as a means of showing how individual expressions are manifestations of collective tensions, struggles, or aspirations. The wholes he dealt with he saw as an indissoluble complex of practical and mental activities, of aesthetic and moral attitudes. Intellectual activity presupposed evaluative acts, which could not be separated from purely cognitive ones, and vice versa. A structure was both an ordered system and a complex of tensions and contradictions.

There is much that is valuable in his contentions, but there is a tendency to connect culture with a single undifferentiated class-interest, to attempt over-comprehensive definitions, and to set cultural expressions too simply and securely in a particular historical situation, so that elements of tradition are ignored and fail to explain why past expressions continue to have interest and value. But what is most instructive for us here is the inability to find any way of effectively relating the cultural and the socio-economic or political levels except by homologies, by seeing them in a sense reflecting one another in a system of correspondences. Thus Goldmann escapes reductionism, but at the cost of failing to link the levels in any dynamic or dialectical interplay.

Althusser now comes into the picture through Gaston Bachelard, the philosopher of science under whom he studied.[11] Bachelard set out the idea of the epistemological break that must come in the process of acquiring knowledge if a radical advance is to be made. The break is between the pre-scientific and the scientific world of ideas; it is a break with the existing pattern and frame of reference, which makes possible the construction of a new pattern or problematic.[12] It is above all a break with any theoretical constructions based on social and practical experience in the real world, which are condemned as empirical. The production of science comes about through such a rupture, not through any accumulation of facts or ideas. Perception is quite different from knowledge. The building-up and working-out of abstract concepts derived from observation is a basic obstruction to the emergence or development of science, which occurs through the reflection of scientific concepts on their theoretical object. Science is autonomous and its concepts have no connection with those based on observation (the use of analogy or metaphor also create an epistemological obstacle.) So science develops solely through a critique of previous ideological thought; it works on existing concepts, not on facts or objects. Its guarantees and criteria are wholly internal.

Bachelard held that to understand a text meant to identify the theory at work inside it. To find the theory one ignored any particular proposition or the author's intentions; one looked only for the structure, at the level where it posed the problems that its function was to solve. There lay the theory's *problematic*, the objective internal reference-system of its particular themes, the system of questions determining the answers given. The concept of the problematic is that of an underlying structure making possible the raising of certain questions in a specific form, while excluding others.[13]

How then do we get at the problematic? Here Bachelard, like so many structuralists, has recourse to psychoanalysis, which is seen as the study of the unconscious. As the analyst extracts from the patient's statements a theory of what he is suffering from, so the structuralist uses a Symptomatic Reading to bring out what is latent, silent, absent, in a text, and to construct its problematic. Althusser argues that there is an unconscious in theory as in the mind or psyche, 'Listening reveals beneath the innocence of speech and hearing the culpable depth of a second, quite different discourse, the discourse of the unconscious.' There will be contradictions in a problematic, dislocations between the levels, gaps, lapses, absences. These are determined by the way the contradictory levels of a text or theory are articulated upon each other. Such a reading 'divulges the undivulged event in the text it reads, and in the same movement relates it to a different text, present as a necessary absence in the first'. So Althusser is able to read into Marx what he did not write. It all depends on how we read the text of *Capital*, and interpret its problematic, which is to be discovered solely through the inner structure of the text, not at all through the text's relations to the real object it considers.[14]

There are further debts to Freud, in the notions of displacement, condensation, over-determination. The first two of these are used in the analysis of contradictions to denote the over-determination of contradictions in the Marxist theory of history. Freud deals with dream-images; Althusser is concerned with the relation between the parts and the whole of a social formation, and the effects of a contradiction in the parts (levels) and the whole there. Thus he defines the pattern of dominance and subordination between parts of a social formation at any moment. The contradictions are never simple; they are always over-determined. The sciences of history and the unconscious, says Althusser, both validly use the term 'over-determination' through their common need to find a way of conceptualising the determination of an element in a system by a structure. Althusser also admits that he owes to Freud the idea that each element in a mode of production has its own history, its own time-scale; the totality that results is a conjunctural fusion of elements which are developing independently, not evolving on a common time-base. He considers Over-determination to be the most profound characteristic of the Marxist dialectic, merged as it is with the concept of the Structure in Dominance. It is 'this reflection of the condition of existence of the contradictions within itself, this reflection of the structure articulated in dominance that constitutes the unity of the complex whole within each contradiction'. He is trying to say something more than that various factors or forces powerfully converge in some level. Over-determination is the mark of a structure in which the complexity, the mutual distinction and interdependence of its elements, is expressed by the way the economy displaces the dominant role within the structure to a particular instance, at the same time organising the other instances in terms of this structure-in-dominance. (The phrases are endlessly repeated, but we get no examples or working-out of just what is meant.)[15]

Althusser also drew much from Spinoza, in whose thought he claims to find many elements of structuralism and its epistemology. Spinoza had an essentially synchronic view of reality, posing the problem of the determination of its elements by the structure as a whole. Cause is seen as immanent in its effects, so that there is a possibility of synchronic explanation. Development of knowledge is seen as discontinuous rather than cumulative, and there is a conviction of the 'opacity of the immediate'—the manifest completely hiding the latent and the object of knowledge absolutely distinct from the real object.[16]

In order to build up his own picture of Marx Althusser has to decide where his epistemological break came. He sees in his thought first (1840-2) a rational liberalism closer to Kant and Fichte than to Hegel and then (1842-5) a Feuerbachian humanism. In 1845 comes the rupture. The earlier problematic assumed that there was a universal human nature, the essence of humanity: positions defined by Althusser as empiricism of the subject and idealism of the object. With the break came the birth of Historical Materialism, which saw humanism as mere ideology, and which introduced new concepts: forces and relations of production, superstructures, ideologies, determination by the economy, relative autonomy in other levels or spheres of the social formation, and so on. Althusser has no difficulty in explaining why Marx carried on elements of what (in Althusser's view) are pre-rupture elements; he merely says that Marx lacked the terminology for rigorously defining his new concepts. We may add, that he sees the rupture solely as a theoretical change in concepts; he says nothing of its strong political basis. [17]

Colletti comments that in 1973 Althusser once again stated at length his thesis of history as a process without a subject, but was also forced to admit for the first time that the theme of alienation runs through *Capital*.

In fact, the truth is that the themes of alienation and fetishism are present not only in *Capital*, but in the whole of the later Marx—not only in the *Grundrisse*, but in the *Theories of Surplus Value* as well, for hundreds of pages on end. The *Grundrisse* and *Theories of Surplus Value* merely declare in more explicit terminology what the language of *Capital* states more obliquely, because Marx was resorting to a greater extent to the scientific vocabulary of English political economy itself. But the problems of alienated labour and commodity fetishism are central to the whole architecture of Marx's later work. Althusser's admission, however reluctant, of their presence in *Capital*, in fact undermines his whole previous formulation of the 'break' between the young and the old Marx; it also disqualifies the notion of history as a process without a subject. But it is this component of Marxism that Althusser essentially rejects. I think that this is what explains his organic sympathy with Stalinism.

We may agree that any thinker develops at least in part by a series of breaks with existing systems; and there will generally be an important early point where he stands back from accepted values and ideas, and looks at the whole of society with deepened critical insight so that his whole future development is affected. What is objectionable in the doctrine of Bachelard and Althusser is the way in which the primary break is made a sort of mystical illumination determining his whole further development, and one in which the illuminating moment is not seen as dynamically and comprehensively linked with reality, with the historical moment in its fulness. The rupture is made merely with previous epistemological concepts.

In the 1840s Marx went through a series of ruptures; and if we are to select one as decisive we might well look at 1843 and the *Critique of Hegel's Philosophy of Right* (as della Volpe and Colletti do). The essential event was the turning-away from all forms of idealism and the creation of a materialist dialectic out of the critique of Hegel. Though there are diffuse and over-generalised elements in the writings of 1844, there is already the notion of a man as a producer in a definite social formation, of the primary nature of the labour-process. Feuerbachian attitudes are all the while being revalued in terms of a genuine perspective of historical materialism. But Althusser needs his extreme over-simplification of what constituted Marx's rupture in order to foist on him a structuralist system.

One example here of the continuity between the young and the older Marx will suffice. The categories put to work by Marx in *Capital* and in the *Theories of Surplus Value* were also centrally employed in the 1844 Manuscripts. Writing in the Manuscripts of the division between labour and capital, and between capital of land, and of wages, profits, and competition, he said: 'Political economy teaches us nothing about the extent to which these external and apparently accidental circumstances are only the expression of a necessary development. We have seen how exchange itself appears to political economy as an accidental fact.'

Althusser begins with a valid enough distinction between the Marxist and Hegelian concepts of totality. For Hegel everything is dominated by the Idea, so that there is only one major contradiction (between essence and phenomena, Idea and civil society), where the second element is reducible to the first (translated into Marxism, says Althusser, that would make superstructure reducible to base.) In Marxism, on the other hand, there is a complex unity of separate and specific levels, which in any given historical formation may be relatively autonomous, and the asymmetrical totality may be dominated by one of its elements (the structure in dominance). The concept of Over-determination seeks to express the autonomy and independence of the various contradictions.[18] A complex internally structured totality is made of various levels linked by all sorts of relations of determination.*

---

* It follows, says Althusser, that there is no homogeneous continuity of time, as in Hegel, who sees history as the periodising moments of the Idea. Each structural level has its own varying time-system, which is linked to the others by relations of correspondence, non-correspondence, and so on, and which is related internally to the relative autonomy of its level. (Thus the concept of uneven development is turned into an idealist metaphysic, as if each level was cut away absolutely in its own self-sufficient time-system.)

Balibar, working with Althusser, holds that this system is revealed in the analysis of the modes of production as specific combinations of differing elements necessary to all production. Each mode has five necessary elements: (1) worker or direct producer, the labour force; (2) means of production: objects, instruments, means of labour; (3) non-workers appropriating surplus labour. And then two sets of relationships that bring together the three elements: (4) the relation of real appropriation (productive process); and (5) the property relation (exploitation process). No. 4 refers primarily to the productive forces, no. 5 to the relations of production (the relations of property in the means of production). All the terms are structural in that their content varies according to the mode of production in which they come together.*

Further, there are four kinds of production: material, political, theoretical, ideological. Each is a practice with its specified character.[19] *Capital*, being a theoretical product, cannot be verified or compared with everyday experience of the reality of capitalism. The theory is correct, so the application is successful; it is not correct because of the success. The criterion of the 'truth of the knowledge produced by Marx's theoretical practice is provided by the theoretical practice itself'. Theory is not part of a superstructure but is science produced by transforming raw material (ideological or pre-scientific ideas) into knowledge by a particular kind of transformation. (This statement applies to all productions, since they all have analogous characters.) To fit art into the fourfold scheme, Althusser has found more than difficult, having admitted it is neither ideology nor science (theory). The concept of production here set out could be valuable if concretely applied and followed through. But for Althusser with his abstract systematising, 'production' becomes only a word:

---

*Balibar admits that (5) holds an evasion: property and its legal forms, since the latter 'are part of the superstructure and not of the base with which we are dealing here.' But, further, property is the whole system organised to bring about the extraction of surplus value, so its definition implies the analysis of reproduction. The 'comparative analysis' presupposes (does not follow from) the synchronic analysis of the whole of *Capital*. So it is false to claim that work's scientific method, 'generalisable to all the historical modes of production, is characterised by these few general concepts that constitute in principle the beginning of the exposition.' *Capital* had first to be assimilated before the general concepts could be distinguished. Indeed in all the five terms the synchronic analysis of the reproductive process must have been made before the terms could be defined. Althusser admits this point in some remarks about primitive society: (3) 179. Balibar , *Lire*, ii (1966) 209f. See Glucksmann (2) 300f, for comments.

The basis of the whole tripartite Althusserian architecture thus arises fully armed from the simple but somewhat forced use of a dictionary. It 'happens' that everything is production. It 'happens' that every production is divided into three. This conceptual empiricism is never questioned in the Althusserian reflection. (A. GLUCKSMANN)[20]

Everything is done by the system itself. The inner structure does not gain its meaning through the activities of people as individuals or groups. The lived relations of the latter are of no meaning to science, for structures are not consciously built up. The existence of a structure is realised only through its effects or its absent cause. History dissolves into what Althusser calls 'the principle of the variation of the forms' of the combinations worked out by the modes of production. In its place is the mode of production as defined above. An 'immense machine' he describes it, a 'play without an author, the presence of an absence'. The unit of analysis is not people, but the relations of production.[21]

A social formation has three main instances: the economy, the polity, and ideology. Each has its specific practices and relative autonomy. (Ideology here has the meaning of the lived relations of people and the world, and is a necessary part of all societies, even those after the revolution.) All theories based on concepts of human nature, praxis, or alienation, which tend to see theory as superstructure, are rejected. This ban is interpreted to mean that any theory which sees alienation, for instance, as a problem, is thinking solely or primarily in terms of human beings, and so is a humanism: a term of the deadliest abuse. History for Althusser is a process without a subject. That is, it develops according to the particular over-determined configurations taken by the contradictions that constitute it. There is no historical meaning that underlies the meaning of the structure; on the contrary it is the structure which gives history its significations:

Since for Althusser real historical time is only indirectly accessible to us, action for him would seem to be a kind of blindfolded operation, a manipulation at distance, in which we could at best watch our own performance indirectly, as though in a mirror, reading it back from the various readjustments of consciousness which result from the alteration in the external situation itself. (JAMESON)[22]

Classes intervene only as Supporters, *Träger*, of economic inter-course.

The real protagonists of history are the social relations of production, political struggle and ideology, which are constituted by the place assigned to those protagonists in the complex structure of the social formation . . . The biological men are only the supports or bearers of the guises

92

(*Charaktermasken*) assigned to them by the structure of relations in the social formation. (ALTHUSSER)

We may well comment:

Here we see a classic example of structuralist idealism and metaphysics: ideas or concepts make history while people only act out the role that is set for them by the concepts. Althusser makes the categories fight the battles of history in *Reading Capital* . . . M. Althusser, like M. Proudhon, has made ideas produce history, whilst, for Marx, people make history under the conditions in which they live. Althusser has failed to grasp the interpenetration of the opposites, subjective and objective, because of his structuralism . . . Althusser sees only the Structure, social relations (whether they be economic, political or ideological); human practice is erased in favour of the abstract categories which use people as agents. (SUMNER)[23]

Marx in fact in *The Poverty of Philosophy* attacked Proudhon at length for exactly the same sort of abstraction as Althusser carries out with far more rigour:

The economists' material is the active, energetic life of man; M. Proudhon's material is the dogmas of the economists. But the moment we cease to pursue the historical movement of production relations, of which the categories are but the theoretical expression . . . we are forced to attribute the origin of these thoughts to the movements of pure reason.

Marx points out how Proudhon, abstracting movement into a series of logical categories, produces a system that makes the categories of political economy 'look as if they had newly blossomed forth in an intellect of pure reason; so much do these categories seem to engender one another, to be linked up and interwined with one another by the very working of the dialectic movement'.

Althusser again and again makes this sort of statement. 'The truth of history cannot be read in its manifest discourse, because the text of history is not a text in which a voice (the Logos) speaks, but the inaudible and illegible notation of the effects of a structure of structures,' *R.C.* 17. The very notion of human agency is no more than the 'the semblance of a problem for *bourgeois ideology.*' F.M. 126.[24]

An Althusserian inteprets the claim that human beings make history as meaning that it is solely their subjective states that matter: 'You would need to know their subjective states, beliefs, attitudes, prejudices, etc. This is how the Political Economy thought about men. And also empiricist philosophy, utilitarianism etc.' (J. MEPHAM). But men make things—including history—with their hands as well as their minds and emotions. The dialectical concept includes both hands and minds, labour-process and culture, relations and forces of production.

So violent is Althusser's hatred of humanism in any shape or form that he declared in 1975, defending his doctoral thesis at Amiens: 'I would never have written anything were it not for the 20th Congress and Kruschev's critique of Stalinism and the subsequent liberalisation . . . My target was therefore clear: these humanist ravings, these feeble dissertations on liberty, labour or alienation which were the effects of all this among French Party intellectuals.'[25]

We have perhaps now seen enough to show how abstract is Althusser's system, how typically structuralist in its circular movement, its self-sufficiency as a logical mechanism. But there are a few more points we need to look at. First, his epistemology (epistemology being the theory or science of the method or grounds of knowledge.) He sets out a system of theoretical activity and of the production of knowledge. What he has to say is close to what we have already noted of the structuralist idea of how a text is to be read. A central notion is that of the problematic, a defined theoretical structure or specific conceptual framework determining the forms in which questions are posed and what is relevant to those questions. It covers particular theories, concepts, methods, and defines the inner limits as to what is to be studied. One problematic ends and another begins at the point where a rupture appears. The idea that the real is concrete and scientific knowledge abstract is rejected, as is the idea that science is an abstraction from the concrete and observable. Such ideas are taken to be based on empiricism of the object and idealism of the essence. Knowledge is considered the concrete and theory is derived from already existing theory or general concepts, which it transforms.

Unity is not naively sought between thought and being, but in a transcendental correlation that identifies the concepts of thought with the 'conditions of existence' of the real (R.C. 216). This unity is the duplex unity of the 'general essence of production,' in so far as it is this unity that divides to produce a 'knowledge effect' and a 'society effect.' The simple opposition of 'theoretical production' and 'material production' does not exhaust the essence of production. Theoretical production contains the essence of all production since 'through it' one must read 'the essence of practice in general' and of 'the development of things in general''; for its part 'material' production is also the production of the knowledge effect as *Darstellung*. The knowledge aspect and the real causality aspect are thus present in all forms of production: it is not the factual distinction between theory and real production that explains the double aspect of all production: on the contrary, it is the internal division of the essence of production that gives rise to the factual distinction. This internal difference defines production metaphysically. (A. GLUCKSMANN).[26]

Darstellung means presentation, exposition, and becomes a key-term for Althusser since at its deepest, he says, it denotes 'positing presence'—'presence offered to the visible'. In it the structure appears. It lies at the heart of Althusser's anti-humanism, since reproduction appears in it as 'a process without a subject'.*

Marxism is not, says Althusser, a guarantor of the sciences, since that would mean it merely becomes the mouthpiece of ideology. Its function is to be the 'theory of theoretical practice' and to analyse the mechanism responsible for the knowledge-effect, 'which is the peculiarity of those special products which are knowledge'. Theoretical practice is specific; its products and their validity are independent of their relations to the social structure. Theory is a form of production, not distinguished from science, since both produce knowledge through theoretical practice (one of the four levels or practices of the social formation). Each practice has its own way of combining productive means, labour, and material. But together they make up social practice in its totality. What marks theoretical practice off from political or economic practice is its raw material (made up of previous products of the practice and ideology, not of the real-concrete). It uses an apparatus of theoretical concepts and functions in the sphere of ideas to produce knowledge. It attains to truth in so far as it is not empirical or idealistic; and its epistemological formation marks it off from ideology, with which it has only an external relation.[27]

All these practices are apparently equal, yet economic, political, and ideological practices are all included in historical materialism, and their theory is contained within the social formation. But the theory of historical materialism or of science is seen as distinct from the social formation, so in effect there is a differentiation between three of the practices, which exist in the social formation, and a fourth, philosophy or dialectical materialism, which exists outside it, above it. The theory of science is external to society and the history of science is independent of the history of society. There are three stages of production: *Generalities* I, II, III. First comes the material that science turns into specific concepts and concrete knowledge (the third stage); between lies the means of production of the transformation. This second stage is rightly called crucial, but is entirely undefined and unexplained. To stay at I is to carry on at the empirical level; to rely on III is to carry on at a purely speculative one. Within a given problematic, while the same conceptual apparatus is used, knowledge

---

* In *Capital* Marx sets out a theory of the true appearance of the processes of capital, but also one of its false appearance (fetishism etc.). Althusser makes *Darstellung* responsible for both the truth and the falsity in their entanglement. 'These forms of manifestation are just as much forms of dissimulation.' (3a) 62.

may be cumulative. Though there is always a danger of falling into ideology, once science has established its controls, a certain permanence results.

Each science has its specific object, with appropriate concepts and methods. So analogies and borrowings between different sciences are likely to lead to fallacies (Althusser does not explain why it was correct for him to use analogies from Freud, not to mention linguistics.) The various spheres of knowledge are, however, alike in producing works from new material, and they all share an homologous form. Theory is relatively autonomous from other practices in the realm of ideas as well as from the social structure in its origins and forms of validation. What all these definitions and their terms mean is taken for granted; no explanations or descriptions of the ways the practices work is ever attempted.*

As usual with Althusser each system is said to authenticate itself and so is not susceptible to any proof or substantiation from outside. Theoretical practice, as well as being autonomous, 'is its own criterion and contains in itself definite protocols with which to validate the quality of its product, i.e. the criteria of the scientificity of the products of theoretical practice'. The 'radical inwardness' of theoretical practice means that no general criterion of scientificity is possible: 'It would seem that Althusser has been unable to transcend the problematic of bourgeois epistemology. This contradiction, which clearly exists in the texts published in *Reading Capital*, did not arise by chance' (CALLINICOS). The scheme of endless homologies which reflect one another and also somehow reflect reality (as the result of an assumed common structure of all practices) leads Althusser once again into the very mechanist-idealism he is supposed to be refuting and supplanting. Theoretical practice can in knowledge appropriate its real object despite the fact that the whole process takes place in the mind, since they own an identical structure, that of practice (Althusser criticises Colletti for the same trick of assimilating the structure of thought to that of the real.) Thus we are given a guarantee that science can appropriate the real by means of a pre-existing relation of identity between thought and reality. But 'to assert the autonomy of theoretical practice without establishing the specific character of the relation it enjoys with the social whole, is to transform the sciences

---

* They are connected by a general concept of practice, not by any idea of original practice in the past. Science aims at correct knowledge, not productive ability; it works through adequately conceptualising the elements of the social formation. The idea of science and theory as productive practices is A's own: M. Glucksmann, 118.

into an instance above and cut off from social process' (CALLINICOS).[78]

If Althusser 'begins by affirming the universality of knowledge in its content, he ends by denying the historicity of its conditions and processes of production; their autonomy has become, quite simply, absolute' (GERAS). Yet he knows that

the conditions of production of knowledge, though they do not affect its validity, are social and historical conditions and not, as idealism supposes, absolutely independent of social formations and their history. He knows it because he says it: science is *relatively* independent, organically related to the other social practices, its development crucially affected by that relationship. But that is all he says. The nature of the relationship is not spelt out, so that we have once again the gesture of an intention but hardly a substantive theory. At the same time what emerges again and again from Althusser's text, in its ambiguities and silences as well as in its sounds, is a view of science which negates his intention.[29]

But we must look further at his notion of political practice, where he does finally make an attempt to break out of the closed idealist circle. Theory does not derive from the practice; it does not lead into it or fuse with it. It does all the guiding, but the political conjuncture and the history of the class-struggle have strong effects on theoretical practice. After the theorist has arrived at his conclusions, he can try to affect operations in the social formation and thus change the structure in the desired direction. He does this by including his plan, which can be that of a revolutionary party, in his analysis of the total structure. Theoretical practice, being productive, changes by its activity the state of knowledge, while theory can reveal the structure of a social formation which political practice is trying to change.

With *Lenin in Philosophy* he made a strenuous effort to relate his thought indirectly to political struggle by revising his idea of philosophy. With his passion for abstractions he sets up Theory (with a capital T) as the theory of practice in general, 'itself elaborated on the basis of the Theory of existing theoretical practices [of the sciences], which transforms into "knowledge" [scientific truths] the ideological product of existing "empirical" practices [the concrete activities of men]. This Theory is the materialist dialectic which is none other than dialectical materialism.'

But this formulation in fact raises more questions than it solves, in particular the relationship of historical materialism to dialectical materialism on the one hand and to the other practices of the social formation on the other . . . There must be some complex relationship between them, and this is where Althusser's inconsistencies start. (M. GLUCKSMAN)[30]

However, in *Reading Capital*, 1965, he repudiated his initial idea of

97

science, stating correctly that it hypostasised the theory of science and idealistically found the validity of theory in a pre-given logic. So for a while two opposed viewpoints were set out. Then in *Lenin and Philosphy*, 1971, criticising his own 'theoreticist tendencies', he gave philosophy a totally new meaning, though he still upheld the distinction between historical and dialectical materialism. Now philosophy (dialectical materialism) becomes political intervention, being produced in the theoretical sphere by the united influences of class-struggle and scientific practice. It reveals the difference between true and false ideas, science and ideology. But what it means beyond that to see philosophy as a practice we are not told. Does it remain a specific and relatively autonomous level of the social formation, or does it turn into social and political activity in general? In any event the concept of the Theory of theoretical activity, which gave his system coherence, is displaced, and we hear nothing of the theory of the productive nature of theory. If science in general does not exist, neither does epistemology, so what happens to Althusser's epistemological doctrine? Philosophy is now not regarded as a science, so what is the scientific status of his work, which he composed as a philosopher? Previously he held it to be both theoretical and philosophic, since its aim was to derive dialectical materialism from historical materialism. Now it is political intervention or a theoretical practice; it cannot be both. He does not confront this problem, nor does he explain the relation of theoretical practice to other practices.

In his recent writings Althusser is even more adamant than before in maintaining that the production of knowledge occurs entirely within the order of thought, and that this is absolutely free from social determinism and problems of relativism, since theory now contains within itself its own methodological and epistemological apparatus. Yet he also maintains exactly the opposite in claiming that theory depends totally on social and historical conditions. For example, 'it is only from the point of view of class exploitation that it is possible to see and analyse the mechanisms of a class society and therefore to produce knowledge of it.' (M. GLUCKSMANN)[31]

We may note further that even at the point of trying to make philosophy active he betrays his idealist basis. He reduces the whole process by which Marxist theory is produced to a theoretical activity autonomous of the political practice of the working class, autonomous of the class struggle and political conditions, which are its own necessary (if not sufficient) conditions of production. Thus is perpetrated a reduction

as grave as any of those castigated by Althusser himself. Its final effect is to make the relations between Marxist theory and the working class a unilateral and purely pedagogic one: the intellectuals 'give' the class the knowledge it needs. This is only the final consequence of every idealism: elitism. When knowledge celebrates its autonomy, the philosophers celebrate their dominance. (A. GLUCKSMANN)[32]

The very term 'political intervention' gives away the mechanist-idealist attitude. 'Intervene' implies 'a positivistic infra-structure/superstructure notion' (SUMNER). Edward Thompson notes 'the ulterior congruence of Althusserism and positivist epistemology'. P. Piccone shows at length that 'Althusser is not aware of the history of recent positivism so that he does not realise that he has unwittingly appropriated their entire discarded problematic'.

With such positions we naturally find a total rejection of the unity of theory and practice. For Marx the two form an integrated whole. He differed in this position from all previous writers in the social sciences who were concerned with the relation of theory and its object. For him to understand the world was only one facet of an act that also involved the changing of the world; theory was therefore always concerned with the transformation of reality. Althusser claims a complete objectivity for his theory, while rejecting empiricism with its claim to objectivity; at the same time he stresses the strategic significance of theory. As usual he does not bring the two aspects of a formulation together, and he does not define how his objectivity differs from that of the empiricists, or what are the scientific guarantees of its correctness. What he discusses is the particular methodology by which he arrives at his positions or how he achieves objectivity. Since his idea of theory lacks the transformational aspect that is pervasive in Marx's, he cannot tackle the problem. He never clarifies the connections between theoretical and political practice, or the relations between his structure-in-dominance and determination by the economy in the last instance, relations that enable the dominant role in a social formation at a given moment to be held by one of a large number of non-economic elements. (If the economy is dominant in the last instance, why is it not the principal contradiction? and if the dominant role may be so easily displaced between different levels, why is his theory not one of an eclectic pluralism? We see that he uses terms like 'in the last instance' not to solve problems but merely to defer them indefinitely.) Always what concerns him is the relation between real process and thought process. We may add that though he uses the term dialectical materialism, he makes no use of dialectics and is throughout hostile to it, seeing it only as a remnant of Hegelian idealism carried on by Marx despite the rupture of 1845 (the notion of the break or rupture might indeed be linked with that of the qualitative leap on 'to a new level', but Althusser does not seem to have noticed any such connection.)[33]

There is another important matter, that of ideology, in which he tries to modify his earlier positions. Accepting the formulations of superstructure and base, he holds that the way the former intervenes in the latter must be seen from the viewpoint of the reproduction of the relations of production. So ideology is an aspect of the reproductive process.* By it there comes about 'a reproduction of submission to the ruling ideology for the workers and a reproduction of the ability to manipulate the ruling ideology correctly for the agents of exploitation and repression, so that they too will produce for the domination of the ruling class "in words".'[34] Althusser sees the state apparatuses as owning ideological as well as repressive functions. In 1971, in a postscript he made his earlier positions more sophisticated, declaring that *Ideological State Apparatuses*, ISA, exist also under the appearance of private institutions—e.g. churches, legal systems, mass-media, trade-unions, schools, the political parties.[35] But he has still not escaped from his old one-sided notion of reflection. The economic structure gives state-power to the ruling class who control the ISAs and transmit their ideology direct to the ready receivers; the dominated labour-force is then fully equipped for its role in the economy. In his pedantic way Althusser declares that ideology 'constitutes concrete individuals as subjects' and that concrete individuals are 'subjected to the Subject'. People live in 'the trap of a mirror-reflection', centred on themselves as 'subjects'. The ideology itself is centred on the absolute power of the subject (the illusions of the individual as a free agent). There are some 'bad subjects' who draw down on themselves the state's repressive apparatus, though how and why they are bad is not stated. Althusser thus sets out the mechanistic thesis that ideologies simply originate in the mode of production and are given effect by the state. Class conflict is inexplicable.†

---

* Though each practice has a specific character, we are told that 'there is no practice except by and in an ideology ' (1) 159; Sumner 40. So ideology has a special kind of existence, in a sense absorbing and determining the other practices. We are not told how this works out in limiting the specificity of the others and in affecting in particular theoretical practice. *Capital* as a theoretical product is brought about 'by and in an ideology.' (In his earlier period his concept of the relatively autonomous conditions of existence of a mode of production saved him from having to explain the mode of intervention by specific ideologies in the mode of production.)

† It is of interest that Althusser's concept of the total penetration of society by ruling-class ideology has much similarity with the Frankfurt School's concept of universal reification, though the terms used and the explanations of the mechanisms of control are quite different.

His 1971 essay on the ISA defined ideology as an imaginary reflection of the relations of production, located in the ISA, centred on the illusory concept of the free subject, and ensuring the reproduction of the economic structure. But in a postscript he made a sharp turn, declaring ideology to be a weapon used on *both sides* of the class-struggle, and reflecting social practices of all kinds. He carried on these ideas in *Essays in Self-Criticism*, regretted his past formulations, and made class-struggle the main theoretical site for the analysis of ideologies. But he still considered the latter essentially products of economic practice, which were extended and systematised in the practices of the superstructure. So we may say that he is always, in his theories of ideology, 'guilty of (1) class-reductionism and (2) economism' (SUMNER).[36] For he limits the social relevance of ideology to its class-forms as well as 'the relevance of the relative autonomy of the superstructure and its intrinsic ideologies', by the way the latter are linked directly with the economy. He does not follow out his new notion of people as aspects of social practice, and gives no clue as to whence ideologies of resistance come. At best he seems to be thinking in terms of a stimulus-response model of proletarian resistance. He does not go on to say that proletarian ideology expresses social relations as does bourgeois ideology. His passionate anti-humanism, his reluctance to allow human beings any significant activity except as units controlled by a structuralist mechanism, deprive him of any sense of the practical determinants of social forms. 'Both humanism and anti-humanism, I venture to suggest, existed in raw contradiction in Feuerbach's work—Marx's work represents the supercession of that contradiction. Althusser merely takes one side of Feuerbach and Marxifies it.' (SUMNER). That is to say, Marx recognised the dialectical unity of the creativity of human beings as makers of their history, and the limitations or controls imposed on that making by the structures and systems built up in the transformation of nature by societies with varying modes of production. Althusser sees only an either/or issue. Human activity is all, or structural determination is.[37]

What then can we learn from the work of Althusser and its powerful effects in the 1960s and 1970s? First, its success brings out how disastrously undeveloped Marxism has been on all the crucial issues we are treating in this book. The response came in part because Althusserian structuralism with its extended and interlinked definitions filled a definite gap. Its very shortcomings appeared as a strength: due to the extreme rigour with which was worked out a detailed scheme of structuralist inter-connections round the central concept of the Structure in Dominance. But the impact could hardly have come about without the favourable situation of the 1960s: the growing interest in Marxism in universities, the widespread dissidence of the youth that came to a climax in 1968, the revolt against the Vietnam war. Here was a ready audience looking for revolutionary doctrines, but quite divorced from the class-struggle at a working-class level. Such an audience was likely to respond to extreme leftist sectarianism or to intellectual systems with every appearance of being watertight and of providing a superior comprehension of what lay behind the confused world situation.[38]

But once we break the spell of Althusser's structuralist thoroughness and cocksure system-building, and stand outside the edifice, we find that most of his definitions have no living relationship to the realities of history, social process or human development. His system explains everything and nothing. It stands out as the diametric opposite of the Marxist dialectic with its vital fullness. Yet with its neat and dogmatic dovetailings and inter-relationships it challenges us to deepen and make more concrete our grasp of the elements composing the complex social whole. By its narrowing-down of the processes of knowledge it challenges us to find a more dynamic and comprehensive concept of the relations of humanity and nature, of science and natural process. Its extended notion of production is full of suggestions that the abstract (mechanist-idealist) method cannot take up and develop. Its supplanting of the dialectic by a structuralist system raises with fresh urgency, in a widened perspective, the question of just what the dialectic is and how integral it is to Marxism. The value then of Althusser's work is primarily as a challenge.'*

---

* We know what Lenin would have said of the abstract academic jargon of Althusser and others such as della Volpe. When he reads in Deborin that dialectical materialism 'introduces everywhere a fresh stream of theoretico-cognitive criticism,' he underlines the last term and comments, 'There is no point in using "foreign words". Again he underlines the sentence: 'The "immanent" becomes "transcendental" insofar as it acquires objectively real significance,' and comments: 'NB Correct truths are outlined in a diabolically pretentious, abstruse form', *Philosophical Notebooks*, 477, 481. Timpanaro remarks of Althusser, 'His terminological acquisitions are far more numerous than his actual conceptual advances,' (2) 193.

Opponents of Marxism have not missed the easy target, e.g. Parkin: 'Contemporary Marxism is exclusively academic. Diligent bands of scholars are now combing through the pages of *Theories of Surplus Value* in search of social reality. As if to secure its newly-won respectability, professorial Marxism has, in the manner of all exclusive bodies, conducted its discourse in language not readily accessible to the uninstructed. Certainly no one would accuse the Marxist professoriate of spreading the kind of ideas likely to cause a stampede to the barricades or the picket lines.'

7 Dialectics of Nature

The question of the nature of science has kept coming up, but we have not directly tackled it. As usual it was Lukacs who set the lines of the new problematic when in *History and Class-Consciousness* he wrote rather confusedly of science, giving the effect that is was a contemplative practice, not involving transformative activity; he spoke of nature as a chaotic set of blind forces going round in circles, 'repeating the same thing'. Thus he limited dialectical method to the treatment of history and society. He wrote (March 1919):

> . . . Engels—following Hegel's mistaken lead—extended the method to apply also to nature. However the crucial determination of dialectics—the interaction of subject and object, the unity of theory and practice, the historical changes in the realities underlying the categories as the root cause of changes in thought, etc.—are absent from our knowledge of nature.

These views were linked with the 'historicist' positions that he later rejected; however they had a strong effect on readers of his book.[1]

If we look at Marx, Engels and Lenin there is not the least doubt that they held in every way to the position that dialectics applied to *all* process, natural as well as human. When Marx wrote in *Capital* that the system of dialectics was 'nothing else than the material world reflected in the human mind and translated into forms of thought', we know that his 'material' is natural as well as social. He always remained true to his 1844 position: 'Natural science will in time incorporate into itself the science of man, just as the science of man will incorporate into itself the natural science; there will be *one* science.' On 1 February 1858 he wrote of bringing 'a science by criticism to the point where it can be dialectically presented.'[2]

Lenin repeatedly (in his *Philosophical Notebooks*) insisted that dialectical materialism must cover nature as well as society and that it cannot be complete until it does so: 'Nature is itself one whole'; 'the dialectics of things themselves, of Nature itself, of the course of events itself'. Indeed he went so far as to suggest that though there is a leap from the level of inorganic to that of organic matter, inorganic matter 'is not devoid of the basic capacity for "sensation" . . . to an extremely small extent', which is 'totally imperceptible to the investigator'.[3]

Now let us look at some typical comments by Marxists who wish to limit dialectics to human development. A. Schmidt argues that nature only becomes dialectical when drawn into 'the web of human and social purposes', and that 'before the existence of human societies, nature could only achieve polarities and oppositions external to each other.' He holds that 'matter only exists in particular forms of being', so that we cannot make statements about it in general. R. Gunn argues that Marx's references to the dialectics of nature are marginal and isolated. True, but so are his remarks on a large number of crucial matters, e.g. culture in its various forms. Monod thinks that a dialectic of nature involves an 'animist projection'. Jordan says that Engels's theory of nature was sure to become anthropomorphic: 'To describe natural processes in terms of dialectical negation or the negating force is to endow material objects with consciousness and purposiveness which only human beings display.' Gunn puts it as 'the idealist reading back into nature of the teleological purposive structure of human thought and action'.[4]

But Marxism does not have a teleological concept of human thought and action. Animals act in a purposive way. DNA is described as having a code and sending messages (I think this use of language is wrong, an imposition of human devices, cybernetics, on natural process; but it brings out the way in which 'purpose' operates in the only way it can at the physical level of DNA.) Many of the difficulties that the thinkers cited above encounter derive from the fact that the terms or phrases generally used in dialectics have been taken over straight from Hegel, and are indeed often anthropomorphic. But this is merely an accident due to the fact that the dialectic—idealist or materialist—was worked out to deal with human processes, history. There is no need to tie it down to those terms.

Dialectics is not an *a priori* scheme that one superimposes on things and thrusts upon them by forcing them into the Procrustean bed. The laws of dialectics are not a closed system of thought like the logical forms of Aristotle, the categories of Kant, or the logic of Hegel. (GARAUDY)[5]

The terms are valuable only to the extent to which they help in describing process with its contradictions and resolutions. We can validly change and develop them to make them adequate to wider spheres of reference without losing their essential meaning. Not that there is any reason why such a concept as dialectical negation should be taken as necessarily involving human agency, and so on. The attack on the dialectics of nature is largely based on an inability to realise that in dealing with, say, society and the world of particles we are dealing with quite different levels, so that the 'agency' at work on one level cannot be mechanically equated with that at work on another. In order to deal adequately with the different levels, it is however true that we need to find terms which get rid of any anthropomorphic suggestion and which apply to all of them, as does the term contradiction.

First, we may note that to consider human and natural processes as obeying different laws is to split the universe. One of the proponents of that position is brave enough to admit the dilemma:

> I would acknowledge that in an important sense the position adopted is indeed dualist. It insists on a basic distinction between concept and object, between interpreting and changing the world, between action (guided by an interpretation of the world and thus involving the 'teleological' moment of theory or intention) and occurrences in nature, i.e. not 'actions' but purely mechanical or instinctive 'happenings': between in short the teleological or purposive and the causal.
>
> Further I would maintain that Marxist materialism is necessarily dualistic in this sense. Besides the position here adopted there are essentially only two alternatives. These are (a) the reduction of the object to the concept, of the causal to the technological (idealist monism); and (b) the reduction of the concept to the object, of the teleological to the causal (mechanistic materialist monism). There are thus only two coherent monisms: idealism and mechanistic materialism. A dialectical materialist monism is a contradiction in terms: to the extent that it takes the dialectical component seriously it is animistic and derivative of absolute idealism, and to the extent that it takes its materialist component seriously it lapses into mecanistic materialism. (R. GUNN)[6]

This statement cannot imagine a dialectical relation of subject and object, of concept and object, which is neither teleological nor animist not mechanist, and in which the union of conflicting elements brings about the creation of a new level with new potentialities. Further, it cannot even begin to explain how humanity emerged from nature with its dialectical approach.—'How can we explain the emergence of dialectical man out of the void of bleak mechanistic timelessness?' (HOFFMAN). The answer is that humanity lifted on to a new level the dialectical relation of animal and nature. There was a leap, but not a gap. Animals exercise in various degrees what Gunn calls a teleological view; they relate cause and effect and take steps to bring about certain results. Simply to call this instinct is merely to use a word to get out of a problem.

The separation of one thing from another, its qualitative distinctions from everything else, breaks down at a certain point in time and space. So long as the opposing forces are in balance the totality appears stable, harmonious, at rest—and is really so. But this is a transient condition. Sooner or later, alterations in the inner relation of forces, and interactions with other processes in the environment, upset the achieved equilibrium, generate instability, and can eventuate in the disruption and destruction of the most hard-and-fast formations. Dialectics is fundamentally the most consistent way of thinking about the universal interconnections of things in the full range of their development. (NOVACK)[7]

The key question for the full extension of dialectics is this one of stability and instability, symmetry and asymmetry, as we shall see later. It is true, however, that we need to look critically at Engels' formulations. His aim was to attack the way science was being used for reactionary purposes: Dühring with his reformism; Haeckel and the others trying to exploit Darwin's work to exalt 'free competition', white supremacy, and so on. He was concerned primarily to undermine mechanistic materialism with its reductive outlook and Social Darwinism. He needed above all the notions of the leap from one level to another and of historical development — nature as well as man owning a history. His problem has been thus stated:

Was Engels' whole intellectual project to his writings on the natural sciences constituted and determined by this appropriation of Hegel (the materialist inversion of Hegel's dialectic), or was the recourse to Hegel necessitated by intellectual-political problems definable and re-constitutable independently of the concepts of dialectical materialism, yet not soluble by means of any other philosophical instruments available to Engels? (BENTON)[8]

The answer is simply that he used the dialectic because he considered it to provide the only valid argument against his opponents, and that he was right in this idea up to a point. It is unfortunate that he did not possess a better dialectical instrument for the purpose; but with the level reached by science at that time he could hardly have developed the method in the way needed for tackling the question of the dialectics of nature. However,

instead of seeing in this rich collection of notes a reflection by Engels on the science of his time, which sought to bring out the overall picture of nature which seemed to derive from the most general laws of nature, of society, and of thought, as they appeared in the science of his epoch, a claim has been made (notably in Stalin's regrettably well-known compendium *Dialectical Materialism and Historical Materialism*) to extract from it an exhaustive catalogue of 'laws' or 'characteristics' of a dialectic which is universally and absolutely valid. (GARAUDY)[9]

The stage reached by the physical sciences in Engels' period is a crucial point. Marx, criticising Lassalle's attempts to use Hegel, remarked: 'He will learn to his cost, that it is one thing to develop a science to the point where one can present it dialectically and something else to apply an abstract and ready-make logic.' He himself needed bourgeois political economy, with its empiricist working-out on a mechanist or analytical basis, in order to produce his critical science, *Kritik der Wissenschaft*, his dialectical presentation. We cannot lay down any simple law in this matter, but we can state as strongly as possible, that the dialectic is not a given method or logic that can be imposed on any material at will. The analytic grasp of the material's structure and interconnections is necessary in varying degrees before any dialectical revaluation or presentation is possible. In short, dialectics is a method, not a logic, even if it uses logic in its own way. A purely analytic method will only apply validly to a stable state. As soon as the question of inner instabilities or asymmetries becomes important, and there is the potentiality of a qualitative leap, dialectics comes in (a potentiality in a system is not always realised; it can be weakened or defeated.) So it is incorrect to define dialectics as a higher form of logic standing above or replacing formal non-contradictory logic, and capable of being worked out as a complete abstract system (as Hegel attempted). A dialectical formulation or presentation cannot be seen as independent of the specific content of the moment or phase of development it seeks to clarify and define. Hegel was right in saying that the advance of knowledge needed the development of new thought-forms, even if he himself sought to formalise a higher (dialectical) logic which covered fully the forms of development.[10]

To return to Engels, his weakest point was the attempt to use the Hegelian law of the transformation of quantity into quality, as if quantitative changes at a determined stage led by themselves to changes of quality. He clung to the law as a weapon against reductive systems, as though it guaranteed the leap into new levels, though in itself it revealed only a quantitative principle. A strong point in his exposition, however, lies in his sense of the moving interconnected totality of things, which involves a deep realisation of the deadly reductive nature of bourgeois science:

The analysis of Nature into its individual parts, the grouping of the different natural processes and natural objects in definite classes, the study of the internal anatomy of organic bodies in their manifold forms — these were the fundamental conditions of the gigantic strides in our knowledge of Nature which have been made during the last four hundred years . . . But this method of investigation has also left us as a legacy, the habit of observing natural objects and natural processes in their isolation, detached from the whole vast interconnection of things; and therefore not in their motion, but in their repose; not as essentially changing, but as fixed constants; not in their life, but in their death. And when, as was the case with Bacon and Locke, this way of looking at things was transferred from natural science to philosophy, it produced the specific narrow-mindedness of the last centuries, the metaphysical mode of thought.[11]

We have now considered some thinkers who accept dialectics in social science, but deny its application to nature. Next we will look at other thinkers, who deny dialectics altogether yet consider themselves Marxists. Galvano della Volpe, born in 1885, grew up in the Italy of Croce and Gentile, and for a while, rejecting liberalism and social-democracy, followed the latter (who became an adherent of Fascism).[12] During the war he came in some respects under the influence of Heidigger and Nietzsche. In 1944 he joined the Communist Party, made something of a return to Kant and became interested in linguistics. As a Marxist he built up his own line of anti-humanism, proposing a universalistic scientific logic which looked back to Aristotle rather than to Plato. He had a strong mathematical (axiomatic) outlook, which had its affinities with the main lines of scientific methodology developing in the bourgeois epoch, and looked back to the hypothetic-deductive method created by Galileo. In 1962-5 della Volpe was considered a leader of the leftists in the Party: he died in 1968. It is not irrelevant to note that 1956, when he became prominent as a thinker, was the year of Kruschev's anti-Stalin revelations. An appeal to science (in bourgeois terms) had a note of opposition to the dialectical materialism championed by Stalin.*

Della Volpe thus exalted the determinate abstraction, the basic tool of all the prevailing sciences, and argued that the dialectic confused the concepts of things and the things themselves. So in place of dialectical contradiction he set what he called real opposition, which was non-contradictory. He considered that 'the task of Marxist science must be to ensure the reciprocal functionality of logic and history, that is, in securing the dominance of mere facticity by scientific reason. In the real, one could speak only by analogy of "negation": such real, positive contradiction is close to Kant's *Realrepugnanz*', Kant's concept of opposition.[13]

He thus called for the total rejection of dialectics and sought to put in its place the non-contradictory logic of the (mechanistic) sciences. In this conventional logic a thing is defined by what it is and what it is not; in a system each term is defined by its relation to the others. We know things, della Volpe says, through determinate abstraction; our

---

* His ideas had strong political links. 'In particular, the philosophical insistence on the importance of "determinate scientific abstraction," characteristic of della Volpe's work, could be read to imply the need for an analysis of Italian society in terms of the "pure" categories of developed capitalism, with correspondingly "advanced" political objectives to be pursued by the working class within it. This contrasted with PCI orthodoxy, which emphasised the historically backward and hybrid nature of Italian society, necessitating more limited demands of a "Democratic" rather than socialist type.' P. ANDERSON.

knowledge therefore is quite distinct and independent of the things known. But dialectics, with its principle of the unity of opposites, rejects the distinction between things and concepts. (He cannot grasp the point that dialectical unity does not equate the opposites but brings them together in dynamic and transformatory process.)

So his notion of science is simply that of Galilean physics, which first introduced the idea of quantification and measurement, and of the Newtonian system with its law of action and reaction being equal and opposite. His non-contradictory logic is simply logic that deals with a closed or stable system or space, which may be opposed by another system but which has no inner contradictions. Classical physics until recently dealt with stable systems; and so if we take its method as typical of all true science, we can argue as della Volpe does. But if we look at the whole expanse of process now visible to science, from the level of particles to that of the evolving higher species, we do not find only closed and stable systems, but an endless series of qualitative and structural changes going on.

He holds that hypothesis should come from deduction (by inference, by reasoning from general to particular) as opposed to induction (in which a general law is inferred from particular instances). By relating this position to Galileo he links it with mechanistic science. In his *Logic* of 1950 he goes into the 'dialectic of presentation', and deals with the idea that it is the work of theory to approximate to, or copy, reality and to conform to the real. There is thus an admitted split between mind and matter, thought and object; and della Volpe is no more capable of bridging that gulf than others we have considered.[14]

In fact, della Volpe comes, by 1954-5, to use the hypothetico-deductive instance in place of the dialectic. This means that human thought is not self contradictory, but rather non-contradictory (exclusive but conciliatory). The real *does*, however, remain contradictory. From the point of view of thought, the scientist uses a monist method (not a dialectical one), dogmatically and internally consistent. He detaches himself from the diadic, heterogeneous nature of thought-and-reality through the non-dialectical (reconciling) method of logic. Logic, science, produces objective knowledge, is not to be negated, or contradicted by the positive contradictions of the real. In the end, that is, scepticism leaves us with contradiction in the real, and non-contradiction as the condition of thought to be achieved. (FRASER)

Della Volpe's reconciliation of contradiction in theory is merely formal and symbolic. In the *Logic* he provides two radically different solutions to the problem of thought and reality, but both have to make obvious concessions to dualism. However he presents his argument it ends by merely substituting his method of hypotheticdeduction in place of the dialectic. We can claim, then, that despite all his agility he leaves the situation at the dilemma posed above by Gunn.

L. Colletti, who left the PCI in 1964, attacked all the elements of dialectics as Hegelian and idealistic. He and della Volpe brought into the open an attitude present in Althusser but never bluntly stated: science as we know it is not dialectical, so that if Marxism is a science it is not dialectical either.[15]

Colletti turns to Kant as against Hegel, claiming that he strongly asserted the primacy of reality to conceptual thought, its irreducibility, and an absolute division between what he called 'real oppositions' and 'logical oppositions.' Colletti asserts the importance of empirical science to Marxism. 'Unless we are ready to accept dialectical materialism and its fantasies of a "proletarian" biology or physics, we must nevertheless acknowledge the validity of the sciences of nature produced by bourgeois civilisation since the Renaissance' (he has been admitting the limitations of the bourgeois social sciences.) Typical of his method is the attack on Lenin in his book on Hegel. He cites the passage from Hegel's *Logic* which Lenin (as also Engels) saw as the valuable 'kernel' of Hegel's thought: 'Identity is merely the determination of the simple immediate, of dead being; but contradiction is the root of all movement and vitality; it is only in so far as something has a contradiction within it that it moves, has an urge and activity.' Lenin, reaching this page, excitedly noted down: 'movement and "self-movement"' . . . "change", "movement and vitality", "the principle of all movement", "impulse (Treib)" to "movement" and "activity"—the opposite to "dead Being"—who would believe that this is the core of "Hegelianism", of abstract and abstruse . . . Hegelianism? This core had to be discovered, understood, *hinüheretten* [rescued], laid bare, refined, which is precisely what Marx and Engels did.'[16] Colletti comments:

The 'reading' given by Lenin of these pages rests, as one can see, on a basic misinterpretation. He 'tried' to read Hegel 'materialistically' precisely at the place where the latter was . . . negating matter. Haunted by the famous propositions of *Anti-Dühring* and and led astray by the very method that he has laid down for himself—which meant a lapse of attention wherever Hegel talks about God—Lenin did not realise that Remark 3 to Chapter 2, which opens with the statement that 'everything is inherently contradictory' and proceeds in the way above, bears upon one precise topic: the problem of proving the existence of God.*

The lapse of attention is entirely Colletti's. Throughout the 150-odd pages of his notes on the *Logic* Lenin shows himself always aware of what Hegel is trying to prove and the different results to be got from a materialist use of the logical system. What excited him is the way in which the method can be reoriented away from God and the Idea. We must recall that in philosophy before Marx, because of the prevailing separation of mind or soul and body or matter, with mind or soul taken as the superior and active side of the relationship, it was idealism that was able to express the active element in life, in the universe, while materialism could operate only at the level of mechanist analysis. Marx's achievement lay precisely in using Hegel's logic in order to bring together the active principle and the materialist outlook. Colletti attributes to Lenin an incredible naivety, which is at odds with the many explicit statements by him, and by Marx and Engels as to precisely what use they were making of the Hegelian method and logic.

How little indeed Colletti understood dialectics is illustrated by his attempt to make fun of it by asking if a car-crash, 'a typical instance of "real opposition"', i.e. of two opposed forces, constitutes a daily verification of dialectical materialism'. He shows that he cannot grasp the unity of opposites; and he tries to prove that the effects of commodity fetishism and alienation are the only source of capitalist contradiction.[17] He attempts to split Marx into two: on one side the scientific political economist, on the other the moral philosopher who wants the overthrow of capitalism's fetishistic reification of human social relations. 'For Marx, capitalism is contradictory, not because it is a *reality* and all realities are contradictory, but because it is an *upside down*, inverted reality (alienation, fetishism).'[18] For long he held with della Volpe that what the dialecticians

described and describe as *contradictions* in the real world were in effect contrarieties, i.e. real oppositions and hence *non-contradictions*. Consequently Marxism, while continuing to speak of conflicts and of *objective oppositions* in reality, no longer had to claim for itself (and worse, seek to impose on science) a special logic of its own—the dialectic—that was at variance with and opposed to the logic followed by the existing sciences. Further: Marxism could henceforth continue to speak of struggles and of objective conflicts in nature and in society, making use of the non-contradictory logic of science; and better yet, it would henceforth be a science and practise science itself.[19]

---

*Colletti's 'lapses of attention' are considerable whenever he wants to make an anti-dialectical point. Thus he says that Lukacs, in his comments on the reduction of qualitative to quantitative time in the mechanised labour of the capitalist factory, went into the factory armed not with *Capital* but with Bergson's *Essai sur les données immédiates de la conscience*. In fact Lukacs was thinking of the remarks about Time in *The Poverty of Philosophy* and those in *Capital* on the way in which a worker is deformed by being compelled 'to work with the regularity of a machine.' LOWY(2) 181.

111

Yet later on, in an interview published in 1974, he repeated his rejection of dialectical materialism, while being forced to admit:

At the same time, re-reading Marx, I have become aware that for him capitalist contradictions undeniably are dialectical contradictions. Della Volpe tried to save the day by interpreting the opposition between capital and wage-labour as a real opposition—*Realrepugnanz*—in Kant's sense: that is, an opposition without contradiction, *ohne Widerspruch*. If the relationship between capital and labour were a real opposition in Kant's sense, it would be non-dialectical and the basic principle of materialism would be safe. But the problem is actually much more complex. I continue to believe that materialism excludes the notion of a contradictory reality; yet there is no doubt that for Marx the capital wage-labour relationship is a dialectical contradiction. Capitalism is a contradictory reality for Marx, not because being a reality it must therefore be contradictory—as dialectical materialism would have it, but because it is a capsized, inverted, upside-down reality. I am perfectly conscious that the notion of an upside-down reality appears to jar with the precepts of any science. Marx was convinced of the validity of this notion. I do not say that he was necessarily right.[20]

Thus he shows himself to be hopelessly confused. He goes on to say that he has moved from the facilely optimistic position he had held in 1958, which assumed a basic homogeneity between the sciences of nature and those of society: so he does not know where he stands. In 1954 he accepted della Volpe's thesis which identified the two sciences and saw Marx as 'the Galileo of the moral world.' That formulation presupposed that the labour-capital relation in Marx was a non-contradictory opposition, which he now recognises was not the case. Yet if he insists on the heterogeneity of the social and natural sciences, the social sciences tend 'to become a qualitatively distinct form of knowledge from the natural sciences'. They tend to take over the relation to science in general once held by philosophy.

The invariable conclusion of this tradition is that true knowledge is social science, which because it cannot be assimilated to natural science, is not science at all but philosophy. Thus there is either a single form of knowledge, which is science (the position I would still like to defend)—but then it should be possible to construct the social sciences on bases analogous to the natural sciences, or the social sciences really are different from the natural sciences, and there are two sorts of knowledge—but since two forms of knowledge are not possible, the natural sciences become a pseudo-knowledge. The latter is the ideologically dominant alternative.[21]

Colletti thus brings to a head the difficulties and dilemmas of anyone who tries to carry on as a Marxist while denying dialectical materialism, with its applications both to society and to nature.

We conclude this chapter with some comments on science and dialectics. First, to assert that the science of a period is closely related to the historical and social situation, does not imply that the results are something subjective. What it does mean is that the particular direction taken by science, and the methods it uses, are strongly affected—even conditioned—by the social and economic situation. Behind Galileo lies the practical and theoretical work connected with gunpowder and ballistics, as well as other practices ranging from book-keeping to mining, all of which are linked to the emerging bourgeoisie and its basis in the cash-nexus, the reduction of people—and indeed everything else—to things. Hence the quantitative mathematical method and the banishing of all questions of quality. But the results of Galileo's work and that of the other scientists following in the tradition he created are not thereby disproved, or reduced to subjective and illusory reflections of class-positions. They effectively unveil the workings of certain areas of nature, while ignoring other areas, other problems, other possibilities. Broadly speaking the quantitative method, which deals excellently with stable states of matter, carried on almost unchallenged till the twentieth century, when the signs of a deep crisis appeared with Einstein, Planck, and work on particle physics. This crisis is still with us, unresolved, and may be linked socially and economically with the crisis of capitalism in its imperialist and monopoly phases—its inner conflicts, problems and potentialities (which include socialism). Among the new potentialities of science today is that of moving on to a new level in which a much fuller grasp of process, its inter-connections and its movements into new wholes, will be possible.[22]

Our way of thinking of the totality of existence is inseparable from our own deepest and innermost essence. Thus it may be that science, following its natural mode of development as a specialised activity, will bring about its own 'end', in the sense that it will enter into 'higher dimensions of human existence.'

Science may thus merge with other currents which will eventually bring about a new wholeness of life on this planet, in which consciousness of the one ever-changing dance of energy that includes ourselves will be so strong and active that the current dominantly static and fragmentary consciousness will pale into insignificance and cease to be effective. (D. J. BOHM)[23]

Large words, yet they set out a possibility that grows ever clearer as we try to bring into a single focus the discoveries and theories of particle-physics. The key-point is the way we think (and feel) about the totality of existence. The bourgeois epoch of science has been ruled by the empiricist approach with its logic of non-contradiction which della Volpe and Colletti have exalted, and which lies behind much of Althusser's formulations, despite their show of denouncing empiricism. All such thinking lacks any concept of the unity of theory and practice, which enables us to move consciously into transformative action. With the advent of Einstein, Planck and particle-physics, although the bourgeois systems are not overthrown, yet that possibility has appeared. The full emergence of science on to the new level is bound up with the resolution of the terrible and rending contradictions in politics, in social and economic life, that now beset us—that is to say with the supercession and transcendence of imperialism and monopoly-capitalism on a national and international level.

Before we move on we may note that the association of science with the bourgeoisie from Galileo onwards, while resulting in many important discoveries that were objectively valid, also had the effect of steadily and powerfully buttressing the capitalist world-view, and intensifying and interiorising its grip on people. While mating humanity and nature in countless new ways, it also set them in opposition. Man became the conqueror and master of nature, of phenomena considered to be alien and outside him, something merely provided for his use. The conquest of nature, in these terms, meant an increase of the power-sense in people, especially in those who drew profit and authority from the situation. The Frankfurt School, in its criticism of the Enlightenment, said many true things of this aspect of scientific development after Galileo, even if it did so in a one-sided way that ignored the positive aspects—the drawing of people together in common tasks in an unprecedented way through technology; the liberation of aspirations and hopes of harmony despite the dominant power-ethic; the final cohering of resistances in the hope for socialism: new elements of potentiality, new elements of Hope in the Blochian sense.

Marcuse, we saw, was the most eloquent in denouncing science and technology, as providing the bourgeoisie with an ethic of power and the means of riveting that ethic on people in general:

The principles of modern science were *a priori* structured in such a way that they could serve as conceptual instruments for a universe of self-propelling, productive control; theoretical operationalism came to correspond to practical operationalism. The scientific method led to the ever-more-effective domination of nature and thus came to provide the pure concepts as well as the instrumentalities for the ever-more-effective domination of man *through* the domination of nature.[24]

Theoretically he agrees that this power could lead to its own negation, towards the promotion of the 'art of life.' But he has no faith in any class that could further the negation; he speaks only of 'a terminal point' that comes about mechanically 'with the mechanisation of all socially necessary but individually repressive labour'. Thus would arrive 'the possibility of an essentially new human reality—namely, existence in free time on the basis of fulfilled vital needs'. If that ever happened, science too would be transformed.

The methodology of bourgeois science, being essentially reductive, mechanistically analytic, was concerned with breaking things down into their components without any accompanying interest in the integrative processes at work. The logical result was the discovery of nuclear fission with its negative or destructive aspect terribly expressed in the atomic bomb. (I once remarked to Prof. Hyman Levy that bourgeois science began in gunpowder and has ended in the atomic bomb. He chuckled and said, 'Don't be surprised if you find me using that.')

I am of course not saying that nuclear fission is a subjective expression of bourgeois positions (fetishism, reification, reduction of people to things), but that in the complete perspective it is a combination of certain objective aspects of matter and of the subjective pressures upon bourgeois science. Science, on the higher level we have assumed as the expression of a socialist world liberated from bourgeois controls, would take note of such things as nuclear fission but would incorporate them in a different totality, where the integrative aspects of process would play the dominant role. Bourgeois science has finally in its crisis led us deep into the particle world, but cannot develop the new dialectical comprehensions required for following out its full implications and possibilities.

In that world, 'internal antagonisms (that is to say, the assemblage of forces which necessarily evolve in contrary directions) illustrate the nature of contradiction,' says Jean-Paul Vigier. The Unity of opposites at one level is the dynamic force that brings about a higher level with its own inner system. 'The transformation of quantity into quality is interpreted as the sudden rupture of equilibrium within a system (for instance, the destruction of one of the antagonistic forces), which modifies the equilibrium and gives rise to a qualitatively new phenomenon in the midst of which new contradictions appear.' Here again we meet the question of instability, asymmetry, to which I drew attention a short while back. Vigier continues:

The motion dealt with in contemporary micro-physics is not considered as the simple shift of an inert element from one point to another but rather as a violent oscillating movement which develops at one point to the degree that it is destroyed in the immediately preceding position. Each side of this dual process of annihilation and creation reciprocally conditions the other.[2 5]

In other works I have dealt at some length with L. L. Whyte's unitary principle and its concept of development occurring through the re-assertion of symmetry in an asymmetrical situation. This concept goes back to the statement by Pierre Curie in 1894 that an asymmetry in causes may disappear in their effects, so that the symmetry of the effects may be greater than that of their causes. Whyte notes that 'Inequality is a more general relationship than equality in the sense that it covers a wider field and approaches equality when the inequality becomes vanishingly small. This is an example of the fact that the field of an asymmetrical relation, such as greater than, often includes the corresponding symmetrical relation, here equal to, as a special limiting case. Thus the field of inequality includes equality, non-simultaneity includes simultaneity, and spatial asymmetry includes spatial symmetry, each as a logically degenerate limiting case of a wider field of relations.' He sums up:

The science of inequality, succession, and asymmetry—which has still to be created—is more comprehensive than the science of equality, reversibility, and symmetry, and can include the latter as a special branch. The science of quantity and equations is a part of the more general science of order. We have therefore to discover the most general possible relation of inequality between cause and effect which can provide a basis for science. This is equivalent to discovering the necessity and sufficient characteristics of scientific causality.[26]

What seems to be an important development of this kind of approach appears in the theories of the Soviet astronomer, N. A. Kozyrev, who has been deprived by the authorities of his right to work in the field of physics at the demand of the atomic physicists. He declares, in mathematical terms, that cause and effect cannot be simultaneous in time and must be separate in space; and makes an attempt to work out a positive system that will go beyond Newtonian principles, including the quantum modifications. He holds that, whatever the time and distance between cause and effect are in fact, the ratio between these two factors provides a constant. This ratio, a measure of speed, is a universal constant as important as the speed of light; and it may be called the speed of the transformation of cause into effect: He names it the Progress of Time.[27] I will not here go into the mathematics of these ideas, but will only note that Kozyrev embodies the power to express left- or right-handedness in our formulations by determining the sign of time-progress in our system of measurement. He goes on to argue that the time-progress for spinning bodies differs from the usual value by an amount equal to the speed of rotation. The change in the time-progress by virtue of rotation gives rise to unbalanced forces, and so can be used as a source of energy. That is to say, the passage of time release energy. Kozyrev believes that it is possible for us to grasp the moments of real change, in which asymmetry appears in a system, and to harness those moments, to draw out of them the energy which internally would have gone to the re-assertion of the system in some extended pattern.*

How far the details of Kozyrev's formulations can be proved to be correct yet remains to be shown. But we may hold that it is along such lines as his or Whyte's that the movement on to a new level of science, transcending that of the scientists from Galileo to Einstein, will be achieved. Time ceases to be an abstract coordinate, no different in character from space, and we enter the real irreversible universe. This universe can only be grasped in terms of the dialectical leap, now seen as the movement on to a new qualitative level through the re-assertion of symmetry in an asymmetrical situation. It is one in which the totality is realised through a new and ever-widening sense of its interconnections. We may recall the experiment of Einstein, Podolsky and Rosen, which had its significance further illuminated by Bell's Theorem. This brought out the fact that elements, separated by long distances in space and long intervals of time, may still be somehow closely and indissolubly connected: as if the irregularities of particular movements were partial manifestations of a deeper and more inward order, 'capable in principle of involving the entire dancing pattern of energy' (BOHM).

To assert that everything is in the last analysis connected with everything else does not nullify the relative autonomy of specific formations and singular things. But the separation of one thing from another, its qualitative distinctions from everything else, breaks down at a certain point in time and space. So long as the opposing forces are in balance the totality appears stable, harmonious, at rest—and is really so. But this is a transient condition. Sooner or later, alterations in the inner relation of forces, and interactions with other processes in the environment, upset the achieved equilibrium, generate instability, and can eventuate in the disruption and destruction of the most hard-and-fast formations. Dialectics is fundamentally the most consistent way of thinking about the universal interconnections of things in the full range of their development. (NOVACK[28])

---

* It is work such as Whyte's that truly opens the field for dialectical science. Efforts to apply the rules of Diamat to a given field may have a certain interest, but are premature, e.g. the work of the Soviet biologist Oparin. He argues that the random formations and interactions of ever more complex molecules bring about the simplest forms of living matter, which then begin to reproduce at the expense of environing organic material. To define this process he uses principles such as the transformation of quantity into quality, rupture of continuity (evolutionary leap), conversion of chance fluctuations into regular processes and definite properties of matter: Novack (1) 1466. Some valuable points come out, but the whole thing is too like an imposition of Diamat rules, not a living unity of the material and dialectical method or system.

117

Before ending this section we may glance afresh at Marx and Engels. Their sympathies in many ways were with the line running from Bruno and Kepler on to Goethe and the Nature-philosophers, rather than to that begun by Galileo and Newton. This concept of the world, which in many ways we could call alchemical, was one 'in which Marx saw a kinship with that of Jakob Boehme, in virtue of the latter's qualitative view of movement, which Lenin found akin to that of Heraclitus' (GARAUDY)—a concept of 'an organic whole in constant process not only of development, but also of auto-creation'. It is not by chance that Marx, in one of his few accounts of contradiction, looks to Kepler. In *Capital* (I, ch. 3) he deals with the contradictory and mutually exclusive conditions implied in the exchange of commodities. The further development of the commodity does not abolish the contradictions, 'but rather provides the form in which they have room to move. That is, in general, the way in which real contradictions are resolved. For instance, it is a contradiction to depict one body as constantly falling towards another and at the same time constantly flying away from it. The ellipse is a form of motion within which this contradiction is both realised and resolved.' He is recalling Hegel's criticism of Newton's law of gravity as taking no account of the sun's and the planet's quality-endowed matter, and his contrast of Newton's abstracting method with that of Kepler, who saw sun and planets in a concrete unity, as movements that did not exclude quality. For Kepler, the ellipse was not an abstract curve with two foci; it was a dialectical magnitude formed by two real points of the revolving body's reversal of direction.

Marx, we may note, was highly critical of the calculus. In his mathematical manuscript he showed, for instance, that the classical writers had the derivative ready prepared before the process of differentiation really began; he wanted a method that actually followed the process of variation of the variable and in this process itself defined the derivative as O/O, in which case it could be endowed with the new symbol dy/dx. The derivation, he insisted, should be performed by a process of differentiation, not be produced from the outset by the binomial theorem; and he suggested a method avoiding the lack of internal development.[29]

Another important feature was his insistence on the operational character of the differential and on the search for the exact moment where the calculus springs from the underlying algebra as a new doctrine. 'Infinitesimals' do not appear in Marx's work at all. In his insistence on the origin of the derivative in a real change of the variable he takes a decisive step in overcoming the ancient paradox of Zeno—by stressing the task of the scientist in not denying the contradictions in the real world but to establish the best mode in which they can exist side by side. (STRUICK)

I cite these little-known examples of Marx's mathematical work to show how eagerly he would have welcomed the possibilities of an effective dialectic of nature which are now emerging.*

---

* Bloch, as we would expect, had his vision of an integrative science. Capitalism, he says, has fabricated a technology based on a purely quantitative and mechanist concept of nature as opposed to a qualitative one. Socialist technology will be 'non-Euclidian', and will restore to humanity a close harmony with nature, making possible a 'qualitative' attitude to it which 'abstract capitalism' is unable to achieve.[30]

8 Symmetry, Asymmetry, Structure, Dominance

In this chapter I interpose a brief account of some aspects of my attempts in the past to develop Marxist ideas; aspects that are relevant to the themes we have been discussing. I do this partly because I think the account will help to clarify various positions I have been trying to set out, and also because in these writings there appear various formulations that have come up elsewhere in recent times. Thus, it should clear me in certain points from any accusation of merely following or imitating other thinkers.

I begin then with an essay in *Dialectics* (New York) published shortly before World War II. In it I agreed that it was necessary to show how a writer of any significance owned a deep understanding of social reality:

But still the gibe that Marxist has merely missed the aesthetic fact has its sting. For when one has minutely proved that Balzac understood the social relationships of his world, that he saw those relationships with an objective clarity which makes his definition intelligible and moving for readers who have stepped into a world where such relationships no longer exist, one has yet not shown in the slightest why Balzac is Balzac or how he differs from, say, Marx and Engels, who had, as analysts, the same remorselessly objective perception of social relationships.

In short, one has still omitted the aesthetic fact.

The examination has not been irrelevant. On the contrary. The aesthetic fact does not exist in isolation, as the exponents of pure-art would argue. It cannot be separated from its social origins and effects; in the last resort it merges with the human whole of its point in time, with the science, the labour-processes, the nexus of emotional and physical satisfactions, which make up the full human reality. Nevertheless, however they all merge in the 'whole', the building of a bridge is distinct from an equation in mathematics or an orchestral symphony. And it is as important to get at the roots of the difference as at the dynamic of the unity. [1]

These points were to refute an essay which had dealt solely with the social content of art.

The aesthetic fact is an organisational dynamic of experience; it is a rhythmic compulsion; it is an active merging with the reality of movement. But the dynamic, the rhythm, the merging, do not rest at an experience of movement. As with science the process objectifies itself in a Form—science in the abstract formulation of law, art in the concrete expression of experience. The emphasis in that statement is on the term 'concrete,' which at once raises the whole question of Rhythm. Into that there is no space to go here. It must be enough to point out the close dynamic relation between the Form of art and science on one side, and on the other the Rhythm of labour-process and the communal dance, and the Rhythm of organic process and organisation, the phenomenal world with which man as producer dynamically merges.

It is Form then that is the aesthetic fact; concrete and rhythmic form. But again we must hedge this declaration against all pure-art distortions by emphasising that 'concrete and rhythmic' at once include the dynamic relation of individual and productive group, the active and purposeful merging with nature which is the human essence . . .

What is the unfailing basis of continuity throughout human history—a basis that we can imagine as failing only with the utter disappearance of humanity? It is the active relationship to nature, with its dynamic spearhead in the productive sphere.

In *Perspective for Poetry*, written while I was still in the army in 1944, I attempted to define further the nature of Form:

It is common to say that form and content make up a unity, and in a sense it is true enough. But it still leaves the question of content in the air. Why should a purely narcisistic content not be enough, since it will have its own adequate form, the projection in aesthetic act?

This theoretical formulation therefore gives a maximum stimulus to the concept of the isolated poet. The truth of the aesthetic act is, however far better stated if we point out that the content is never simple. The content is always rent by a conflict. It is precisely this conflict of opposites within the content which creates the Form. The Form is the resolution of the inner conflict. It is the act in which the opposites achieve unity. Within the content are always elements of inner and outer, personal and social, self and audience, and so on. These opposites become poetry, become aesthetically realised (as distinct from being intellectually realised, etc.) only through the *the Act which is the Form*. The form can only be conceived, then, in terms of the conflict which it resolves.

Next, I possess duplicated texts of a long discussion-document which was circulated for an evening conference in 1945 organised by the cultural committee of the Communist Party of Great Britain. The theme was the nature of culture, its role in social development, its relation to production. After discussing a number of texts from Marx and Engels, and the tendency of many Marxists to see culture as a mere 'reflection of economic mechanism and the sum total of social relations', the document turned to Plekhanov's essay *The Materialist Conception of History*, which tried to attack reductionism by arguing that the state of the productive forces in the long run determines all social relations, economic class-relations, then legal and moral relations, and lastly and indirectly the arts and sciences, etc. 'What is this *indirect* determination? Does it merely mean that the connection is more tangled?' The term *Reflection* was then further examined and rejected. Engels wrote that the economic factor was not the sole determining factor, but did not specify the other factors or how they worked. He made a positive contribution by insisting on the need for a concept of dialectical reciprocity. His term interaction had relevance if we were thinking of base and superstructure as social formations or institutions (the old conventional psychology saw the relationship of body and mind as one of either parallelism or interaction).

The following quotations will give an idea how the paper worked out its thesis.[2]

PASSAGES FROM THE DISCUSSION PAPER
(1) Consciousness in the individual, we saw, emerges when the quantitative organisation of the body reached a certain point of unity. Then mind, a new quality, develops, and keeps developing in a continual dialectical relation with the body. Culture emerges in the group when the productive activity, with its cooperative basis, develops a certain quantity of superabundant social energy. Then the new unity, the new quality, which we know as culture, appears.* In short, production and culture are in a dialectical relation of conflict and unity, and if that is so, then one is being continually transformed into the other.

Look at the primitive again. His superabundant social energy, based on productive cooperative activity, is transformed into the form of ritual, that is dance and song and painting. This is no mere reflection of labour-process, but a *transformation of productive activity*. It is productive activity on a new level, where it becomes a satisfaction in itself. And yet by the dialectical law the new activity, culture, is continually transformed back into economic activity. For the organisation of personal and social energy on the new level increases enormously human powers: the individual achieves enormously enhanced powers of energisation, powers that he could never possibly have achieved if all his outlets of energy can be conceived as having remained on the economic level pure and simple. These new energies return back into everyday life, giving increased consciousness for his daily task, his economic task. He thus becomes a

---

* *Later comment.* There is a mechanistic touch in the idea of quantity into quality. Mind is present in some degree in the human body from the outset; culture is linked with production from the outset, however embryonic the fusion, it is the early stages of human evolution. (I cite these passages from my paper for their general direction; in detail many formulations can be criticised.)

more efficient, a better organised productive agent; and from the higher level, the level of culture, spring ideas and impulses which are translated into *techniques and new methods*.

It is clear then that as soon as social energy reaches the dialectical point where it is transformed into the new quality, Culture, it has done something that cannot be undone. Something that is essential to all further social and personal development. Culture or the superstructure is not something just added as a kind of extra, a luxury to the sub-structure, the direct productive levels. It is something on which the substructure entirely depends, just as it depends in turn on the substructure: the two make up a dialectical unity. And man can no more get on with his productive task without an ideology, without a release and satisfaction on cultural levels, than he can develop airy structures of the mind without the sustaining productive levels. *For humanity, culture is just as essential as production.* Every advance in production is in dialectical unity with an advance in culture.

Any formulation, then, which states production as isolatedly primary is mechanist and anti-dialectical. Man advances as the whole man, or not at all. He never advances merely as economic man, which is an abstraction without any historical meaning.

(2) What is the way in which the un-realised social relations act as a compulsion on the individual? If they act as an unconscious (un-realised) force—reflected (to use the old mechanist term) in the tensions and conflicts of the ideological levels, where does the transformation-formula come in? I confess that I can only see in this difficulty another form of mechanism. What are unconscious social forces? A Marxist cannot be thinking in terms of Jungian collective-unconscious. If there is a dialectical relation of individual and society, the un-realised social relations and their historical movement must have a dialectical expression in the individual in his personal unconscious and in religious (or idealistic) formulations. Otherwise we are using the term 'social relations' in a mystical vitalist sense. The conflict-and-unity between the elements of knowledge and consciousness in the individual, and the elements of compulsion and unconsciousness, must have a dialectical relation with the conflict-and-unity between the elements of planning and compulsion, of realised and un-realised cause-and-effect in society.

The significance of class-conflict in class-society is not thereby lessened. There the struggle of men to master the world and to know themselves is entangled in class-relations which are understood in a narrow sense but are not understood in relation to the movement of society *as a whole*. Therefore a man's intuition of a cooperative whole is in conflict with his experience of a divided society. The productive pattern, transformed into the levels of culture, carries with it this tension, this conflict between co-operative content and class-forms. The result is certainly a very complicated series of conflicts and transformations. There is no common body of culture because there is no common activity on the productive level. Differing class-positions will tend to bring about a different pattern of tensions and resolutions.

(3) Before we understand what the problem is we must begin to understand the part played by the genetic factors in the individual (Caudwell began to attack this issue, but confusedly.) Jung has tried to isolate the infantile patterns of experience as mystical symbols, and the Gestalt school has tried out a method for defining the reality of mental process in figurations of movement. We must know and analyse these attempts for what is valid and invalid. We will then begin to see how the tension between self and society, between the organic functioning of the body and the transformed patterns in the mind, enable us to grasp reality. Freud has given us the key to the dialectical movement between conscious and unconscious in the individual. We must sift his work, to get rid of the mechanist classifications, and must find how this process in the psyche which Freud has shown is dialectically linked with the conflicts between realised and un-realised social forces and relations . . .

The genetic basis of individuality, and the unity-and-conflict of family and social relationships, must then be kept in mind in evaluating what goes to form a man. In a class-society the pattern is liable to become very complicated. The reduction to simple economic motivation becomes a mechanist absurdity.

(4) 'Men, developing their material production and their material intercourse, change along with this their real existence, also their thinking and the products of their thought. It is not consciousness that determines life, but life that determines consciousness.' Note that he (Marx) does not say in any way at all that the superstucture is a reflection of production. He relates both super and sub-structure to the larger whole which he calls the life-process: which can only be what he called in *The Holy Family* 'the Total Human Being'. He deliberately used an active term to express the work of the spirit: *Production.* He thus makes the work of the spirit as real as the work of any economic activity. He does not say that it is economic or social activity or relations which determine consciousness. He says it is *Life.* That is, he makes consciousness and economic activity both part of a larger whole, the life-process, the human whole.

His statement is thus quite antagonistic to what now masquerades in the name of the Marxist theory of the superstructure. It also explains why he and Engels did not go further than they did in analysing the superstructure. The term *production* is here used to cover all human activity, economic, social, or cultural. It is clear that Production always had something of this larger sense for Marx, but he was not concerned to work out the dialectics of the relation between sub- and superstructure. After his early work he turned for practical reasons to political economy. We can now proceed to the further task because of the great demolishing work done by Marx and Engels: work in which the dialectical analysis was applied widely to nature (the transformation of energy) and to the economic levels of society. Once the primary stages of consolidation are passed, however, the problem of Culture comes to the fore. It is found that men do not act on the over-simplification of motive which the concentration on economic mechanism and social relation implied. Men become men by a fuller process. And reasons imbedded in that process can make them cling to an outworn scheme of things long after it has become political suicide and economic disaster. Because of the lack of any scientific psychology much of eighteenth-century rationalism still clung to the first attempts of Marxism. Lenin knew that Rosa Luxemburg was wrong when she drew up her theory of spontaneity, which is logically impeccable if economic mechanism plus social relations is the whole dynamic of society. He knew just that things didn't work out that way, that the workers didn't become automatically revolutionary, etc. But he had no theoretical justification.*

I may mention that with one exception everyone present at the conference condemned my views. The exception was Edward Thompson, who came in travel-worn, having arrived an hour or so earlier from a youth-camp in Yugoslavia. I have given the above citations because, though many of the formulations are much over-simplified, there are, I think, several positive points which were new in Marxist controversy in Britain at the time. First, there is the general scepticism about the thesis of base and superstructure, and the concept of cultural activity as a form of productive activity. Productive activity is seen always as a transformation, so that while economic activity directly transforms nature, culture transforms the

---

* *Later note.* These remarks do not do full justice to Rosa Luxemburg, though she did see a sort of steady organic rise of political consciousness in the working-class at each new confrontation with the bourgeoisie. Her strength lay in her faith in the energies that could be developed in workers at each intensification of struggle: a position that led her to oppose anything like bureaucratic centralism.

relation of people both to nature and to one another. The two activities combine to create the individual, endowing him with richer energies and wider scopes. Further, there is a strong attack on reductionism in all its forms; while stress is laid on the totality of factors or processes in a given situation, and on the fact that what composes the totality is a complex of processes, not elements that can be taken apart, added up, or treated as things. Long before Timpanaro the question is raised of the genetic basis of the individual and of the continuous unity-and-conflict of biological factors inside the social situation. Also the question of the family, its nature and role, and the fact that it must be seen as more than a mere microcosm reflecting social relations outside it.

The main weakness lies in the over-generalised concept of the unity in society which makes possible the emergence and development of conflicts. No clear differentiation is made between the imposed unity that expresses the outlook and needs of a ruling class, and the dynamic elements emerging from the cooperative forms and processes of production. In an actual situation, these two aspects can become closely entangled and, indeed, their co-existence has never been properly noted and analysed by Marxists (apart from Bloch with his concepts of Hope and Block). It constitutes one of the deepest problems in the question of hegemony, which has been raised by Gramsci (of whose work at this time I knew nothing).

In this paper was set out—I think for the first time—the concept of culture as productive activity. Recently Raymond Williams has written in much the same terms: 'My aim was to emphasise that cultural practices are forms of material production, and that until this is understood it is impossible to think about them in their real social relations—there can only ever be a second order of correlation.' He uses the term production in a very wide sense, covering in effect all forms of human activity. Rejecting the distinctions of base and superstructure, he speaks of 'a single and indissoluble real process' simultaneously integrating economic, social, political and cultural activities.[3] He thus lays himself open to the charges that Suchadolski, as we shall see, made against my positions. The attacks on Williams were made by the *New-Left-Review* critics in 1979:

Now you are certainly right to emphasise the dangers of an idealist account of culture as a sphere of intangible notions and values, and to point out the way culture is composed of real, physical processes of communication and reproduction. But can we say that it is therefore 'wholly beside the point to isolate production and industry from welfare, entertainment and public opinion'? We earlier criticised your tendency, to miss the importance of causal hierarchies in historical analysis, in which far from being beside the point, it is absolutely essential to be able to isolate the forces which have a superior capacity to induce large-scale social change; and argued that in your previous writings you were inclined to overlook the fact that economic production becomes cultural production in a way which is not symmetrically true of the relation of cultural production to economic production. Your latest emphasis now seems to produce a new circularity in which all elements of the social order are equal because they are material.

I cite this at length because it brings out the way in which any attempt to give some measure of autonomy to cultural processes finds that the link with the economic base is hard to define, and is liable to produce some sort of 'circularity'. Gramsci comes up against this problem and fails to solve it theoretically, though without real damage to his concept of hegemony in society.

One direct result of the discussion was my book *Song of a Falling World* (1948), which dealt with culture during the breakup of the Roman Empire, 350-600 A.D. Here I examined the poetry of the period for the ways in which it revealed the collapse of the old imperial culture, expressed the changing situation and the new attitudes of people, and brought out in various ways in which the new potentialities were emerging and looking into the future. Culture did not merely facilitate the growth of new modes of production; it helped to create the full human situation out of which the modes grew. The concluding chapter tried to formulate more clearly the positions set out in the document and to apply them.*

In 1949 I published *Marxism and Contemporary Science*. Here I argued that the idea of unity was an essential aspects of dialectics, since it was inside an enveloping unity that conflicts and contradictions arose, developed, extended, and finally brought about the movement into a new level, a new unity. Without the unity the conflicts would have no basis on which to arise and develop. Without it the nature of the conflicts could not be understood. At the same time I examined various fields of science for what seemed positive elements capable of being used and developed by Marxists. Using the work of L. L. Whyte, I sought to get rid of what mechanist or limited elements in Hegelian terminology had been taken over by Diamat (a convenient term for the orthodoxies into which Marxism had largely settled). I sought to apply and work out the concepts of symmetry-

---

* In all my works since 1936 I have sought to use a Marxist methodology according to the different fields, e.g. in my lives of writers and artists. However, because I have not obtruded the method abstractly but have tried to bring together concretely the historical, socio-economic, personal, and aesthetic elements in a living unity, this point has hardly been noticed.

asymmetry, stability-instability, as defining in the most general form the ways in which development, breakdown or disintegration, renewal or movement on to a new level, came about.

The book was at once condemned by all the Marxists of the time into whose view it came. The one exception was Bogdan Suchadolski, who wrote a long and detailed review in the Polish *Mysl Wspolczesna* in 1951. He accepted as valid a great deal of my exposition, but made some strong criticisms. For example,

Dialectical thinking that loses sight of the wholeness and unity of developing processes ceases to be, according to Lindsay, genuine dialectical thinking. It leads to the rigid opposition of rigid and immobile conceptions, to the understanding of contradictions as being separate things completely alien to each other. Dialectical thinking spoilt by dualism becomes incapable of understanding developing processes, of understanding movement, because dialectical understanding of them is only possible as long as we understand contradictions to form a definite whole. Otherwise the contradictions become independent and grow into separate, mutually alien and disconnected beings. This produces a complete series of fictitious philosophical problems and reduces philosophical thinking to the traditional position of dualism.[4]

He found the most important part of the book the 'attempts to prove on the basis of examples taken from the fields of art, ethics, biology, anthropology, psychology, and history, that all progressive materialistic thought uses unitary dialectics and is constantly striving to strengthen it'. But he correctly condemned the failure to develop any clear structure or hierarchy inside the dialectical system described. He defined this as a lack of true materialism in the system.

[That is] why Lindsay formulates his attitude as a conception of 'everything being connected with everything,' why he seems to see all reality as a kind of globe hanging in a void, within which everything is linked and interdependent, in which everything is struggling and achieving harmony, but in which nothing forms a basis for all the others, in which nothing is 'first'.

However, I would like to cite here some passages from the book which, though not providing the required firm structure, do suggest lines of approach, terminology, which could be used for that purpose. Oddly, they anticipate the terms that were to be devised by Althusser some 15 years later.

PASSAGES FROM MARXISM AND CONTEMPORARY SCIENCE

(1) Form *is* Content. This, as Abercrombie pointed out, is true of creative activity in all its stages, conscious or unconscious. The final Form, reached according to the *Prägnanz* formula, is the final objectification of the inner conflict, the degree of unity between energy and organisation which prevailing conditions (inner and outer)

allow. Can we advance from that definition? Art, we can say, is the *Structure* of human process arrested and objectified at a certain point (the *Prägnanz* point): the *Pattern* or *Form* is the projection of the structure. *Rhythm* is the movement of the process employed in bringing about this projection, and is revealed in the *Pattern*. The moment of projection reveals further a *Dominance*, the keypoint in the development leading to the work of art, which expresses the particular relation of inner and outer, organism and environment, individual and history.

The keypoint, expressing and revealing the Dominance, is *integrative*. It expresses 'the arrangement of organic structure and tension so that *a single characteristic form* is developed'. (I use this terminology because it relates the creative act to general evolutionary process.) Development may be defined as *Decrease in Asymmetry* and the Dominance is *the relation of the Form to the Process it facilitates.*[5]

That is, the artist, seeking to unify a confusion and conflict which is going on inside himself and which is dialectically one with confusions and conflicts going on outside, strives to develop the conflict in organised expression. He grapples with the discordant (asymmetrical) material—himself and the world—and seeks to overcome its asymmetry. In doing so he creates a new form. He reaches forward into the potential and makes it the actual. He is not at all concerned with reflecting the present, with being realistic. He is concerned with facilitating the life-process. To bring about his aim, he must however embrace the actual: otherwise he will lack the essential conflict out of which creativity proceeds, and will be dealing with simple wish-fulfilments. The more he can embrace of the actual, the stronger the conflict and the greater the drive forward into the levels where present conflicts and asymmetries are resolved in an extended symmetry. The stronger his drive to harmony, the greater his need to embrace more and more conflict, in order to overcome it. He judges life always in terms of the potential, and his aim is one of integration. His acceptance and comprehension of the world and himself are only in terms of the resolving harmonies which he intuits and which he brings into existence by his creation of Form.

(2) In such a (biological) situation the maintenance of anything like equilibrium between organism and environment is clearly a highly complex affair; and men keep 'extending their structure' by the continual projection of gestalts, which express the tension of organism and environment, and stabilise it by powerful symmetries. Therein lies the active symbiosis between men and nature. Among the gestalts—supreme among them— are the social and cultural

formations by which men keep their life stable.

But If the stability is being forever disturbed by changing tensions between men and nature, which are dialectically one with changing tensions and conflicts inside the group, we need a further concept to explain the relation between the stable system and the processes of its development. This concept is that of the Dominance: the relation of a structure to the processes which it facilitates. A system of processes connected by relations of dominance is a hierarchy. Among men it is productive activity which facilitates process, which maintains and extends the stable relationship between men and nature on the one hand, and which maintains and extends the stable relationships within society on the other.

But by the very virtue which makes men into men, we must not abstract productive activity as a thing in itself, a matter of statistics and measurable relationships. Statistics and measurable relations exist, and for certain purposes it is necessary to know them; but we misunderstand the concept of Dominance if we think the situation can be reduced to them. The economic situation can never really be isolated from the cultural and social situation, and vice-versa. For the Dominance which alone makes human productivity possible involves an Organising Process (the dominant process in the hierarchy of an organism or stable system); and for men the Organising Process is fundamentally spiritual as well as social. That is, it is related to the facilitation by the brain of the formative aspects of organic process and to the record in the brain of organising processes which facilitate delayed responses.

Therefore the whole human tradition, which we roughly call Culture, is inherent in the Dominance; and out of the complex instability of the whole social system (in its relation to nature) and its internal tensions and conflicts there comes a ceaseless formative process which it is the aim of men to facilitate. In so far as they succeed, they succeed in achieving stability. Because of the dominant and integrative function of the brain, men can plan and invent. They can project organic symbols in art or science, and separate off gestalts as techniques. They are never closed in by the actual, the immediate relations. They can look forwards and backwards; and out of a situation of stress and disequilibrium they can wrest the potential form, the form which will create a higher stability in the future.

(3) The unitary approach enables us to make sense of the relations between the economic and the cultural levels in society. We can trace as aspects of a single process the prevailing scientific ideas and the forms of technique, the cultural forms of self-expresion and the social formations. In dealing with class-societies we see class-forms as

simultaneously providing the basis of cohesion (since they are the most effective modes at that stage for a maximum control of nature) and the basis of tension and antagonism (since the changing forms of techniques and exploitation shift the emphasis of Dominance and put new potential virtues of human advancement in the hands of one section or class to the detriment of others). As one class finds that its forms and methods are in increased harmony with the Organising Process, the opposed class loses its effective relation to Dominance and sinks towards static formations more and more out of key with the formative process. The clue to new active differentiations and dominances passes into the hands of the newly emerging class, who then control and develop productive techniques and methods, and play an essential part in facilitating new cultural formations.

These words must be taken only as a brief sketch of the way in which a process-logic will tackle the various aspects of social and cultural development, and relate them to a single human process. But the whole direction of my argument will have been missed if it seems that in all this we are merely considering and playing about with ideas on the abstractly intellectual level. The ultimate dynamic of all these concepts of unity lies in the movement of the peoples of the world at this moment into unity, into socialism; a movement against all the divisive factors of capitalism in its present bloodily convulsive state, which threatens the destruction of the earth by nuclear fission. The form of thought I am putting forward is alive and will prevail to the extent to which it realises that unity, that unity of men with men, and of man with nature. To that extent it is the form of thought of Marx and Lenin. The release and co-ordination at which it aims can reach their first full activity only in that world-unity, that revolution of the hand and the spirit against all that seeks to reduce men to things. But, to the extent to which it apprehends reality, it must work to facilitate that revolution.

All development, it will be clear, involves transformation of some sort, large or small. But we must distinguish on the one hand the normal facilitation of a system, its tendency to extend its form by a repetition of the process by which it was formed; and on the other hand the Critical Points, the moment of decisive shifts in integrative levels.

The terms *Structure* and *Dominance*, and so on, I took from biological and physical process. But they were not clearly worked out. In the first passage I seek to analyse the way in which an artwork is created. The controlling idea-image is the Dominance, which exerts a pervasively formative influence on the Structure that represents the moment of life (with elements both inside the psyche and outside it, in nature and society) arrested by the artist, taken over and recreated in Pattern or Form. Rhythm is the vital movement of process which produces the integration of inner and outer in the Form. The projection of the artwork itself happens with the coming-together of Dominance, Structure, Rhythm, Form. The Dominance determines the precise union-and-conflict with life, the coherence and meaning, which compose the Structure; the Rhythm releases into Form. Rhythm appears in a sense of vital proportions, in organisation of meaning and emphasis, in mathematical relations, and so on.[6]

I meant to infer that the same sort of system was at work in any cultural expression that laid hold of reality, revealed it, transformed it. But in the later use of the term I was raising a much wider issue: that of the means by which a group (class) or individuals maintain themselves and develop. The same general pattern is seen at work, but the Dominance is now the central or most comprehensive of the various factors controlling and directing life, society, history. The Structure in Dominance is here the socio-economic system which brings about production and reproduction. It is defined as dominating a hierarchy of processes, which are all related to it in varying degrees of closeness and completeness. I claimed that 'one obvious advantage of this approach is that cultural and economic forms and forces are at once brought together in real act—whereas a theory of interrelated structures keeps them apart. Social relations, economic formations, and technical methods are seen as dialectically one, and there is no division between them and the whole cultural field implicated in the release of human potentiality by production.' That may be so, but by making this kind of integrative inter-connection one is liable to be left in the end with the situation that Suchadolski described. One is omitting the whole question of hierarchy, which was stated as a necessary part of the system but was not developed. In the next chapter we shall discuss the problem of preserving the idea of the mode of production as the structure in dominance of the social totality, without losing sight of what has been called the relative

---

* Facilitation is the tendency of structures to extend their form by repetition of the process by which they were formed. A structure facilitates a process if its tendency to develop internally implies the recurrence of that process. (The tendency may not be realised.) Facilitation holds an important *asymmetry*. The record of the past formative process held in the structure tends to determine the future. This asymmetrical relation we call dominance: the relation of a structure to the process that it facilitates. Structure is process nearing a symmetrical form.

autonomy of the other structures. Relative autonomy, we must not forget, implies also relative dependence.

In *Origins of Alchemy* (1970) I attempted, among other things, to show the links of labour-process and methods with ideas about natural process and about critical or nodal points of change, a triadic movement—ideas that foreshadow the later philosophical concepts of dialectical process in thinkers like Heraclitus and Plato or the alchemists themselves (right up to the days of men like Boehme). [7] Then in *Blastpower and Ballistics* I dealt at length with ancient concepts of force and energy (compared with modern ones) and with the ancient concentration on quality rather than quantity. From one angle the problem of science today is to bring together the lines of approach based on quantity and quality, disintegration and integration. Engels intuited something of all this. 'Among the Greeks,' he wrote, 'just because they were not yet advanced enough to dissect, analyse nature, nature is still viewed as a whole, in general. The universal connection of natural phenomena is not proved with regard to the particulars; for the Greeks it is the result of unmediated, intuitive perception.' So, if today science is to change over from 'empirical science' into a theoretical 'natural science', it will be 'forced to go back to the Greeks'.

In *Blastpower and Ballistics* I made a detailed attempt to show that nuclear fission and its bombs are the final expression of blastpower fantasies, starting at a shamanist level and gradually actualised in various war-devices, finally in gunpowder leading on to the present fiendish systems of destruction. From the analysis of the consequences of the Galileo-Newton system we come to the question of alternative lines of research into physical reality such as have been suggested by Whyte and Kozyrev for the post-Planck world.*

---

* The triadic concept of change (life, death, rebirth; primary state, critical point of breakdown, transformation on a new level), found in alchemic systems, is also that of initiation-ritual, which leaves an extremely powerful imprint on all early levels of culture.

I may add that in the 1960s I wrote two large works on Alienation and allied problems, but could find no publisher for them.

9   Some Conclusions

There are some other post-1917 Marxist thinkers whom we might have examined, as well as some near-Marxists such as Sartre; but in general it may be claimed that the field covered gives a representative picture of the struggles that have been going on in the advanced levels concerned with theoretical and cultural issues, rather than with the direct problems of political action. The title *Crisis in Marxism* is surely justified by the lack of any substantial agreement among the main thinkers. Althusser, for example, has attacked Lukacs, Korsch, Goldmann, Sartre, Gramsci and della Volpe as all duped by historicism, which in his definition is 'an ideology in which society becomes a circular "expressive" totality, history a homogeneous flow of linear time, philosophy a self-consciousness of the historical process, class-struggle a combat of collective "subjects", capitalism a universe essentially defined by alienation, communism a state of true humanity beyond alienation.' This is a definition that tells us much more about Althusser than it does of the thinkers he criticised.

But despite the controversies, there are certain points of agreement. Though Lukacs took a very different view later, in 1923 he tended to convey the effect of bourgeois society, working-class and all, as hopelessly reified, things in a non-human world. In the case of Adorno, Horkheimer and Marcuse the concept of a total reification became the central motive, with other thinkers such as Goldmann concurring. As with Althusser, though in a different way, humanity as a subject in effect disappeared; people were manipulated puppets; for Althusser they were units or ciphers in a structural system. The Frankfurt School accepted the importance of dialectical materialism, but reduced it to a critical theory of non-identity thinking which at most could give the reified world a few minor shocks. The movement to new levels became impossible except by some sort of miracle. Dialectics, though formally accepted by Althusser, was displaced by his structuralist system. Della Volpe and Colletti completed this trend by denouncing dialectics altogether and considering Marxism to be an empiricist materialism with the non-contradictory logic that rules in bourgeois science. Bloch alone stands out as giving a positive lead; but he can define his utopian movement of resistance against all that obstructs and divides, only by more or less ignoring the actual historical situation and its more direct forms of struggle.

In the field of literary or artistic criticism, Lukacs wants socialists to attempt to carry over all the positive, integrative, and critical elements of the great works of the bourgeois epoch, to realise them on a new level: a task that would be possible only in a socialist society in which full liberation had been achieved—though inevitably the complex struggle by which the state of liberation had been won would have involved all kinds of different and new forms of art-activity, so that the problem could not be confronted in the more or less simple way in which Lukacs formulates it. Thus, he attacked Toller in 1926 for 'abstract and romantic utopianism.' True enough to a considerable extent, but it ignores the forceful impact of the expressionist plays, the extent to which they were valuable at a given stage of the struggle to transform culture and people. On the other hand, Adorno or Goldmann see virtue only in the works that directly reflect the utterly alienated state of bourgeois man, in the hope that the unrelieved presentation will stir in people an awareness of their predicament. We may contrast with both Lukacs and Adorno Gramsci's attitude to the Futurists. He saw them (before their drift to Fascism) as embodying a counter-hegemodic potential that the Italian communists failed to recognise and mobilise. [1]

It is hard, then, to find common areas in the thinkers examined, areas that can be directly developed to deal with the problems confronting us today. We can argue that in many important points the thinkers show the weaknesses in what had become the conventional forms of Marxism, the problems which had been insufficiently faced and explored. They can thus stimulate us to tackle these problems afresh, learning from both what was effective, and what was inadequate in their presentations. We may perhaps agree that the nature and role of culture in its manifold forms is an issue that has continually come up in direct or indirect ways. The failure of so many political activities brings home the lack of sufficient understanding of what forms people, what attaches them to a given system or detaches them in critical resistances of various kinds, and finally leads them to desire deep-going or revolutionary change. So the question of culture, as has been brought out by Gramsci in particular, is also a political one, often a crucially political one. The failure of any break-through after 1917 in the areas of advanced industrialism has steadily put a question mark against many of the assumptions about the way in which capitalist crisis works and affects people , the way in which the contradictions of capitalism operate in the highly integrated societies that it has brought about. There the oppositions of highly socialised work-systems and monopoly-ownership do not in the least automatically create a broadly-based movement for the completion of the socialising process. On the contrary. As can be seen in the United States, the result can be to integrate the working-class into the system: a development that so badly upset Adorno and Marcuse. The idea that sooner or later capitalism will come to the end of its resources is a hopelessly mechanist and incorrect idea. It will always keep on finding further resources if it is not confronted and challenged by a mass-force which has severed its ideological roots in bourgeois ideas and emotions, and which understands at least certain fundamental aspects of socialist democracy.

Gramsci is the one thinker who has raised points of this kind in a consistent and comprehensive way.[2] He may not have said the last word on the subject, but he *has* said many of the first ones. In raising the question of hegemony, the means by which a ruling class consolidates, extends and stabilises its domination, he did not go explicitly into the question whether the superstructure and the cultural spheres were ultimately dependent on the economic base. It is possible to argue that he attributed causal primacy to civil society over political society, and to both these aspects of the social whole over the economic system or base; or that in the last instance he accepted economic determination. In some ways the question did not seem highly relevant to the situation he was examining, the ways in which the superstructural and cultural aspects of the social whole affected people and gained their willing or unwilling acceptance of the way things were constituted. He certainly was opposed to reducing superstructure and culture to the economic base, either in a direct mechanistic way or in more devious ways. He enlarged the concept of the State so that in effect it represented all the ways in which people were drawn into seeing the existent situation as the natural, or best, or only practicable way of organising a society. The State, indeed, does appear as the wielder of power and repression, but also as the organiser of consent and thus the begetter of the harmonious inter-actions without which any society must break down. At the same time he brought out the role of culture as a dimension of politics. He saw hegemony as involving moral, intellectual and aesthetic elements as well as representing political leadership in the obvious sense. It has been said that he developed a gnoseology of politics. That is to say he gave a dialectical account of the effects that philosophy has in all practices, including all the aspects of daily life. Philosophy is shown to have pervasive effects on thought, feeling, action, even when this is

137

quite unsuspected. In other words, all members of society share certain deep notions about the nature of life, people, and so on, the origins of which they mostly do not understand or know.

In his discussions Gramsci continually returns to the point that he is dealing with a unitary system, in which no part can be simply cut away from another. He differentiates between a methodological distinction and an organic one. 'In actual reality civil society and state are identified.' Again, 'State = political society + civil society, in other words, hegemony protected by the armour of coercion.'

Material forces are the content and ideologies the form, though this distinction between form and content has purely 'didactic' value, since the material forces would be inconceivable historically without form and the ideologies would be individual fancies without the material forces.

For the assessment of a social situation it is necessary to attend to the level of development of the material forces of production.

Rejecting any economist or metaphysical concept of the 'structure—Unknown God,' he comments:

Is structure therefore viewed as something immovable and absolute and not, on the contrary, as reality itself in motion, and doesn't the assertion put forward in the *Theses on Feuerbach* that 'the educator must be educated' pose a necessary relation of active reaction by man on the structure, which is an affirmation of the unity of the process of reality.

He wrote a text with the title: 'Unity in the constitutive elements of Marxism':

Unity is provided by the dialectical development of contradictions between man and matter (nature—material forces of production). In the economy the unitary centre is value which is to say the relation between the worker and the industrial forces of production; in philosophy—praxis—which is the relation between human will (superstructure) and the economic structure; in politics—the relation between the state and civil society, which is to say the intervention of the state (centralised will) to educate the educator, the social milieu in general—(Develop and state in more exact terms).[3]

Throughout, we may claim, he was struggling to develop a coherent theory of structures and forces dialectically linked in a unitary process.* He thus laid the basis for a Marxist theory which refuses all

---

* I think I may claim that the attitudes to the unity of society and to the problem of transforming culture in my *Marxism and Contemporary Science*, if developed politically, would lead in Gramsci's direction, e.g. 'One obvious advantage of this approach is that cultural and economic forms and forces are at once brought together in real act—whereas a theory of inter-related structures keeps them apart', 243. But this working-out is not attempted. At the time I knew of Gramsci only his analysis of Croce (*cited*, 206).

forms of reductionism while keeping a central perspective of the class-struggle. He saw that it was necessary to understand the way in which the State (in his broad sense of the term) continually reorganised and extended its concepts and methods to meet the challenges emerging from the inner conflicts of the system—the crises and difficulties which if not re-interpreted, revalued, so as to re-integrate people and to overcome the fears, doubts, antagonisms that they produced, would become dangers to its stability. A successful socialist struggle necessitated a counter-attack which at every level broke down the forms of established hegemony and kept on transforming life in a socialist direction. Politics and philosophy must come together and keep on coming together. The transition to socialism needed the construction of a new common sense (good sense), a new culture in all spheres, a new philosophy, a new consciousness which in the end would express organically all the positions and attitudes necessary for a socialist way of life.

There are some points here that we should examine more closely. First his comments on the shortcomings in Marxist theory. He notes that Marx had very little to say about the way that the transition to socialism would be effected, seeming to infer that the inner contradictions would themselves bring things to a resolving climax. He notes too that Marx did not ever examine systematically the origins and nature of differing kinds of working-class consciousness, so that it was easy for the theorists of the Second International to assume that the whole problematic of consciousness was a remnant of bourgeois idealism. Ideas like 'class', 'state', 'party', 'mode of production', were taken as abstract entities, with no realisation of their real origin and existence through human action. So political initiative was transferred from human beings to structural systems which were expected to do the whole historical job. On the theoretical level this led to views such as those held by Plekhanov and Bukharin, who tried to turn Marxism into a pseudo-science which explained history by a formal system of causal laws. The economist attitude, which saw the struggle of the workers as limited to direct economic issues, was in fact a mere reflection of the premises of bourgeois society, incapable of truly contesting bourgeois hegemony.

Gramsci wanted attention paid to every kind of stirring of discontent or resistance—populism, social banditry, forms of mysticism or millenarianism in the countryside, utopian socialism, urban insurrection and cultural revolt. People restless in the first pangs of awareness as to the nature of their society were more than likely to find rebellious forms or idioms that were 'impure', fragmentary and contradictory. The Marxist must patiently seek to develop and 'demystify' such beginnings so that they truly eroded bourgeois hegemony. At the same time the embryonic stirrings must not be over valued.

Throughout he underlined the role of consciousness in bringing about and shaping revolutionary change; and he was the first Marxist to do so. Concepts are brought down fully into the mellay of the social situation from which they grew; they do not exist on some level above the ceaseless entanglement of struggle and change, they are part of an historically-evolving socio-political process and refuse to fit into simple determinist models. In turn material forces gain meaning only through human definition and involvement, which includes a variety of possible mediations and individual realisations. Gramsci thus sees human activity as shaped or 'determined' by social structures, yet at the same time, as subject, creating new forms that challenge and overturn those structures. 'Structure,' he says, 'ceases to be an external force which crushes man, assimilates him to itself, and makes him passive, and is transformed into a means of freedom, an instrument to create a new ethical political form and a source of new initiatives.'[4]

We find here the answer to the pessimisms of Adorno and Marcuse with their conviction that the reified consciousness inevitable with an expanding market structure of exchange had destroyed the proletariat as subjects in an all-enveloping domination. Gramsci recognised the power of the advanced capitalist state; he saw the United States as creating an historically new type of individual, the 'trained gorilla', so crushed by rationalised work-process that pleasure, sensuality, critical thinking could be expressed only in a very restricted (often guilt-ridden) way. But he saw that this development was only one aspect of what was happening. The question was the degree of equilibrium set up between civil society and the state, which could be either stable or precarious, thus determining the extent of the resources that ruling groups could call on at moments of crisis. Though advanced industrial societies had great resources in this way, the last word went to the disequilibrium that Gramsci recognised as asserting itself through most of European history.[5]

Indeed, in his *Prison Notebooks* he predicted an increasing complexity in civil society in the advanced areas that would raise the ideological cultural struggle to a new level, a new importance, since the state would more and more base its authority on establishing a consensus of support rather than relying on force and coercion. He saw this development as breaking down the relatively simple division of base and superstructure, state and civil society, which had worked in the past: the situation would result in a broad 'ensemble of relations'. To meet it the revolutionary would need to drop all ideas of a shattering crisis sapping the state and its repressive powers, and making possible a movement of the socialist forces into the vacant or broken sphere of power, as happened in 1917. The struggle for change must go on at all levels, all areas, of society. Gramsci distinguished organic movements (long-term and deeply-rooted trends in society) from conjunctural ones, 'which appear as occasional, immediate, almost accidental'. In a prolonged crisis, when deep structural contradictions have actually emerged, the ruling powers make every effort to hold up and alleviate the effects 'within certain limits'. These efforts represent the terrain of the conjunctural. Commonly, in historico-political analysis, there is a failure to find the correct relationship of the organic and the conjunctural. Gramsci's presentation of these issues leads him to the idea of the historical bloc when the objective and the subjective forces combine to bring about a truly revolutionary situation, with people possessing the knowledge and the will to use it: 'the conception of the historical bloc, in which precisely material forces are the content and ideologies are the form'—structures and superstructures come together to form the bloc. Gramsci stresses the full dialectical content of the situation, and uses the term 'historical bloc' to describe the 'unity between spirit and nature, structure and superstructure, unity of opposites and of distincts'.[6]

He is saying that the revolution can come about only when people are already moving into the unifying or integrated cultural viewpoints of socialism so strongly that the new social forms are already implicated, clarified as objectives: 'The principle must always rule that ideas are not born of other ideas, philosophies of other philosophies; they are a continually renewed expression of real historical development'. Looking back on the *Ordine Nuovo* movement of the early postwar years, Gramsci summed up what he felt was its positive achievement which he wants to lift to a new stable level of illuminating consciousness. The leadership

applied itself to real men, formed in specific historical relations, with specific feelings, outlooks, fragmentary conceptions of the world, etc . . . This element of 'spontaneity' was not neglected and even less despised. It was educated, directed, purged of extraneous contaminations; the aim was to bring it into line with modern theory [Marxism]—but in a living and historically effective manner. The leaders themselves spoke of the 'spontaneity' of the movement, and rightly so. This assurance was a stimulus, a tonic, an element of unification in depth . . . It gave the masses a 'theoretical' consciousness of being creators of historical and institutional values, of being founders of a state. This unity between 'spontaneity' and 'conscious leadership' or 'discipline' is precisely the real political action of the

141

subaltern classes, insofar as this is mass politics and not merely an adventure by groups claiming to represent the masses.[7]

To carry on the division between élitist or superior theory and passive or directionless mass-consciousness was to deny the creative popular energies without which a sustained cultural revolution, leading directly into full democratic socialism, could not come about.

Clearly the intellectuals have a new and essential role to play in such a situation. Gramsci saw the key-step as the formation of what he called groupings of organic intellectuals, who were both leading and representative, shedding their isolated positions by becoming part of the daily social existence of the working-class. Part of their function was to win over the more traditional intellectuals, but their work had a very much wider scope than that.

New ideas would not be introduced or 'propagandised' as extraneous inputs into mass politics but would be integrated into the very fabric of proletarian culture, life-styles, language, traditions, etc. by revolutionaries who themselves lived and worked within the same environment. Only this could ensure the dialectical relation between theory and practice, the intellectual and the spontaneous, the political and the social, which could lay the foundations of an authentic *Marxist* subjectivity in popular consciousness itself. (BOGGS)[8]

A counsel of perfection perhaps, but certainly a goal to be worked towards.

It will be clear that generally the positions set out by Gramsci are in accord with those that this book has been attempting to clarify and develop, even if he uses terms with different emphases. Thus he speaks of the state being enlarged when we might prefer to speak of the state's control of the rest of the superstructure being more openly and closely exercised, and so on. He uses the terms base and superstructure in the conventional way, being concerned with the dialectics of the hegemonic structure in general, and the way in which a counter-structure is built up in the struggle to clarify what a revolutionary change constitutes. But though he does not try to solve the vexed question of just how much autonomy, how much dependency the cultural spheres have in total structure (which has the economic base or mode of protection as its dominance), his presentation, and the whole problematic it raises, helps powerfully to bring out the importance of the various cultural practices. He demonstrates clearly that any attempt to reduce the latter to the base or to make them ancillary in any obvious or drastic way is a dire error in both the theoretical and the practical fields.

The effects of a simple one-way relation of base and superstructure, which reduces the latter to a servant or stimulator of the former, as was done under Stalin, has disastrous effects in both the cultural and the political fields. Such views are still accepted in the Soviet Union, and strongly obstruct the evolution of a socialist democracy with a maximum of popular participation in all spheres and at all levels. For the superstructure has become in many ways a synonym for the state-bureaucracy, which in turn is indistinguishable from party-controls at all levels (exercised from above). Cultural activity, though not wholly dominated by any means, is severely limited in its range and effects, in its powers of renewal and extension.

In advanced bourgeois communities Marxist parties with a purely political programme, which leave cultural and moral hegemony unchallenged in the control of the ruling class and its exponents, have no hope of success. The struggle must go on at all levels. The direct economic and political struggle must be conducted in union with a struggle to change ideas, emotions, sensuous responses—indeed every aspect of life—in the new direction. As a result of Gramsci's work, these assertions are indisputable.

But we can now turn and ask if more precision is possible in the attempts to relate the cultural spheres to base and superstructure, to establish to some extent the degrees of autonomy and dependency.

First let us look again at the conventional terms; base and superstructure. Earlier we objected to base as a question-begging word which suggested something solid and impermeable, not a sphere of productive activities and processes. The Mode of Production, in which the forces and relations of productions came together, was proposed as a more suitable term. The one point in which base is superior is that it suits as a descriptive term for elements that include factories, workshops, all sorts of installations. Perhaps it would be best to keep both terms, to be used according to the angle from which one approaches the issues. Base goes better with superstructure; but if one is using these two words together it must be understood that the superstructure is essentially the state and the various institutions that serve it, and that includes the law, army, police, and so on, not to mention schools, colleges, universities and the like. In such a sphere of reference the term also suggests rightly enough something solidly constructed. But the cultural spheres cannot be enclosed in either base or superstructure, for they are too fluid and free-ranging. It is best to define them as forms or structures of productive activity, producing science, literature, art, philosophy, etc. Insofar as they involve organisations such as publishing firms, learned and other societies they have links with both base and superstructure. Education above all, and the mass-media are fields where base, superstructure and culture are closely interwoven.

We have agreed that the base or productive mode is the structure in dominance of the totality of human activities, of the essential human process. But this does not mean that it stands in a fixed relation of domination to each of the manifold activities that make up human life. The relationship will vary first of all according to the kind of activity in question, and indeed to each particular activity of the given sphere. Thus, there is the general question of the relation of science to the base, to the mode of production, a relation that will continually vary according to the moment of history, the stages of science on the one hand and of the base on the other; and it will vary again in each particular instance of scientific theory and practice. We can make a fairly thorough examination of, say, the relation of science to the economic situation in Newton's day, and go on to relate Newton's hypothesis of gravitation to that situation in particular ways. Not that there will be any simple equivalence or one-way traffic here or elsewhere. If the economic situation makes the science possible, the science assists in the consolidation and expansion of the economic system. The workings in a cultural sphere at any given moment include what is going on actually, the tradition behind the practices, and the potentialities opening up and lighting the way forward. If the interactions and mergings functioned automatically, or with anything like precise equivalences, there would be no space for the emergence of the truly new, of positions opposed to the reigning systems. The dynamic inter-relations have the effect of tending to prevent any closed systems, which go on merely repeating themselves.[9]

Here then the Blochian principle of potentiality emerges. We can translate it at a certain level into terms of symmetry and asymmetry. Facilitation, we noted, requires a measure of asymmetry, which can be however, at least temporarily, overcome by the repetition or extension of the structure in dominance. Where the asymmetry grows greater than the facilitating process can control, the emergence of the truly new becomes possible. Therefore the relation of base and superstructure, mode of production and cultural structures, is never a simple stable one. Elements of instability, large or small, continually intrude and make possible developments on both the quantitative and qualitative levels. How far and how strongly those elements appear can only be estimated by concrete analyses of definite occasions.

It may well seem that our formulations are not precise enough; but we are dealing with highly complex processes and much damage can be done by over-simplification. At the same time we must carry on as thoroughly as we can with the task of clarifying the relationships. We need to stress the entanglement, while at the same time showing how the tangle comes about.

It is obvious, given our definition of 'relations of production', that elements of 'consciousness' embracing a wide range of higher-order cognitive and psychological activity—perception, belief, desire, decision-making, emotions, etc.—are all to some extent included in the base, since they are part and parcel of relations of power and control . . . Historical materialism is not intended to be any form of technological determinism. Social relations of production include relations of domination, subordination, and control among humans in the work process and between human and non-human productive forces. (HELLMANN)[10]

The relations of domination and subordination are further highly important for the superstructure centred on the state and including legal relations.

The cultural spheres are affected by both base and superstructure, and have links with them, at times even merging with them, yet they remain distinct and specific spheres in structures of production. In each of them the structure in dominance is complex and fought out (symmetrical-asymmetrical), and it will be affected by the structure in dominance in the mode of production (linked as that is with the dominations in the superstructure). But the two structures will not be in any way identical. At times, in extreme situations, the structure in dominance in a cultural system may resist and fight that in the base or superstructure. As we noted, the fields of education and the mass-media belong largely to the superstructure, yet are linked with the cultural structures, without which they could not exist. Here the cultural structures and the superstructure merge, harmonise, conflict. The last word is with the superstructure (linked in turn with base), but because of the elements of independence in the cultural systems there can be deep and prolonged conflicts and contradictions in the fields of education and the mass-media.

We see, then, that the cultural structures, while dominated in the last resort by the base-superstructure, have considerable areas of freedom in which to develop: areas that vary with history, with the particular phase of social development at a given moment, with all sorts of lesser elements—e.g. the forms of tradition still effective—and with the state of the class-struggle. The latter effects the base through strikes and other forms of resistance; it affects the superstructure insofar as it modifies or changes the forms of class-domination, but it has an even greater likelihood of affecting the cultural spheres. The degree of fluidity, of potentiality, in those spheres marks them off from the areas we have seen as directly linked with the superstructure.

A primary element in the relative autonomy of a cultural product lies in the Form. This is true whether we are considering a poem, a picture, a scientific concept and the experiments connected with it, and so on. The poet, for example, is working in a specific field, all his own, with its material (intellectual activity, emotional responses, sensuous experiences) gathered into the poem in a specific kind of unity. The discipline thus inherent in the Form sets certain limits, but also liberates potentialities which are quite unlike anything operative in the mode of production or the other cultural spheres.

We must emphasise that dominance in the term structure-in-dominance does not simply imply some form of domination. The essential point in dominance here is a facilitation of the process in question. In a sense the structure-in-dominance is directing the process, but not in some external way as if it were issuing orders or imposing a merely restrictive control. It is helping the process to be ever more itself: which involves the absorption of elements from outside without upsetting the internal balance. That is, while all goes well: if the structure in question comes up against difficulties that it cannot solve, the process is arrested or breaks down. The essential point again is to realise that dominance inside a given organisation (the system of dominance-relations in an organism or group of organisms) is not a mechanistic matter made up of controls or limiting pressures. It is a highly complex matter of controls and facilitations, of limits and liberations. When we have got this point clear, we can reconsider the question of relative autonomy afresh. We are mistaken if we phrase it as implying that a particular cultural structure (say, that of a poem) is free in some respects, controlled in others. Rather, what we mean is that its rich complex of direct impulses and struggling potentialities has certain limits in the Form it achieves. These limits are tied up with the over-all dominance exerted by the structurations of the more comprehensive system in which it functions (the cultural sphere of literary expression in general), and by the effects of the structure-in-dominance of the mode of production on the superstructure and all the cultural systems.

Along some such lines we can begin to grasp how the various dominances work together in facilitating process at different levels. It becomes clear that the term 'relative autonomy' impedes rather than helps our exploration of the relation of the cultural spheres to the productive mode. It suggests some sort of external controlling force, a master-system, which dominates the expression in question, while the latter resists and manages somehow to find an area in which it can carry on without reference to the master-system (the economic base). Our inquiry cannot but make us feel that we need a radically new line of approach, new terms. I suggest that we see the cultural spheres as composed of a Freedom (the release of constructive energy) and a Situation (providing the possibilities and also the limits of the release).

The two terms are also applicable to the mode of production, which has its own area of free expansion and development in a situation determined by the past (tradition, inherited lores and methods, etc.), and by the stage reached in the dynamic transformation of nature. The mode must always be understood, not as a self-sufficient system of productive forces and relations, but as a system of processes, based on those forces and relations but set in a particular stage of union-and-conflict with nature.

If we turn back to the spheres of cultural production, to art and science, we see that at any given moment there is a release of energy through the specific Form in question, a release that occurs in a situation which expresses the stage reached by humanity in transforming nature through the productive mode. In art that situation involves on one hand the level of tradition, of craft-skills, of forms of reproduction; on the other hand the whole complex socio-economic development which makes possible the achieved stage. By analysing in its essentials the situation of any particular artist we can assess the limiting and releasing elements there present. We can show what he starts with in his art, what he adds, how he makes his breakthrough or rupture into a new level of integration (simultaneously aesthetic and social). The freedom won by his expression can be estimated by the degree and range of his definition, by the way in which the ceaseless union-and-conflict between his Form and the diverse forces making up his Situation works out. His freedom is not an abstract matter (the capacity to do anything he likes). It is born from the dialectical union-and-conflict of his individuality and the entangled situation out of which that individuality grows, and reveals itself triumphantly in his Form. The question of relative autonomy thus simply does not arise, provided one is looking at the actual situation of creative transformation and is not seeking to arrest it for the imposition of mechanist measurements.

What we have called the Situation may be equated with the Content of a work of art, or rather, it provides the content. By that one does not mean that the whole of it at any given time is crammed into a single work. The situation of the artist includes both the socio-economic world of his period and his personal experiences (through which he refracts and takes in the larger whole), the two elements struggling in a dialectical union-and-conflict. In the creative act the aspects of the situation which are most strongly affecting him (and which thus constitute a structure-in-dominance for him) provide him with his material and with the need to reorganise it in aesthetic terms. In the process of achieving Form he resolves the inner conflicts and contradictions that gave a dynamic and significant force to the

147

material. The Form restores his harmony with the life-process; it restores his spiritual balance in a disturbed and challenging situation.

In science the procedure is essentially the same, with different elements of the situation assuming the role of structure-in-dominance. Again we meet among the elements the levels of tradition, inherited lores, present activity, the link with the transformations of nature going on in the economic productive sphere—this time through technology and applied science. Out of the particular problems comes the resolving Form, the theoretical structure with its new orientations.

It will be clear how different is the picture that emerges from the type of analysis and correlation we have been attempting, from that which was inherent in the old concepts of base and superstructure, with areas of activity owning a relative autonomy. A perfect example of how not to tackle the problem was the method advocated by Luperini (cited above in chapter 2), in which the cognitive dissection of an artwork was seen as decomposing 'its various components and placing it face to face with the real (socio-economic) base from which it is born.' As if the artwork itself was not real or as if its reality resided in some sort of remote-control structure on which the living material of the art-process had been superimposed. But transformation is the key-aspect of all productive activities. The economic system transforms nature, using methods and systems that are themselves miming some kind of natural activity or process. Art in its various forms carries over the transformative power in its re-creations of nature and society. Science seeks to grasp the secrets of movement in nature so as to penetrate the inner laws or systems of process and reproduce them on a new level. Productive activity in all its forms reproduces, transforms, re-creates systems of movement, change, organic patterns: not mechanically in flat reflections, but in new extensions or concentrations that reveal the hidden potentialities of the systems, their possible development into higher forms of themselves. Art, for instance, transforms its material in terms of the potentialities of that material, which merge with the liberated potentialities in the artist himself. Here we are moving into the terrain explored by Bloch, but at the same time we are giving his concept of Hope a concrete basis which he himself could not postulate. By grasping the potentiality in a situation the artist deepens sensibility, sensuousness and emotion, and though he may not at all speak directly of social change, he keeps implying, defining even, a higher stage of human development in which people are more authentically themselves, and society is somehow capable of greater harmony with human needs and aspirations. A brief work that tackles these issues is Marcuse's *The Aesthetic Dimension*, first published 1977. He argues strongly against all reductive analyses and stresses the liberating function of Form.

In contrast to orthodox Marxist aesthetics I see the political potential of art in art itself, in the aesthetic form as such. Furthermore, I argue that by virtue of its aesthetic form, art is largely autonomous vis à vis the given social relations. In its autonomy art both protests these relations and at the same time transcends them. Thereby art subverts the dominant consciousness, the ordinary experience . . .

A work of art can be called revolutionary if, by virtue of the aesthetic transformation, it represents, in the exemplary fate of individuals, the prevailing unfreedom and the rebelling forces, thus breaking through the mystified (and petrified) social reality, and opening the horizon of change (liberation).

Again he states:

The radical qualities of art, that is to say, its indictment of the established reality and its invocation of the beautiful image (*schöner Schein*) of liberation are grounded precisely in the dimensions where art transcends its social determination and emancipates itself from the given universe of discourse and behaviour while preserving its overwhelming presence. Thereby art creates the realm in which the subversion of experience proper to art becomes possible: the world formed by art is recognised as a reality which is suppressed and distorted in the given reality. This experience culminates in extreme situations (of love and death, guilt and failure, but also joy, happiness, and fulfilment) which explode the given reality in the name of a truth normally denied or even unheard. The inner logic of the work of art terminates in the emergence of another reason, another sensibility, which defy the rationality and sensibility incorporated in the dominant social institutions.[11]

But he simply keeps on asserting that art is autonomous, without making any effort to relate the freedom to what I have called the situation. There is thus an idealist note in the argument, and in the end he is driven back to a kind of élitism and pessimistic doubt that an audience for art worthy of the word can be found in our unfree or reified society. Nevertheless the stress on Form and the attack on reductionism are valuable.

We are near the end of our inquiry: before we finish it would be well to go further into the question of alienation. We may note the three main meanings that have historically grown up round the term. Alienation, say the dictionaries, is (1) the action of estranging or the state of estrangement; (2) the act of transferring ownership of property to someone else; (3) the loss or derangement of one's mental faculties. It can thus equally mean the loss of property, of things, and the loss of mental faculties, one's inner self. The alienated person is cut off from both his essential self and from the outer world in which he should have his share, his fulfilling activity and place.

Hegel made the crucial step of seeing that human beings are alienated because their labour is alienated. Their needs are always a step or more ahead of available economic resources; and they lay hold of the world and make it theirs in thought or act by a process of objectification, which imprisons them in the objects they produce. Marx replied that the tension between needs and productive activity is the result of an historical situation which can be overcome, transcended, and that people are not limited and oppressed by their objectifying powers, but by the social situation of division and exploitation that cuts them off from their productions. Objectification itself lies at the heart of human creativity. The gap between human needs and resources on the one hand, and the exploiting or dividing system on the other, are historical products that can be overcome. Socialism as the transition to communism begins the overcoming of both the sources and causes of alienation.

The two aspects of alienation however still dominate our world, as they have dominated societies in the past, though the way they have operated has been determined at each historical phase by the existent conditions and by the extent to which people have successfully transformed nature to meet their needs. Thus the particular form and range of alienation at any given moment has been determined by a number of factors, indeed by the total activity of the society in question: a totality that includes the science, art, thought, and the organisational forms developed at all levels between economic base and State.

Here we can only glance at the ways in which alienation arises and operates in primitive societies and carries on as systems grow more complex, arriving finally at the class-state, which itself goes through a number of profound changes. This important subject has been totally neglected by Marxists. It will help here, then, to consider briefly how alienation works among the Australian tribes, who are still at the hunting and food-gathering stage. There is nothing like class-division, though there may be varying levels of status through which all individuals pass, and there is already a deep division between the sexes. We find that clear systems of thought and practice express the way in which the members of a group feel their separation-out from nature, their insecure place in a dangerous world. Take the churinga of the Arunta tribe. When a spirit enters a woman , so that she conceives, the churinga is dropped. At the child's birth she tells her husband the site of the Nanja tree or stone where she believes that the event occurred. He and one or two of the elders go there and find the churinga (perhaps provided by paternal grandfather or made from a bit of wood close to the Nanja tree and carved with a device relating to the Totem). The Nanja tree or rock is organically related to the child, and the churinga is his churinga nanja. When the Alcheringa or Dreamtime Ancestors went into the earth, the churinga stayed behind and with it the spirit-part. From the Nanja tree also issued a spirit, the Arumburinga of the Alcheringa individual; and at each totem-centre is a group, the Iruntarinia, linked with the churinga or the Arumburinga. The Iruntarinia are thought to be organised in local totemic groups just like the members of the tribes. The churinga is put in a cave Ernatulinga, with the other churingas in bundles. 'Spirit-land is the land of doubles, and it is the doubles of the natives that are projected into space and materialised in the Churinga.'[1][2]

Many more details might be added to show how the individual is thought to have an external-soul or otherself, and how this otherself is both located in an object and in the spirit-world. A complex system of ideas and rites express both the separation-out of the individual and his reintegration with the life of the group and of nature. With the advent of agriculture and settled modes of existence new strains emerge, new forms of the external-soul: Private property and forms of exchange-value (as distinct from the gift-exchanges which had helped to bind the group together), embryonic forms of money (sacred at first), systems of taboos sanctifying ownership, medicine-bags, talismans, fetishes. Concepts of privately-cornered spirit-power at all points accompany the growth of division and personal property in the group. Finally, helped by the advent of the war-chief, class-society is born. The inner division in the individual is defined as a division of body and soul; religion proper appears with its priesthoods. The ancestral world ceases to mediate between the group and nature. It becomes a separate spirit-world, with heaven and hell, places of bliss or torment. The religious sanctions are bound up with the sanctions of power and property inside the society. (At the same time social conflicts can intrude into the spirit-world. The climax of such developments occurred in Christianity, when, stirred by the civil wars under Caesar and Augustus, the oppressed or dispossessed broke in with their claims to salvation, to freedom. As the church developed, elements of dissent and conformity merged and struggled in highly entangled ways.)

In such a very compressed account the complicated shifting and endlessly involved fusion of inner and outer factors is drastically oversimplified and reduced to a few over-riding patterns. But along these lines, with full attention paid to the large number of transitional forms in all their unstable and changing diversity, their extensions and breakdowns, their reassertions and combinations, we can show how there is a dialectical continuity of development that leads from the churinga of the Arunta to the commodity production of capitalist

151

society, with varying but persistent forms of alienation. Not that we must infer any simple dominance of the alienating factors. We saw how the Arunta devised systems of thought and practice to balance or offset the sense of inner division. All through the many stages, right up to the capitalism of today, there are liberating factors based in concrete labour, in creative productive activity. These bind people together humanly and stimulate the struggle towards a fuller humanity, which is in effect a struggle against alienation. Otherwise the human race would have been tied down at the outset to a paralysing sense of division between the existent social self and the otherself, a dead thing.

We need to realise how long the problem of alienation has been with us to appreciate that its overcoming cannot be a simple matter. It is of much interest that Marx realised that alienation had a long prehistory, even though the anthropological material for anything like a full analysis was not yet available. Early in *Capital* (I,4) he sets out the Mystery of the Fetishistic Character of Commodities showing how fundamental was the connection in his mind:

To find an analogy [for capitalist process], we must enter the nebulous world of religion. In that world the products of the human mind become independent shapes, endowed with lives of their own, and able to enter into relations with men and women. The products of the human hand do the same thing in the world of commodities. I speak of this as the fetishistic character which attaches to the products of labour, so soon as they are produced in the form of commodities. It is inseparable from commodity production.

The first volume of *Capital* was published in 1867; in 1871 Tylor in his *Primitive Culture* wrote as follows about Fetishism:

Centuries ago, the Portuguese in West Africa, noticing the veneration paid by the negroes to certain objects, such as trees, fish, plants, idols, pebbles, claws or beasts, sticks, and so forth, very fairly compared these objects to the amulets and talismans with which they were themselves familiar and called them *feitico* or charm, a word derived from the Latin *factitius*, in the sense of magically artful . . . The President de Brosses . . . introduced the word *Fetichisme* as a general descriptive term (1760), and since then it has obtained great currency by Comte's use of it to denote a general theory of primitive religion, in which external objects are regarded as animated by a life analogous to man's.

Tylor himself preferred the term Animism 'for the doctrine of spirits in general', confining 'the word Fetichism to that subordinate department which it properly belongs to, namely, the doctrine of spirits embodied in or attached to, or conveying influence through, certain material objects.'

Marx would certainly have known Comte's use of the term. His concept of alienation has four main aspects. A human being is alienated from nature; from himself or herself (from his or her activity); from his or her species-being (his or her existence as a member of the human species); from other men and women. All the aspects are linked with alienated labour. The first aspect expresses the relation of worker to the product of his or her labour (which is also his or her relation to the sensuous external world, the objects and processes of nature). The second expresses labour's relation to the productive act within the labour-process: that is, the worker's activity is alien activity that offers satisfaction, not in or by itself, but only through the act of being sold to someone else. (The satisfaction lies, not in the activity itself but in an abstract property of it: its saleability under certain conditions. The first aspect reveals 'estrangement of the thing', the second, 'self-estrangement'.) The third aspect derives from the fact that the object of labour is the objectification of human species-life; for a man 'duplicates himself, not only, as in consciousness, intellectually, but also actively, in reality, and therefore he contemplates himself in the world he has created'. But alienated labour turns his species-being, 'both nature and his spiritual species property, into a being alien to him, into a means to his individual existence. It estranges man's own body from him as it does external nature and his spiritual existence, his human being.'

Both the third and fourth aspects are implied by the first two. But in the fourth Marx considers the effects on the relation of each human being to his or her fellows:

If a man is confronted by himself, he is confronted by the other man. What applies to man's relation to his work, to the product of his labour and to himself, also holds of man's relation to the other man, and to the other man's labour and object of labour. In fact, the proposition that man's species nature is estranged from him means that one man is estranged from the other, as each of them is from man's essential nature.

Alienation is thus seen as 'man's estrangement from nature and from himself', and also the expression of this process in the relation of the individual to the species, of man or woman to other man or men or women.[13]

The core of alienation in capitalist society lies in commodity-production, commodity-fetishism. We have seen this concept developed in the work of Lukacs and the Frankfurt School, and need not go further into it here. The mass of the people have been denied access to the means of production and subsistence. They have been deprived of the land, driven off it. The products of labour become the property of the employer; and the person selling his or her labour cannot find in work a means of self-expression. Work becomes merely a means for gaining money with which consumer-goods can be bought. The consumer-society of post-1945 years, linked in turn with a worsening internal crisis of the system expressed in monetary terms by inflation, is the logical conclusion of commodity-production. The increasing contradictions can only be overcome by socialism.

Socialism may be defined as the transitional period between capitalism and communism, under which alienation is steadily undermined and finally eliminated. The ending of the private ownership of production and distribution does not by itself overcome alienation, though it is a first necessary step in that direction. It is not true that

> the domination of an alien power over men is done away with when private property is abolished by the proletarian revolution and the building of communist society, since here men find themselves freely facing their own products (JAHN)

unless we mean a lot more things by the term 'the building of communist society'. Nor is the problem much advanced if we define alienation as

> estrangement of workers against capitalist employers because, although selling their own labour, they have no control over the use and over the goods and services they produce. Alienation may also appear under Socialism in the case of highly centralised economic planning and administration and a weak or arbitrary system of material incentives. It leads to the indifference and even hostility of workers to enterprises and of the local management and administration to higher authorities. (WILCZYNSKI)[14]

Certainly bureaucratic centralism is a key-factor in maintaining alienation under socialism; and unless it is broken down there can be little substantial advance. But there are many other alienating factors at work, many other goals that need to be striven for. Under the limited socialism we are considering there is still no advance being made towards the stage when the division of labour is ended, especially that between manual and intellectual work. Labour-power is still exchanged for a limited and externally-controlled wage, and the worker has no choice but to accept the system. Further, his needs as consumer will be imperfectly met. There is still little question of the freedom of each worker to develop in an all-round way. The goal of socialism is communism, and each stage it moves into must be judged by the extent to which it begins to realise that goal. Communism implies the ending of the State and of all coercive mechanisms, the ending of money and the division of labour, the full creativity of labour and an harmonious union with nature, from which all the old fears and balances are banished. It implies the ending of the gap between productivity and human needs (in the process needs are themselves changed; they express the requirements of human creativity, not the endless quantitative expansion characteristic of the consumer-society which is the bourgeois culmination.)[15]

Therefore, for socialism to function truly and stably as an active process realising its full potentialities, the public ownership of the means of production and distribution must be made the basis of a system steadily developing in the direction of communism. The moment it halts or evades such a development it cannot but grow malformed, intensifying alienation. Obviously communism cannot be reached at a stride, but it must always be kept in mind or as a goal, a criterion for judging each step taken. There must be a ceaseless effort to break down all forms of bureaucracy and centralisation as far as is possible at a given stage, and to devolve all organisational systems on to free groups emerging to meet the particular problems of that stage. The breaking-down of the divisions built up between the sexes is also a primary need. The solutions in all matters can be found only by people working together, aware of the claims and needs of the individuals composing the group, and striving always towards the ideal of a world without compulsions. There must be the fullest possible extension of democracy in all spheres, self-management of the economy by the workers, and so on. Collective ownership of the means of production and socialist planning overcome in principle social helplessness in relation to the movement of society as a whole, but do not obliterate that helplessness for all the individuals involved. Not only are there the manifold carry-overs from the past, persisting inequalities in education and opportunity, and so forth; there is the fact that the helplessness can be transcended in practice only when individuals realise their unity with society through activities implicating a large number of free decisions.

As the production of material goods grows ever more adequate, the essential aim of the productive system becomes the creation of fully developed individuals. This development is linked with the extension of automation, and the devising of such new forms of automation as cybernetics and micro-chips. 'The domination of "dead labour" over "living labour" disappears and freedom is "restored" in material production.' Such formulations are not in any way utopian since the first technological stages necessary for such a development are already with us. What is lacking is the right kind of aims, the right kind of organisation.

Further, there is the point that the kind of socialist society which emerges out of capitalism, transcending it, will in many ways, at least in its initial stages, be strongly influenced by the forms of struggle that have brought it about. The more that the leap on to a new social level

155

has been accompanied or achieved by an extension of democratic rights and practices, the more stable will be the result, the greater the potentialities for a rapid advance to communism. On the other hand if the new society comes about, according to the narrow ideas which have ruled Marxists for so long, by a capture of power, a sudden and rapid overthrow of the bourgeois state, the more likely is there to be a rigid power-structure imposed from above. In such a situation the problem of extending freedoms and engaging people more and more thoroughly, at all levels, in the working-out of the new political, social, and economic forms, will be more difficult and delayed.

We must discard the idea of a rather strict equivalence between a given economic system and its state-form, which we find at times in Lenin's thought. As we noted earlier, 1917 saw the taking over of state-power by the Bolsheviks in something of a political vacuum. The semi-feudal tsarist state had been broken down by Germans, while the bourgeoisie was not mature enough to step into the gap and develop forms relevant to their needs. So the socialist revolutionaries had in many ways to start from scratch, in the extremely difficult situation of civil war, economic breakdown, and attack from outside. The socialist state was thus built up in years when invasion by the capitalist enemies was always possible, and there was an inevitable drive to strengthen that state so as to cope with the inner and outer situation, with all the consequences of centralised bureacracy and harsh party-control from above, which soon resulted in Stalinism.

We can see how little was Lenin prepared to meet the situation of 1918-19 if we look at *State and Revolution*, written on the eve of the revolution. He sees no political, social, or economic problems as liable to result from the seizure of power:

Accounting and control—these are the principal things that are necessary for the 'setting up' and correct functioning of the first phase of communist society. All citizens are transformed into the salaried employees of the state, which consist of the armed workers. All citizens become employees and workers of a single national state 'syndicate.' All that is required is that they should work equally—do their proper share of work—and get paid equally. The accounting and control necessary for this have been so utterly simplified by capitalism that they have become the extraordinarily simple operation of checking, recording and, issuing receipts, which anyone who can read and write and who knows the first four rules of arithmetic can perform.

When most of the functions of the state are reduced to this accounting and control by the workers themselves, it ceases to be a 'political state'.[16]

The position in a new socialist society would clearly be very different if the breakthrough had been accomplished on Gramscian principles, with a maximum of possible changes along democratic lines in the cultural, social, political and economic spheres, giving more power at all levels to the workers, the common folk. Then the further extension of democratic activities, or self-government in full socialist terms would appear the natural thing and would be much more easy to achieve. The limitation and final elimination of bureaucracy would be a central principle from the outset.

We may, then, glance at Gramsci's concept of a transitional phase, what it involves on the part of the resistant bourgeoisie and of the advancing proletariat. He reconsiders the two points made by Marx: that no social formation disappears while the productive forces developed within it have space for further expansion, and that a society does not set itself tasks for the solution of which the necessary conditions have not been incubated. He insists that these principles 'must first be developed *critically* in all their implications, and purged of every residue of mechanicism and fatalism.' The bourgeois resistance he calls a passive revolution. It works through a 'conservatism or moderate reformism', which tends to undermine the free political dialectic of class contradiction and to weaken the popular drive for change by its concession of reform in small packets. So the problems of change and of hegemony are diverted from the real issues of democratic advance, and treated in ways that help to strengthen the state as dominating with its administrative and coercive apparatus. (An example is the way in which the U.S.A. has managed to develop a conforming society of the kind which we saw the Frankfurt School defining as hopelessly reified. A sharper example is the way in which fascist systems have been favoured and taken over to save the bourgeois state.)[17]

To defeat the passive revolution we need the building-up of the historical bloc through the movement to a socialist consciousness, a socialist kind of activity (as far as is possible in a class-society), through ever-widening struggle. Such a struggle involves the rejection of the simple view of the state as a mere instrument of domination, an instrument of class-oppression. The development of a new system of hegemony involves a steady transformation of the state as of every component of the class-society where the struggle goes on. We thus discard the economistic view of the state as a mere monolithic repressive organisation devoid of socio-political contradictions. The 'enlargement of the state' brought about by the strengthening and consolidation of the historical bloc has its roots in the form of a democracy of the base. It is linked with the democratic creativity of the masses and the extension of their hegemony by ceaseless struggle and transformation of the social situation. The stress on the state here is the opposite of the Stalinist position, for it sees the state as providing the basis for a ceaseless 'socialisation' of politics, a continuous reconsideration and revaluation of the role of social factors and the hegemonic struggle during the phase of transition, with the withering-away of the state as the final criterion and aim. Precisely in order to ensure that they will not be replaced by the centrally bureaucratic state, the revolutionary class and its allies must gain hegemonic unity in cultural, ideological and political fields before the decisive transfer of political power.

Gramsci is thus one of the few Marxists who kept in mind that any given moment of process is dialectically both one of unity and contradiction or conflict. In the continual moments of imbalance or asymmetry in the process the struggle is both to increase conflict and to take over as much of the unifying elements (revalued and transformed) as is possible. The historical bloc, in its achievement, involves a grasp of the living unity of society, of the productive base and the superstructure, of the diverse elements of culture and ideology, of objective and subjective conditions. That is to say, it involves a grasp of the endlessly complex ways in which hegemony expresses itself and the ways in which the revolutionary class can draw more and more elements over to itself. It tests out the principles of transition set out by Marx, using them as a guide to action, a clarification of the situation through its transformation. The result is a self-regulation and expansion of civil society at the expense of political society, with the ultimate aim of the withering away of the state. (Exactly the opposite process occurs in the building of the totalitarian state.)

This means that the dialectic of state-civil society, far from being a neo-crocean-hegelian regression in comparison to the Marxist analysis of the mode of production, as Althusser has thought, is really the opposite. This is because, in the first place, this dialectic underpins Marx's political thought, his critique of the superstitious view of the state as something separate and centralised, engulfing all social forces in a monstrous bureaucratic and parasitical mechanism; but above all it is because this dialectic permits an anti-economistic approach to the economy itself, a re-evaluation of the role of the social in its relations with the political and an analysis of political forms from which to conduct a 'left' critique of Stalinism in terms of 'passive revolution.' (BUCI-GLUCKSMANN)[18]

These summaries of the Gramscian position are compressed and could be much more extended. But they sufficiently bring out the way in which the analysis of the passive revolution and the historical bloc grasps concretely the nature of struggle in our world. The stress is on the way in which the socialist struggle for hegemony already begins to transform the state before the winning of socialism, and ensures that the movement of the new society will be along democratic antibureaucratic lines in the direction of communism. In the struggle to bring about and develop the historical bloc the first crucial steps towards the ending of alienation are made, and the road opened to its full defeat.[19]

We have now completed what we set out to do: to look at the difficulties and problems that have beset Marxism since 1917, and in particular since 1923 when Lukacs published *History and Class-Consciousness*. Behind the problems lay the fact that history seemed in no haste to repeat 1917—on the contrary. It became ever clearer that what was needed was not a mere reassessment of political strategies, but a comprehensive revaluation of what capitalist crisis meant: an analysis that could not be carried out without going into the whole question as to what forms and transforms people. Hence the question of the nature and role of culture grew ever more important.

We have looked at several typical thinkers—Lukacs, Bloch, Adorno, Horkheimer, Marcuse, Althusser, della Volpe, Colletti, Gramsci—and have attempted to clarify what was effective, what was confused and limited, in their thinking. Finally we have tried to assess what we have learned; how far we are better equipped to deal with the question of culture, its nature and role; and what is involved in overcoming the world-crisis of bourgeois society. Out of our explorations several new points have emerged, or points made elsewhere have been given a new emphasis and fullness of relationship. These may be briefly summarised as follows:

(1) Stress has been laid on the fact that all productive activity, whether economic or cultural, involves a transformation of nature as well as of society, of people. Only by keeping this point in mind can we consistently avoid the various reductions that arise out of a limited application of Marxism. The nature in question is both outer and inner, the world of objective nature and the biological world of the individual being: both have been continually transformed throughout history, but both survive as essential factors in human development. While we keep the relation to nature in mind, we cannot succumb, say, to economic reductionism; we are driven to attempt to grasp the dialectical fullness of human existence.

(2) We decided that the conventional use of the terms Base and Superstructure led to a narrow form of analysis, to mechanised and oversimplified notions of what constituted society despite the complex interaction and fusion of activities at a large number of levels. We thought however it was useful to keep the terms for a limited and definite use: Base for forces and relations of production in a directly economic perspective, and Superstructure for the State and its allied

159

institutions, especially that of the Law. Though the terms could thus be used for certain abstracted elements of society, we must keep on recognising the way in which Base and Superstructure affected one another, affected other spheres of activity (such as art and science), and were in turn themselves affected.

(3) Instead of seeing the various forms of cultural activity as merged with the Superstructure and as direct ideological expressions of the ruling class (the State), we decided that they should be defined as Productive Activities linked with both Base and Superstructure, but with their own kind of life and development.

(4) In this connection the term Mode of Production seemed better to express the complex of economic forces and relations in the productive sphere than did the term Base.

(5) We needed to clarify the relation of cultural activities to the sphere of economic production and to the superstructure (the State). Each sphere of activity or practice was seen as a system of structures with a varying structure-in-dominance—the Mode of Production appearing as the structure-in-dominance of society, of the whole human system.

(6) The term Relative Autonomy (to express the relation of the various cultural spheres of the superstructure itself to the base or mode of production) was discarded as derived from a mechanist type of analysis. Instead of using it, we decided to treat each kind of productive activity as possessing its own inner Freedom, which was linked with Rhythm as its mode of expression or liberation and with the Form in which its activity culminated. The limiting factor lay in the Situation in which the activity went on, a situation that included the mode of production and the superstructure as well as the elements of the system in question. The Form expressed the successful resolution or overcoming of the conflict or contradiction which initiated the activity. The Content, with its conflicting elements, came from the Situation; it was the aspect of the Situation that was the structure-in-dominance there at the given time.

(7) Finally there was the question of Dialectical Materialism. Though Marx drew on a tradition reaching from Heraclitus to Hegel, his great contribution lay in bringing dialectics down to earth in a truly materialist system, and in thus providing a powerful example of the way in which the question of development in human society could be tackled and understood. But that did not mean that Dialectical Materialism was thenceforth tied down to the terms he used, and so on. This issue comes up particularly in the next point.

(8) One of the most vexed questions in Marxism has been that of the Dialectic of Nature. We examined the way in which a negative answer

160

has been given through an inadequate grasp of the nature of dialectics and of the relation of science to history, to social development. We found that the broadest set of terms as yet available for a dialectical system embracing both nature and society was one concerned with questions of stability/instability, symmetry/asymmetry. We glanced at the way in which the course of science is conditioned by the socio-economic situation, and the link of nuclear fission with the analytic method developed after Galileo, and the way in which physics since Planck and Einstein is providing the basis for a fully organic use of dialectics in scientific method—a development of thought which is bound up with the problem of overcoming the world crisis of capitalism today.

NOTES

Chapter 1: The Crisis in Marxism
1. Gramsci took term hegemony from Lenin who used it to express the leadership assumed by the proletariat in a revolutionary situation. In general: Perry Anderson (2), also *Dialectics* no. 24/5
2. See fuller account in Perry Anderson (1), Kalakowski etc.

Chapter 2: Man and Nature
1. Timpanaro (1) 17.
2. E. Thompson (1) 270-2, 332, 267; Marcuse (10) 151-3; Althusser (2) 22, 27 and (3) 133.
The idea of the negation of the negation disappeared as the State was assumed to solve non-antagonistic contradictions: Philipov, 37.
Objective laws: Iovchuk (cited) 40 (1) 4.
3. E. Thompson, 307. Marx remarks (*Capital*, 1972, 791) that the mode of production reveals the secret of any social formation.
4. R. Williams (6)
5. Soper, 78: see the rest of her essay, esp. 97, 93. See also Sève and Althusser (2) 242-8, Soper 98f; Collier 42-4.
6. Chomsky: language not necessarily innate, see Collier 44. Voghera: Timpanaro, 20f.
7. A. Schmidt 80f. The term 'laboratory' occurs in Paracelsus. In general: Venable and Gould.
8. See Schmidt, ch. 4.
9. Hoffmann, 17-9; Coulter (1) 134; Petrovic, 23.
10. Lefebvre, 38.
11. Harris, 38-40, 206. See also Flannery, Ucko, Gross, Harner.

Chapter 3: Georg Lukacs
1. Laing, 47; MacDonough, 40-3; Löwy, 156-8.
2. 'The strength of every society is in the last resort a spiritual strength,' *H. & C. C.* 262.
3. Althusser (3). McLellan, 87, is taken in by Althusser.
Engels in *Anti-D.* seems to argue that movement in the real order dictates change in the logical order; that is to make the latter a mere reflection of the former.
4. Rose, 30 n.30.
5. Rose, 31.
6. Rose, 32-5; Lukacs (2) 156f for the only passage where Simmel uses reification.
7. Novack, 122; *H. & C. C.* 129-33
8. Lewin, 113. Totality: cf Lenin (*Coll. Works*, XVI 348-9) on dialectics: a full "definition" of an object must include the whole of human experience, both as a criterion of truth and as a practical indicator of its connection with human wants.
9. Jameson (1) 172; Lukacs, *New Hung. Q.*, 47, 1972; Laing, 55, 57.
Brecht: NLR 80, 1974, 48-50; Benjamin, *ib.*, 1973, 118. Kolakowski 301-5, 279.
10. Raulet.

11. Jameson, 191-5. The typical fuses universal and particular: Kolakowski, 291f.
12. In general, Meszaros, Jameson, Stedman Jones, Lichtheim, Revai, Gallas, J. L. (5).

Chapter 4: Ernst Bloch
1. Habermas (1) 634. In general, Jameson (1) 116-59, Kellner, Negt, Jones, Kolakowski, Howard, Paetgold.
2. Jameson (1) 120f.
3. Bloch (2) 231.
4. J. L. (5) essay on Joyce.
5. Kellner, 31-3
6. Jameson (1) 147.
7. The existentialist present is for Bloch a real emptiness, a void without the redeeming and transforming wish, hope, aspiration. See Lichtheim in attack on Bloch's ideas as merely wishful-thinking aimed at making it easier to live.
8. Jameson (1) 141f; Bloch (5) ii 46f. Art, religion: Bloch (5) 49-208, Jameson, 142. Images: Bloch (5) 151, Jameson 147f; Bloch (2) 908, 980.
9. Jameson, 129 on Goethe and concept of the Demonic.
10. Negt, 24f; Bloch(5) 106.
11. Lenin, 372f (written 1914-6).
12. Bloch (1), 'K. Marx, Death and Apocalypse'.
13. Kellner 23f, nn. 46f.
14. He tries to assess the revolutionary potential of dissatisfaction in essay, '*Marx als Denker der Revolution*' in (4).
15. Negt, 13; Fetscher.
16. Bloch (2a) ii 269.
17. Bloch(1) 59, (2a) 8. Kellner, 21-4.
18. Jameson, 118ff. Have not gone into his concept of hermeneutics by means of which the full and hidden truth-content is revealed in expressions of the past, the 'unredeemed aspects'. Also his struggle with the fact of Death (overcome in collective emotion, devotion to a revolutionary cause, but still remaining as a defeat): Jameson 135-40.
19. Fetscher, 117ff; Lowy (3) 43; Negt, 49; Bloch (19) and (20).
20. Kolakowski, 442-5.

Chapter 5: Adorno and the Frankfurt School
1. Adorno (11) 159. Rose 55 n21, also 23 n125 and n114, 22 n15; Adorno(11) 23. In general, Rose 18-26; Pütz, 175-91; Jay (1): Habermas (4); A. Schmidt in Horkheimer (2) 115-32. Adorno (10) 119, the only place where he concentrates on Reason and Domination of Nature.
2. Therborn, 52-4. Cf. Weber's thesis of increasing rationality in the organisation of capitalism.
3. Adorno(19) 6ND, 151, 33, 34, (11) 23 and (10) 4, 9; Rose, 123f. Hegel: Adorno (11) 158; Ruben, 39. Fisk, 142. Hegel, *Logic*, 194, 219.
Critical Theory sees itself as humanity's self-knowledge, so cannot and must not have a structure (formally) logical and systematic; that would mean that human beings systematised themselves: Therborn, 98, Formal logic the expression of 'indifference to the individual', Adorno (10) 202.

4. Adorno uses Hegelian terminology only on basis of Nietzschean inversion, Rose, 21f, n112. Adorno stresses the 'antinomial character of systems'. (11) 26-8. Concept: *ib.* 13; Rose, 24. Adorno (11)5; Rose 15f.
5. Adorno (17) 282, (18) 211, Horkheimer (5) ii 195 (the following quotation). *Prisms*, 27. Adorno says, 'Irony says: such it (Ideology) claims to be, but such it (reality) is'. Irony thus works at doing the 'immanent' procedure that takes the 'objective idea' of a product (philosophical, literary, etc.) and 'confronts it with the norms which it itself has crystallised.' He defines the immanent procedure in the same terms as irony, 'the difference between ideology and reality.' It 'takes seriously the principle that it is not ideology in itself, which is untrue, but rather its pretensions to correspond to reality.' His method is the same whether looked at from the subjective or objective viewpoint.
6. Jameson, 56; Rose, 13-5.
7. J. L. (5) 389-92.
8. Adorno (18); Jameson, 57.
9. Adorno (10) 6f; (19) 8 Posstreit 317f; (17) 107 and (18) 86. Quotations: Adorno (11) 406, 31, 5 and 141. Kolakowski, 364.

   At times Critical Theory is taken as the same as philosophy; at times, not—and philosophy is seen as non-dialectical. Critical Theory is not a theory in the sense of a set of interrelated propositions aimed at exploring observed (observable) facts; it is a method.
10. Kolakowski, 367.
11. Adorno (19) 8 Postreit, 347, 302. Also (19) 14.
12. Adorno (11) 149. Marx: Rose, 46f. Reification is a social category; it refers to the way consciousness is determined. It is not a concept (like society, subject, freedom); to see and understand it is to gain a change in one's whole perspective of reality. It determines consciousness, but like commodity-production is not in origin a fact of consciousness. Some concepts (e.g. theoretical like value, or non-theoretical like money) have no non-reified application. Rose, 47.
13. Utopia: Rose, 48, 24, 61. A concept would be concrete if it really covered its object (rational identity): this is its utopian sense. Refs., Rose, 48.
14. Adorno (19) 8 Sol, 369; 14 Diss FUR 25, and 6 ND, 314. Adorno deals with ideological domination without refs. to class-consciousness, alienation etc. Exchange as fundamental reality: Horkheimer (5) ii 173. Adorno (10) 104. Productive forces are not part of a structural contradiction, but represent a stage of human evolution that now enable the Negating Subject to wipe out poverty and misery from the human condition: Therborn, 117. In this sense they are neutral, a raw material of potentiality. Later this potentiality is denied. But in neither case are the forces seen in their Marxist structural context. The Negating Subject remains a philosphical concept, not a social one.
15. Again, the natural sciences and their empiricist counterpart in epistemology are more disastrous than the market: Therborn, 103.
   Form: Jameson, 55. Quotations: Adorno (3) 16; Rose 118f. Detective story: *Prisms*, 32, 129f, 41.
16. Rose, 119f.
17. Adorno (17) 119; (18) 95.

18. Rose, 120; Jameson, 38-40.
19. Laing, 63f; Adorno (7) 43 and (13). Compare ideas of surrealism. There are links of his irony etc. with Dadist attempts to shock and wake people up. Also Benjamin: 'shock as the key-notion'. Laing, 5; Jimenez, 168.
    Note the changing terms for Fascism: 'the truth of Liberalism,' 'abstract internal community,' Authoritarian Personality, 'the truth of modern society.' Enlightenment becomes mass-deception and Fascism is the self-destruction of the Enlightenment. Therborn, 99-103; Marcuse (8) i 63, 93; Horkheimer (6) 116). Not a word of Fascism as a specific form of monopoly-capitalism.
20. Jimenez, 254, 453.
21. Laing, 65f; Adorno (14).
22. Jimenez, 255; Swingewood (1) 14f.
23. Marcuse (4) 16f. Fromm (*Crisis of Psychoanalysis*, 1973, 30-3) sees M., like many avantgarde writers and artists, 'attracted by infantile regression, perversion, and—as I see it—in a more hidden way by destruction and hate'.
24. Laing, 17; Marcuse, *Essay on Liberation.* He rejects the term elitist, puts stress on Women's Liberation: Magee, 71f. Habermas: Therborn, 120ff; Rose, 141f, 146.

Chapter 6: Structuralist Marxism: Althusser

1. In general, M. Glucksmann, A. Glucksmann, Geras, Anzias, Callinicos, Sumner, Jameson, D. Sayer, E. Thompson, Piccone, Karsz, Hall (2) 6, McLellan. In order to gain a broad basis to my critique of Althusser, I have cited passages in the text from writers with whose positions I agree. Saussure; Jameson (2) 5, and 3-43; Scholes, chap. 2.
2. Jameson, 32, contrasting sign with symbol (as in Ogden and Richards).
3. Jameson, 109f, 35. Binary: *Ib*. 35, 109; Summer, 103, Sperber, 23f, 46-50, 48 (Chomsky's critique), footnote, 40.
4. Barthes (1) 41; Sumner, 132. Barthes (2) 111; Sumner 135. Marx: Sumner, 135.
5. Also Sumner, 103, 106, 143f (cited). Burgelin, 154. Hall (L) 25.
   For Barthes an artwork is 'not like the effect of a cause, but like the *signifier* of a *signifiant* ,' (3) 158. It is not a product.
6. Summer, 106f and 114; Burgelin, 154. Sumner, 147 (cited).
7. Summer, 147f, 153. Culler (1) 243, 251 (Kristeva). Burniston 212, 218.
8. Culler; Burgelin.
9. Sturrock, 14f
10. Sumner, 160 (Kristeva). Goldman: Kolakowski, ch. ix; Hall (2) 13; Macherey. He is interested in totality like Lukacs; holds empirical fact gains significance when brought into whole or structure; sees understanding as an intellectual approach based in a description as exact as possible of the significant structure (not empathy or a matter of imitative experience: Dilthey), explanation as the integration of the structure as a constitutive and functional element in the structure that directly comprises it. Goldman (5) 65f; M. Glucksmann, 146. Barthes' system is also homologic (3) 150.
11. Both Glucksmanns; S. Clarke on Althusser and structural functionalism.

12. M. Glucksmann 97f; Callinicos, 34, 115; Lecourt. Born in Algeria, 1918. A. was educated as Catholic, joined CP 1948, Problematic: Callinicos, 34f; Geras 244-7 (Break); Bheskar (2) 471.
13. Althusser (2) 67n; Geras 244-6.
14. A. (3) 16; Callinicos, 34f.
15. A. (2) 28 and 205f. Callinicos, 51. A. (3) 188 and (2) 205f.
16. M. Glucksmann, 102f; A. (3) 40 and (2) 210, 78 n40; Ollman, App.2.
17. Marx: M. Glucksmann, 103-5; A. Glucksmann (2) 308-14. Also M. G., 125f. D. Sayer on A. collapsing Marx's method of inquiry into his method of presenting the economic categories of capitalism.
    On Times: G. M., 108f: Geras, 252-4; Callinicos, 46f; E. Thompson, 285; A. (2) 213.
18. Meikle, 30. Contrast Marx's idea of 'different moments' (1857, intro. to *Gundrisse*; *Grundrisse* (1953) 99f: *Theories of Surplus Value* (Moscow) pt. ii, 87f. Conjuncture: used by A. to express the necessary co-existence of necessarily uneven instances at a given moment. It is the specific complex unity, which is revealed by analysis in a social formation at any point of time. Callinicos, 47. Overdetermination: Thompson, 299, 304; Barthes 178, 183.
19. A. Glucksmann (2) 295; M. G., 110f.
20. A. (3) 59. Dictionary: A. Glucksmann (1) 71. For attempt to provide A. with a concept of the individual: Molina.
21. A. (3) 177.
22. A. (3) 267; Thompson, 299; A. Glucksmann 292: Jameson (2) 108; Thompson, 275f.
23. A. Glucksmann (2) 312; A. (3) 252. 183ff, 320. Sumner, 185f.
24. Thompson, 297-9 and 309-12 (Marx and Proudhon).
25. Thompson, 394, notes 134, 137, 139, Report in *Le Monde*, cited Thompson. Also Garratone. Thompson, 302, passage from Sartre. Both Barthes and Foucault feel it necessary to get rid of the human being from any consideration of literature: Barthes (3), Foucault, 353; Culler (2) 156f.
26. A. Glucksmann, 309f.
27. A. (3a) 62. Footnote: A. (3a) 148; A. Glucksmann, 303-5; Rancière. Dàrstellung: A. (3a) ii 170 (omitted 2nd edition). For A.'s relation to the metaphysical tradition from Aristotle to Kant, Nietzsche to Heidigger, *Western Marxism*, 274.
28. Callinicos, 58f; A. (3) 59 (Callinicos, 60). Callinicos, 77.
29. Geras, 264; A. (3a) i 29 (Rancière); (3) 122. A. (2) 167, 229 (3) 41f, 58, 60, 99f, 133, and (2) 168.
30. M. Glucksmann, 121, and 123f.
31. M. Glucksmann, 125, citing A. (1) 8; also on similar inconsistencies in A. (2).
32. A. Glucksmann, 268. Sumner, 42f. Thompson, 386; Piccone, 27f; Gillian (positivism).
33. Pluralism: M. Glucksmann, 129. Thought process: Poulantzas (3). Dialectics: Thompson, 393 n119, and 303-6. Ideology: Mepham (1); K. Russell; On Ideology. For A., ideologies' function is to create Subjectivity in Culture.

34. A. (1) 127f and 142.
35. Sumner, 37-9.
36. A. (4). Sumner, 44, 45f, 47.
37. Sumner, 49. See Hirst (1); G. McLennan.
38. A.'s stress on rigour: (2) 37, 116, 164, 193 (3) 74, 77, 90, 114 (1) 23-5, 76. *One—Dimensional Marxism,* S. Clarke and others (1980): an excellent dissection of A. which reached me too late for use here.

Chapter 7: Dialectic of Nature
1. A. Schmidt, 210. *H. & C. C.*, 24 n6, also 4, 18.
2. *Coll. Works*, iii 304. He hailed the *Origin of Species* as giving 'the natural scientific basis of the class-struggle in history,' 16 Jan. 1861 to Lassalle. There is no basis in Marx for an attempt to distinguish two types of dialectics, critical and systematic (first involving only the relation of theory to the social production in which it is rooted; second as the ordering of dialectical concepts through a focus in social analysis on human productive agency as the source, origin, essential reality of the society in question).
3. Lenin, 461, 111, 91, 445, 222, 155, 181. Negation of negation is 'the kernel of all dialectics,' 229. Also 228, 202, 'criterion of truth the unity of the image and reality'. Consciousness: 521. He stresses totality, e.g. 159.
4. Schmidt, 57-60; Gunn (2) 47; Monod, 210; Jordan, 176. Also Schmidt, 195; Gunn, 48; Kojève.
5. Garaudy, 59. Aims and purposes arising out of human activity, the whole 'potential' thus created, are not teleological in any abstract sense: Howard (1) 10; von Wright; Howard (3).
6. Gunn (2) 49f.
7. Novack, 237.
8. Benton for discussion of Engels' strengths and weaknesses. See also Timpanaro, Jones.
9. Benton, 103; Fraser, 23. Garaudy, 54. Also, McLellan (1) 61. Quantity-quality: Benton, 122; Gramsci, QC 1446-7 and PN 469. M. Shirikov, *Textbook of Marxist Philosophy* (Left Book Club) 211-315 for Stalinist view.
10. Meikle, 10, 15, 9, 29, 12-4. Marx to Engels, 1 Feb. 1858. Edgley sees dialectical materialism as a general fusion of logic and ontology, where logic 'must become ontologic': an overstatement unless he merely means that the thought-forms of the dialectic grasp reality in movement and change as formal logic cannot.
11. *Anti-D.* (1939) 27. The question whether a given sphere of natural reality is organic in essence or not resides in the philosophical error generated in the bourgeois epoch that natural reality could be anything else: Meikle, 28f.
12. In general, Fraser; D. Howard; M.Montano. Relation to Stalin: Merker, Cherubini.
13. Cited, Fraser, 52f. P. Anderson, 41; Cassano, 7f, 14-9, 180f.
14. Fraser, 75.
15. Colletti (1) 326; (2) 24f.
16. Colletti (2) 25f. Kant; Novack, 193-6, 203 (Colletti).

17. Novack, 211f; Colletti (3) 11.
18. Colletti (3) 29; Novak, 223f for Marx.
19. Colletti (3) 19.
20. Colletti (1) 337f.
21. *Ibid*, 338f
22. See J.L. (1); B. Hessen in *Science at the Crossroads*, 1931, etc.
23. Bohm, rev. Zukay, TLS 15 Feb. 1980.
24. Marcuse (4) 130, 181.
25. Novack, 238f.
26. J. L. (1) 424f; and Whyte (1) (2) (3).
27. J. L. (1) 425-7.
28. Bohm, see n 23 above; Zukay; Novack, 287. See Fisk for consideration of 'complexity, contradiction, essence'. But these notions cannot alone constitute a dialectical theory.
29. Kepler: J. L. (1) 402; Meikle, 25, 14f. Mathematics: J. L. (1) 99, also for Struick. For the relation of the Galilean concept of inertia and the exchange abstraction; Sohn-Rothel, ch. 25.
30. Bloch (2) 775ff.

Chapter 8: Symmetry, Asymmetry, Structure, Dominance

1. *Dialectics* no. 8, n.d., 28-32. *Perspective* (Fore Pubs, 1944) 18.
2. I have two copies of the duplicated document.
3. R. Williams (5) 351, and (1).
4. *Mysl W.*, September 1951, 8(63), 155-63.
5. J. L. (4) 143f, 240f, 246f. See Whyte (1) Glossary for terms.
6. J. L. (1) 243.
7. Engels, *Anti-D.*, old preface (Moscow, 19 47) 395. Colletti (2) 42. Initiation: J. L. (6) 100f. 238, 209, 295f.

Chapter 9: Some Conclusions: Gramsci again

1. Lowy, 194. Gramsci on Futurism: L'Ordine Nuovo, 5 Jan . 1921; Joll, 20.
2. Useful is C. Mouffe; also Boggs, Buci-Glucksmann, Fiore, Joll, Merrington.
3. Texier, 64, 58, 61. *Prison Notebooks*, 377; Gramsci (7) 231. *Oeuvres Choisies*, 97; PN 363f. Hegemony: Poulantzas (2) 137-9, 204f; Hall (1) 48, 66; Merrington 148.
4. Boggs, 55, 63f, 11, 26; 110 (economism), 60; 64, 72 (PN 272f); PN 367, Merrington, 144.
5. Boggs 44, 47. Section of PN, 'Americanism and Fordism.' Boggs, 40, 45f. His analysis of Weber, Boggs, 96, 45.
6. Boggs, 120, 85-7, 80f; PN 377, 366. The Bloc is not a temporary matter. PN 201, 9f, 339; Joll, 86. Conjunctual: QC 1879, PN 177.
7. PN198. How people create their own personalities; QC 1338, PN 360; QC 1550f, PN91.
8 Boggs, 77f, Joll, 101f, Merrington, 168.
9. See the differential method suggested by Hellman, 1x 161-2; against 'strict organicity.' (Bernard Smith, *The Antipodean Manifesto*, Melbourne, 1976, has interesting suggestions on art systems—craft, fine-art, industrial—and their methods of production and reproduction.)

10. Hellman, 146f. For law: G. A. Cohen, *Aristotle Soc. Suppl.* xliv (1970) 121-41.
11. Marcuse (9) pp. ix. xi, 6f.
12. See Roheim. 168ff for reference and further details. What I set out here about the otherself and its trails, the systems that develop round it, is extremely compressed and schematic, but it indicates the lines along which a fuller exposition could be made.
13. Meszaros (2) 14f. See the whole of the work for the development of the ideas. The ideas set out in the 1844 MSS. in their essential meaning underlie all Marx's formulations.
14. Jahn. 864. See Mandel in Novack (4) 32ff. Wilczynski, 13. 213.
15. Mandel 42; Dawydow; Mandel (2) ch. 7 for basis in Marx's *Grundrisse*. Helplessness: Heise and Mandel (1) 39f. See C. Johnson, 'Reformism and Commodity Fetishism'—*NLR* 119.
16. See J.L. (4) 197-9.
17. See Buci-Glucksmann (1).
18. *Ibid*, 225.
19. See further De Giovanni (1) and (2) , Salvadori, etc.
    For the inability of Soviet philosophers to learn anything whatever from the developments we have discussed in this book, see for ex. Iovchuk (2). 'The use of a complete and definitive theory is nothing but a phantom of the bureaucracy,' Castoriades.

I must thank Paul Grenville for obtaining many books and periodicals for me.

BIBLIOGRAPHY

ADORNO, T. W. (1) *Philosophie der neuen Musik* (Frankfurt) 1958 (2) *Negative Dialektik* (Fr.) 1966 (3) *Aesthetische Theorie (Fr.)* 1973 (4) *Gesprach über die Utopia*, with Bloch (Zollikerberg) 1973 (5) *Prisms*, 1967 (6) *Dialektik der Aufklarung Philosophische Fragmente* (Amsterdam) 1947 (7) *Philosophy of Modern Music* (NY) 1973 (8) *Noten zur Literatur* (Berlin) 1958-61 (9) *New German Critique*, Fall 1975 (10) *Dialectic of the Enlightenment* 1973 (11) *Negative Dialectics*, 1973 (12) *Aesthetics and Politics*, New Left Books., 1977 (13) On Commitment in *New Left Rev.* 87/8 1974 (14) Letters to W. Benjamin, *ib.* 81, 1973 (15) Sociology and Psychology , *N.L.R.* 46-7, 1966-7 (16) *Salmagundi* no. 10-1 (Fall 1969, Winter 1970) (17) *Minima Moralia*, 1951 (18) transl. E. P. N. Jephcott, 1974 (19) *The Jargon of Authenticity*, 1973 (20) *Aspects of Sociology*, 1973.

ALTHUSSER, L. (1) *Lenin and Philosophy*, 1971 (2) *For Marx*, 1969 (2a) *Pour Marx*, 1965 (3) *Reading Capital*, 1970 (3a) *Lire le Capital*, 1968 (4) *Essays in Self-Criticism*, 1976 (5) *Réponse à John Lewis*, 1973 (6) *Theoretical Practice*, 7/8 Jan. 1973.

ANDERSON, PERRY (1) *Considerations on Western Marxism*, 1976 (2) *New Left Rev.* 100, Jan. 1977 (Gramsci). (3) *Arguments within English Marxism*, 1980.

ANZIAS, J. M. with others, *Structuralisme et Marxisme* (Paris) 1970, 85ff.

ARONSON, R. in *Western Marxism*.

ARTHUR, C. *Issues* i 87-116 (Dialectics and Labour).

BADALONI, N. in Mouffe.

BADCOCK, C. R. *British J. of Sociology* xxvi, 2, June 1975, 156-68.

BAHR, E. (1) *La Pensée de G. Lukacs* (Toulouse) 1972 (2) revised (NY) 1972.

BAHRO, R. *Je continuerai mon chemin* (Paris) 1979.

BARTHES, R. (1) *Elements of Semiology*, 1967 (2) *Mythologies* (Paris) 1973 (3) *Sur Racine*, 1963.

BATES, T. A., *J. of History of Ideas*, xxxvi, 2, April-June 1975 (Gramsci).

BENTON, T., *Issues* ii 101-42.

BHASKAR, R. (1) *A Realist Theory of Science* (Leeds Books) 1975 (2) *New Left Rev.*, 94, Nov-Dec. 1975.

BLACKBURN, R. (1) *Ideology and Social Science*, 1972 (2) ed. with Cockburn, *Towards Socialism*, 1965.

BLOCH, ERNST (1) *Geist der Utopie* (Frankfurt) 1964 (2) *Das Prinzip Hoffnung* (Fr.) 1959 (2a) the same, 3 vols. 1973 (3) *Spuren* Fr.) 1960 (4) *Verfremdungen* (Fr.) 2 vols. 1963 (5) *Tübinger Einleitung in die Philosophie* (Fr.) 2 vols 1963-4 (6) *Auswahl aus seinen Schriften* (Fr.) 1967 (7) *Marx und der Revolution* (Fr.) 1968 (8) *Die Kunst Schiller zu Spreche*, 1974 (9) *Erbschaft dieser Zeit* (Fr.) 1973 (10) *On Karl Marx* (NY) 1971 (11) *Atheism in Christianity* (NY) 1971 (12) *Philosophie Aufsätz* (Fr.) 1969 (13) *Das Materialismusproblem* (Fr.) 1972 (15) *Avicenna und die Aristotelische Linke* (16) *Subjekt-Objekt* (GDR) 1951 (17) *Revision des Marxismus* (Berlin) 1975 (18) *A Philosophy of the Future* (NY) 1970 (19) *Vom Hazard sur Katastrophe* (Fr.) 1972 (20) *Politische Messungen*, 1970.

BOBBIO, N. in Mouffe.

BOGGS, C. *Gramsci's Marxism*, 1976.

BOTTOMORE, G. in Meszaros (1) 49-64.

BUCI-GLUCKSMANN, C. (1) *Gramsci and the State,* 1980 (2) in Mouffe. (3) *Gramsci et l'état* (Paris) 1974.
BUCK-MORSS, *Telos* 14 (Winter 1972).
BURGELIN, *Studies in Broadcasting*, Nippon Hoio Kyokai, Tokio (Radio and TV Cult. Research Inst.) 1968.
BURNISTON, S. with C. Weedin, in *On Ideology*, 199-229.
BUTTERS, S. *Issues* iii 175-83.

CALVEZ, J. Y. *La Pensée de Karl Marx* (Paris) 1956.
CAMMETT, J. M. *A. Gramsci and the Origins of Italian Communism* (Stanford) 1967.
CASSANO, F. ed *Marxismo e Filosofia in Italia* (Bari) 1973.
CASTORIADES, C. *Socialisme ou Barbarie*, no. 35 (see Howard (1)283).
CHERKESOV, *Voprosy Filosofi* (Moscow) 2, 1950.
CHERUBINI, G. *Società* 1-2 (Jan-June) 1953.
CLARKE, S. *Capital and Class* (Summer) 1977, 'Marxism , Sociology, and Poulantzas' Theory of the State'.
COLLETTI, L. (1) Interview in *Western Marxism* (1a) *New Left Rev.* 86 (July-Aug.) 1974. (2) *Marxism and Hegel*, 1973 (3) *N.L.R.* (Sept.-Oct.) 1975, Marxism and the Dialectic (4) *From Rousseau to Lenin* (NY) 1972.
COLLIER, A., *Issues* ii 35.60.
CORNU, A. (1) *The Origins of Marxist Thought*, 1957 (2) *La Jeunesse de K. Marx* (Paris) 1934 (3) *La Pensée* × 1946.
COULTER, A. *Socialist Register* 1971: The Engels Paradox.
COZENS, P., *Twenty Years of A. Gramsci* (bibliog.) 1977.
CRANSTON, M. ed. *The New Left,* 1970.
CULLER, J. (1) in Sturrock 154-80 (2) *Structuralist Poetics*, 1975 (3) in Robey, 'The Cybernetic Basis of Structuralism' (4) *Language and Style*, 5:1, 1971, 53-66 (Jacobson).

DAVIDSON, A. (1) *A. Gramsci, towards an intellectual biography,* 1977 (2) *Political Studies* 1972.
DAWYDOW, J. N. *Freiheit und Entfremdung* (Berlin) 1964.
DERRIDA, J. (1) *Écriture et la différence* (Paris) 1967 (2) *Positions*, 1972.

ECO, H. (1) *La struttura assente* (Milan) 1968 (2) *Le forme del contenuto* (Milan) 1971.
EDGLEY, R. *Critique*, vii (Winter) 1976-7 (Colletti).
EHRMANN, J., ed. *Structuralism* (Yale) 1966.
ENGELS (1) *Ant-Dühring* (Moscow) 1969 (2) *Dialectic of Nature* (Moscow) 1964 (3) *L. Feuerbach* (Moscow) 1969.
ENZENBERGER, H. M., *New Left Rev.* 64, 1970.

FEMIA, J. *Political Studies* xxiii 1975.
FETSCHER, I., *Marx and Marxism* (NY) 1971.
FIORI, G., *A. Gramsci*, 1970.
FISCHER, E. *Auf den Spuren der Wirklichkeit* (Reinbeck) 1968.
FISK. M. *Issues* i 117-40 (Dialectics and Ontology).
FLANNERY, M. In Ucko, 73-100.
FOUCAULD, M. (1) *Les mots et les choses* Paris) 1966 (2) *Cahiers pour l'analyse*, 9, 1968, 9-40 (3) *L'Ordre du discours*, 1971 (4) *The Order of Things,* 1970.

172

FROMM, E. ed. *Socialist Humanism* (Anchor) 1966.

GABEL, J. *False Consciousness*, 1975.

GALLAS, H. (1) *Marxistische Literaturtheorie* (Neuwied) 1971 (2) *Working Papers in Cultural Studies* 4 (Birmingham) 1973.

GARAUDY, R. *Marxism in the Twentieth Century*, 1970.

GENOVESE, E., *Studies on the Left* (March-April) 1967: Gramsci.

GERAS, N. (1) in *Western Marxism* 231-72 (2) *New Left Rev.* 65 (Jan-Feb.) 1971 (3) same, 71 (Jan-Feb.) 1972.

GERRATANA, V. *New Left Rev.* 101-2 (Feb.-April) 1977.

GILLIAN, H. *History and Theory* xv, 3, 1976 (Dialectics of Realism and Idealism in Modern Historiographical Theory).

GIOVANNI. B. DE (1) in Mouffe (2) *La teoria politica delle classi nel 'Capitale'* (Bari) 1976.

GLUCKSMANN, A. (1) in *Western Marxism* (2) *New Left Rev.* 72 (March-April) 1972.

GLUCKSMANN, M. *Structuralist Analysis in Contemporary Thought*, 1974.

GOLDMANN, L. (1) *The Human Sciences and Philosophy*, 1969 (2) *The Hidden God,* 1964 (3) *Pour une sociologie du roman* (Paris) 1964. (4) *Towards a Sociology of the Novel*, 1975 (5) *Marxisme et sciences humaines*, 1970 (6) in Meszaro (1) 65-84.

GORZ, A. in *Western Marxism* (Satre).

GOULD, C. C. *Marx's Social Ontology* (MIT) 1978.

GOULDNER, A. W. *The Two Marxisms* (NY) 1980

GRAHAM, L. R. *Science and Philosophy in the S. U.* (NY) 1972.

GRAMSCI, A. (1) *The Modern Prince and Other Writings*, 1957 (2) *Letters from Prison*, ed. Lynne Lawner, 1975 (3) *Selections from Prison Notebooks*, ed. Q. Hoare and G. Nowell-Smith, 1971 (4) *Selections from the Political Writings 1910-20*, ed. Q. Hoare, 1971, 1977 (5) *New Edinburgh Rev.* Gramsci numbers), ed. C. K. Maisels, 1974 (6) *Scritti Politici* (Rome) 1967, ed. P. Spriano.

GREGORY, F. (1) *Scientific Materialism in Nineteenth Century Germany* (Boston) 1977 (2) *Isis* lxviii, 242 (Jan.) 1977, 206-23.

GROSS, D. (1) *American Anthrop.* 77, 1975, 526-49 (2) *Towards a New Marxism* (St. Louis) 1973.

GUNN, N. (1) *Marxism Today* 1973, 215 (2) same, Feb. 1977, 45-52.

GUTZMORE, C. *Marxism Today*, 1972, 267.

HABERMAS, J. (1) *Salmagundi* 10-1 (Fall 1969, Winter 1970) 633-54 (2) *The Legitimation Crisis* (Boston) 1975 (3) *New German Critique*, Fall 1974.

HALL, S. (with B. Lumley, G. McLennan), *Politics and Ideology*, 1977, 45-76: Gramsci (2) *idem*, 9-32.

HARNER, M. *Southwestern J. of Anthropology*, 26, 1970, 67-86.

HARRIS, M. (1) *Cannibals and Kings*, 1978 (2) *Cows, Pigs, Wars and Witches* (NY) 1974 (3) *Culture, People, Nature* (NY) 1975.

HEGEL, *Logic.* transl. Wallace (Oxf.) 1972.

HEISE, W. *Deutsche Zeits. f. Philosophie*, 6 (1965) 700-11.

HELLMAN, G. *Issues* ii, 143-70.

HESSEN, B. *Social and Economic Roots of Newton's Principia* (Kniga, England) 1931.

HIRST, P. Q. (1) *Economy and Society* v. 6, Nov. 1976 (2) *Problems and Advances in the Theory of Ideology* (Communist Univ. of Cambridge) 1975.

HOBSBAWM, E. (1) in Blackburn, *K. Marx's Contribution to Historiography* (2) in Mesvaros (1) 5-21 (3) *NY Rev. of Books,* xxi, 5, April 1974 (Gramsci).

HOFFMAN, J. (1) *Marxism and the Theory of Praxis,* 1975 (2) *Marxism Today* Jan. 1977, 11-8.

HORKHEIMER, M. (1) *Critical Theory,* 1972 (2) ed. *Zeugnisse T. W. Adorno,* 1963 (3) *The Eclipse of Reason* (NY) 1847 (4) *Zeits f. Socialforschung,* Heft 2, 1937 (5) *Kritische Theorie* i-ii (Frankfurt) 1968 (6) as (4) 1939: The Jews and Europe (7) *Diogenes,* no. 53 (Paris) 1966.

HOWARD, D. (1) *The Marxist Legacy,* 1977 (2) with K. Klare, ed. *The Unknown Dimension* (NY) 1972 (3) intro. to Rosa Luxemburg. *Sel. Political Writings* (Monthly Rev. Press) 1971.

HUGHES, H. STUART, *Consciousness and Society* (NY) 1958.

IOVCHUK, M. T. (1) *Voprosy Filosofi,* 1, 1955 (2) *Philosophical Traditions Today* (Moscow) 1973.

Issues: Issues in Marxist Philosophy, 3 vols., ed. J.Mepham and D. H. Ruben (Harvester) 1979.

JACOBSON, R. and M. HALLE, *Fundamentals of Language* (Hague) 1956.

JAHN, W., *Wirstschaftswissenschaft,* 6, (1957) 864.

JAMESON, F. (1) *Marxism and Form* Princeton) 1971 (2) *The Prison House of Language* (Princeton) 1972 (3) *PMLA* 86, 1971, 9-18: Metacommentary.

JAUSS, H. R. *New Literary History,* vii (Autumn) 1977: The Idealist Embarrassment

JAY, M. (1) *The Dialectical Imagination,* 1973 (2) *Social Research* xxxix 1972, 285-305.

JESSOP, BOB, *Marxism Today,* Feb. 1980, 23.5.

JOLL, J. *Gramsci,* 1977.

JONES, G. S. (1) in *Western Marxism:* Early Lukacs (2) *New Left Rev.* (May-June) 1973, 17-36: Engels.

JONES, M. T. *New German Critique,* ix (Fall) 1976, 180-6.

JORDAN, Z. A. (1) *The Evolution of Dialectical Materialism,* 1967 (2) *Philosophy and Ideology* (Dordrecht) 1963.

KARSZ, S. *Theorie et politique: L. Althusser* (Paris) 1974.

KAY, G. *Critique,* vii: Labour.

KELLNER, D. with H. O'HARA, *New German Crit.* 9 (Fall) 1976, 10-34.

KIERNAN, V. G. *Socialist Register,* 1972: Gramsci.

KIRALYFALVI, B. *The Aesthetic of G. Lukacs* (Princeton) 1975.

KLINE, G. L. *Amer. Acad. of Political Sc.,* Annals ccciii (Jan.) 1956, 126-38.

KOJÈVE, A., *Intro. to the Reading of Hegel* (Basic Books).

KOLAKOWSKI, L. *Main Currents of Marxism: The Breakdown,* 1978.

KORSCH, K. (1) *Marxism and Philosphy,* 1970 (2) *Political Theory,* ed. D. Kellner (Texas) 1977.

KRIEGER, L., *J. of Hist. of Ideas,* xiv, 3 (June) 1953, 396ff.

KRIPKE, in *Naming, Necessity and Natural Kinds,* ed. SP. Schwartz (Ithaca NY) 1977.

KRISTEVA, J. (1) *Semiotica* 1, 1969, 196-204 (semiology as science of the ideologies) (2) in *Théorie d'ensemble* (Seuil, Paris 1968, 298-317 (3) *Tel Quel,* 44, 1971, 17-34 (4 *Languages,* 24, 1971, 107-26.

LACAN, J., in *New Left Review,* 51 (the Mirror Phase) (2) *Écrits* (Paris) 1966 (3) in Macksey, 186-95.

LAING, D. *The Marxist Theory of Art* (Harvester) 1978.

LAURETIS, T. de, *Clio,* iv, 129-34.

LEACH, E. (1) *New Society,* 16 May 1974, 371-3 (2) Levi-Strauss, 1970.

LECOURT, D. (1) *L'Épistémologie historique de G. Bachelard* (Paris) 1969 (2) *Pour une critique de l'épistémologie* (Paris) 1972 (3) *Une crise et son enjeu* (Paris) 1973.

LEFEBVRE, H. *The Sociology of Marx,* 1972

LEFEBVRE, H. (2) *Critique de la vie quotidienne,* ii (Paris) 1961, 209 (3) *Intro. à la modernité* (Paris) 1962, 146.

LENIN, *Coll. Works* (Moscow) 1938: *Philosophical Notebooks,* vol. 38.

LEWIN, M. *Lenin's Last Struggle,* 1968.

LEVI-STRAUSS, C. (1) *Anthropologie structurale* (Paris) 1958 (2) *Word* (J. of Linguistic Circle of NY) i. no. 2.

LICHTHEIM, G. (1) *History and Theory* iii, 2, 1963-4, 222-481 (2) *From Marx to Hegel,* 1971.

LILLEY, S. *Marxism Today,* Nov. 1969.

LINDSAY, J. (1) *Blastpower and Ballistics,* 1974 (2) *Origins of Astrology,* 1971 (3) *Origins of Alchemy,* 1970 (4) *Marxism and Contemporary Science,* 1949 (5) *Decay and Renewal,* 1976 (6) *Short History of Culture,* 1962.

LUKACS, G. (1) *Aesthetik* (Berlin) 1963 (2) *History and Class-Consciousness* 1973 (3) *The Young Hegel,* 1975 (4) Lenin, 1970. (5) *The Theory of the Novel,* 1971 (6) *Prolegomeni a un' estetica Marxista* (Editori Riuniti, Rome) 1957 (7) *Conversations with Lukacs,* ed. T. Pinkus, 1974 (8) *The Historical Novel,* 1962 (9) *Kunst und Objectiv Wahrheit* (Leipzig) 1977.

LUPERINI, R. *Marxismo e Letteratura* (Bari) 1971.

LUPORINI, C. *L'Homme et la Société,* 7 (Parls) 1968 (Intro. to *German Ideology*).

MACDONOUGH, R. in *On Ideology.*

MACHEREY, P. (1) *Pour une théorie de la production littéraire* (Paris) 1966 (2) *Littérature,* no. 14, with Balibar.

MACKSEY, R. with E. Donato, ed. *The Language of Criticism and the Sciences of Man* (Baltimore) 1970.

MCLELLAN, D. (1) *Engels,* 1977 (2) K. Marx, *Selected Writings,* ed. 1977.

MCLELLAN, G. with Molina and R. Peters in *On Ideology.*

MACINTYRE, A. (1) *New Reasoner,* 7, Winter 1958-9 (2) *Marcuse,* 1970.

MAGEE, B. *Men of Ideas,* 1978.

MAISELS, C. K. ed. *The New Edinburgh Rev.* (Gramsci numbers) 1974.

MANDEL, E. (1) in Novack (4) (2) *The Formation of the Economic Thought of Karl Marx,* 1971.

MANN, M. *Consciousness and Action among the Western World Communists,* 1973.

MANNHELIM, K. *Ideology and Utopia,* 1936.

MARCUSE, H. (1) *New Left Rev.* 74, July-Aug., 1972 (2) *Eros and Civilisation,* 1968 (3) *Essay on Liberation,* 1969 (4) *One Dimensional Man,* 1964 (5) in Fromm, *Socialist Humanism* (6) *Reason and Revolution,* 1969 (7) *Negations,* 1969 (8) *Kultur und Gesellschaft,* i-ii (Frankfurt) 1965 (9) *The Aesthetic Dimension,* 1980 (10) *Soviet Marxism,* 1958.

MARX K. (1) see D. McLellan (2), (2) *Texts on Method,* ed. T. Carver (Oxf.)

1975 (3) *Grundrisse*, tr. M. Nicolaus, 1976 (4) *Critique of Hegel's Philosophy of Right*, ed. J. O'Malley (CUP) 1970(5) *Capital* , I. B. Fowkes, 1978.

MARZANI, C. *The Open Marxism of A. Gramsci,* (NY) 1957.

MEIKLE, SCOT, *Issues,* i 5-35.

MEPHAM, J. (1) *Radical Philosophy*, 6 (Winter) 1973: Who makes History (2) *Issues*, iii, 141-174 (3) *Essays in Marxist Philosophy*, with Rubin, 1978.

MERKER, N. *Società* xii, 5 (Oct.) 1956.

MERRINGTON, J. in *Western Marxism*, 140-75.

MESZAROS, I. (1) ed. *Aspects of History and Class-Consciousness*, 1971 (2) *Marx's Theory of Alienation*, 1970.

MILIBAND, R. (1) *The State in Capitalist Society*, 1969 (2) *Marxism and Politics*, 1977.

MOLINA, V. in *On Ideology*, 230-58.

MONOD, J. *Chance and Necessity*, 1972. (Note discussion: J. Chiari, *The Necessity of Being*, 1973; *Beyond Chance and Necessity*, ed. J.Lewis. 1974).

MONTANO, M. *Telos*, 7 (Spring) 1971.

MOUFFE, C. ed. *Gramsci and Marxist Theory*, 1979.

NEGT, O. (1) *New German Critique*, 9 (Fall) 1976, 47-60 (2) same, Winter 1975.

NOVACK, G. (1) *Polemics in Marxist Philosophy* (NY) n.d. (2) *Intro to the Logic of Marxism* (NY) 1969 (3) *Internat. Socialist Rev.* (Summer) 1964: Is Nature dialectical? (4) with Mandel, *The Marxist Theory of Alienation* (NY) 1973.

OLLMAN, B. *Alienation* (2nd ed. Cambridge) 1976.

On Ideology (Centre for Contemp. Cult. Studies, Univ. of Birmingham) 1977.

PAETGOLD, H. *Neumarxistische Aesthetik*, i. Bloch-Benjamin, ii, Adorno, Marcuse (Dusseldorf) 1974.

PAGGI, L. (1) in Mouffe (2) *Gramsci e il Moderno Principe* (Rome) 1970.

PARKIN, F. *Marxism and Class Theory*, 1980.

PARKINSON, H. R. (1) *G. Lukacs, the man, his work and his ideas* (Reading Univ. Studies of Contemp. Europe, 4) 1970 (2) *G. Lukacs*, 1977.

PETROVIC, *Marx in the mid-Twentieth Century* (NY) 1957.

PHILIPOV, A. *Logic and Dialectics in the S. U.* (NY) 1952.

PICCONE, P. *Radical America* iii, 3 (Sept.) 1969: *Structuralist Marxism*.

POULANTZAS, N. (1) *Classes in Contemporary Capitalism*, 1975 (2) *Political Power and Social Class*, 1973 (3) *L'Etat, le pouvoir et le socialism,* 1978.

PÜTZ, P. *Nietzsche Studien* 3 (Berlin) 1974.

RAPHAEL, MAX, *Proudhon, Marx, Picasso*, 1980.

RAULET, G. *New German Critique*, 9.

RAYNER, S. *Marxism Today*, May 1977 153-5.

REED, C. A. *Origins of Agriculture* (Hague) 1977.

REMMLING, G. W. *The Sociology of Karl Mannheim*, 1969.

RENNER, R. G. *Aesthetik Theorie bei G. Lukacs* (Bern) 1976.

REVAI, J. *Theoretical Practice, i (London) 1976.*

RICOEUR, P. *De l'interprétation* (Paris) 1965.

ROBEY, D. *Structuralism*, 1973.

ROHEIM, G. *Australian Totemism*, 1915.

ROSDOLSKY, R. (1) *Zur Entstehungsgeschichte der Marxschen Kapital*, 2 vols. (Frankfurt) 1973 (2) *The Making of Marx's Capital*, 1977.

ROSE, G. *The Melancholy Science*, 1978.

ROUSSEL, J. *New Left Rev:* No. 51: Intro to Lacan.

ROWBOTHAM, SHEILA (with L. Segal, H. Wainwright), *Beyond the Fragments,* 2nd ed. 1980.

RUBEN, D. H. *Issues* i 37-85.

RUBIN, I. *Essays on Marx's Theory of Value* Detroit) 1972.

RUSCONI, G. P. (1) *La Teoria critica della Società* (Bologna) 1968 (2) revised ed. 1970.

RUSSELL, K. *Issues* iii 185-06.

SALVADORI, M., in Mouffe.

SAID, E. *Times Lit.Supp.,* 6 Feb. 1976 (Lacan).

SANDER, H. D. *Marxistische Ideologie and allgemeine Kunsttheories* (Tubingen) 1970.

SAYER, D. (1) in Mepham (3): Science as Critique, Marx v. Althusser. (2) *Marx's Method*, 1979.

SCHAFF, ADAM (1) in Fromm (2) *Marxismus und des menschlich Individum* (Vienna) 1966.

SCHILPP, P.A. ed, *The Philosophy of Rudolp Carnap.*

SCHMIDT, A., *The Concept of Nature in Marx,* 1971.

SCHMIDT, J. *Telos*, 24 (Spring) 1975, 2-40.

SCHOLES, R., *Structuralism in Literature* (New Haven) 1974.

SCHROYER, T. *The Critique of Domination*, 1974.

SELIGER, M. *The Marxist Concept of Ideology* (CUP) 1977.

SÈVE, L. (1) *Man in Marxist Theory and the Psychology of Personality*, 1978 (2) *Marxism and the Theory of Human Personality*, 1975.

SIMMEL, G. (1) *Philosophie des Geldes* (2nd ed. Leipzig) 1907 (2) *Schopenhauer and Nietzsche* (Leipzig) 1907.

SMITH, A. *The Shadow in the Cave*, 1976.

SOHN-RETHEL, A. *Intellectual and Manual Labour*, 1978.

SOLOMON, M. *Telos* 13 (Fall) 1972.

SOPER, KATE *Issues* ii, 61-99.

SPERBER, D. in *Sturrock*.

SPRIANO, P., *A. Gramsci and the Party: the Prison Years* 1979.

STRUICK, D. J., *Science and Society*, xii, 1, 1948, 1181-96.

STURROCK, J. *Structuraliism and Since* (OUP) 1979.

SUCHTING, W. *Issues* ii: Theses on Feurbach.

SUMNER, C. *Reading Ideologies*, 1979.

SWINGEWOOD, A. (1) *The Myth of Mass-Culture*, 1977 (2) *Marx and Modern Social Theory*, 1977.

TEXIER, J. *in Mouffe.*

THERBORN, G. (1) in *Western Marxism (2) New Left Rev.* 63, 1970.

THOMPSON, E. T. (1) *The Poverty of Theory*, 1978 (2) *Past and Present*, 38, 1967.

THOMPSON, J. *Marxism Today*, Aug. 1975, 250-4

TIMPANARO, S. (1) *New Left Rev.* 85, 3-32 (2) *On Materialism*, 1975 (3) *The Freudian Slip*, 1976.

TOMICH, D. (1) *Radical America*, iii, 5, 1969 (2) same, iv, 6, 1970.

UCKO, P. in C. W. Dimbleby and R. Tringham. ed. *Man, Settlement and Urbanism*, 1972.

VASQUEZ, A. S. *Art and Society*, 1973.
VENABLE, V. *Human Nature: the Marxian View*, 1946.

WEIMANN, R. *Structure and Society in Literary History*, 1977.
Western Marxism A Critical Reader (New Left Review) 1977.
WETTER, G. *Der Dialektische Materialismus* (Frieburg) 1952.
WHYTE, L. L. (1) *The next Development of Man*, 1944 (2) *The Unitary Principle in Physics and Biology*, 1949 (3) *Critique of Physics*, 1931.
WILCZYNSKI, J. *The Economics of Socialism*, 1977.
WILLIAMS, G. A., (1) *Proletarian Order: A. Gramsci, factory councils, etc.* 1975.
WILLIAMS, RAYMOND (1) *Marxism and Literature* (OUP) 1977 (2) *New Left Rev.*, 82, 1973 (2) *Keywords*, 1976 (5) *Culture and Society*, 1958 (6) *New Left Rev.* 109 (May June) 1978, 3-18.
WOLFF, K., ed. *G. Simmel* (NY) 1950.
WRIGHT, G. H. VON *Explanation and Understanding* Cornell 1971.

ZITTA, G. V. *G. Lukacs' Marxism* (Hague) 1964.
ZUKAY, G. *The Dancing Wu Li Masters*, 1979.

Index

180

181

relationship of socio-economic Base, 14

Storm, T., 38

Stravinsky, Igor, 76-7

Structuralism, 84-5
use of Symptomatic Readings, 87

Structure concept, 130-1, 132-3, 146

Struick, D. J., 119

Subject/object concept
empiricist viewpoint, 36
Lukacs' treatment, 34

Suchadolski, Bogdan, 127, 129, 133

Sumner, V., 101

Superstructure
Althusser's use of concept, 100
links with cultural structure, 145
see also Base and Superstructure theory

Thompson, Edward, 8, 99, 126

Thomson, George, 8

Time, Progress of Kozyrev's theories on, 116-17

Timpanaro, S., 13-14, 20, 21, 127
criticism of Marxism, 61

Trotsky, Leon, 7

Tylor, Sir Edward Burnett, 152

Unity of opposites theory, 15

Use value, 71-2

Utopian philosophy, 72
drawbacks in Bloch's thought, 136

Value, Adorno's Theory of, 71-2

Vigier, Jean-Paul, 115

Voghera, Guido, 22

Weber, M., 38

Whyte, L. L., 115-16, 117n

Wilczynski, J., 154

Williams, Raymond, 20, 127

Youth movement, contribution of Althusser to, 102